Adobe®
Illustrator® 9.0
Illustrated Introductory

Ann Fisher

COURSE
TECHNOLOGY

Thomson Learning™

25 THOMSON PLACE, BOSTON, MA 02210

Australia • Canada • Denmark • Japan • Mexico • New Zealand • Philippines
Puerto Rico • Singapore • South Africa • Spain • United Kingdom • United States

Adobe® Illustrator® 9.0—Illustrated Introductory

is published by Course Technology

Managing Editor:	Nicole Jones Pinard
Product Manager:	Rebecca Berardy
Production Editor:	Christine Spillett
Developmental Editor:	Sandy Kruse
Associate Product Manager:	Stacie Parillo
Editorial Assistant:	Emeline Elliot
Technical Reviewer:	Colleen Case
Composition House:	GEX, Inc.
QA Manuscript Reviewers:	John Freitas, Burt LaFountain, Jeff Schwartz, Ashlee Welz, Andrew Sciarretta
Text Designer:	Joseph Lee, Black Fish Design
Cover Designer:	Doug Goodman, Doug Goodman Designs

For more information contact:

Course Technology
25 Thomson Place
Boston, MA 02210

or find us on the World Wide Web at: www.course.com

ISBN 0-619-01750-3

Printed in the United States of America

1 2 3 4 5 6 7 8 9 BM 05 04 03 02 01

Exciting New Products

Try out Illustrated's New Product Line: Multimedia Tools

What are Multimedia Tools?

Multimedia tools teach students how to create text, graphics, video, animations, and sound; all of which can be incorporated for use in printed materials, Web pages, CD-ROMs, and multimedia presentations.

New Titles

- Adobe Photoshop 5.5—Illustrated Introductory (0-7600-6337-0)
- Adobe Illustrator 9.0—Illustrated Introductory (0-619-01750-3)
- Macromedia Director 8— Illustrated Introductory (0-619-01772-4)
- Macromedia Director 8— Illustrated Complete (0-619-01779-1)

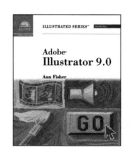

Master Microsoft Office 2000

Master Microsoft Office 2000 applications with the Illustrated series. With *Microsoft Office 2000—Illustrated Introductory*, students will learn the basics of Microsoft Office 2000 Professional Edition. *Microsoft Office 2000— Illustrated Second Course* focuses on the more advanced skills of Office 2000 applications, and it includes coverage of all of the software in the Premium Edition.

Illustrated also offers individual application books on Access, Excel, Word, and PowerPoint 2000. Each book covers basic to advanced skills for the application and meets Microsoft Office User Specialist (MOUS) Expert certification.

Other titles include:

- Microsoft Access 2000—Illustrated Introductory and Complete

- Microsoft Publisher 2000—Illustrated Essentials
- Microsoft Publisher 2000—Illustrated Introductory
- Microsoft Outlook 2000—Illustrated Essentials
- Microsoft FrontPage 2000—Illustrated Introductory
- Microsoft FrontPage 2000—Illustrated Essentials
- Microsoft FrontPage 2000—Illustrated Complete
- Microsoft Office 2000—Illustrated Introductory and Second Course
- Microsoft Office 2000—Illustrated Brief
- Microsoft PowerPoint 2000—Illustrated Brief and Introductory
- Microsoft Word 2000—Illustrated Introductory and Complete
- Microsoft PhotoDraw (version 2) —Illustrated Essentials

Check Out Computer Concepts

Computer Concepts—Illustrated Brief and Introductory, Third Edition is the quick and visual way to learn cutting-edge computer concepts. The third edition has been updated to include advances to the Internet and multimedia, changes to the industry, and an introduction to e-commerce and security.

Create Your Ideal Course Package with CourseKits™

If one book doesn't offer all the coverage you need, create a course package that does. With Course Technology's CourseKits—our mix-and-match approach to selecting texts—you have the freedom to combine products from more than one series. When you choose any two or more Course Technology products for one course, we'll discount the price and package them together so your students can pick up one convenient bundle at the bookstore.

Preface

Welcome to *Adobe Illustrator 9.0—Illustrated Introductory*. This highly visual book offers users a hands-on introduction to Illustrator 9.0 and also serves as an excellent reference for future use.

Adobe Illustrator 9.0—Illustrated Introductory is the latest edition to Illustrated's product line: Multimedia Tools. These books teach students how to create text, graphics, video, animations, and sound for use in print publications, CD-ROM products, and Web-based applications.

▶ Organization and Coverage

This text is organized into eight units with three appendices. In these units, students are introduced to vector-based objects, learn how to plan, create and enhance an illustration, work with paths, layers, and tools, and edit artwork using advanced features. This book also included three appendices: Appendix A covers the various formats for exporting Illustrator documents; and Appendices B & C list helpful keyboard shortcuts.

▶ About this Approach

What makes the Illustrated approach so effective at teaching software skills? It's quite simple. Each skill is presented on two facing pages, with the step-by-step instructions on the left page, and large screen illustrations on the right. Students can focus on a single skill without having to turn the page. This unique design makes information extremely accessible and easy to absorb, and provides a great reference for after the course is over. This hands-on approach also makes it ideal for both self-paced or instructor-led classes.

Each lesson, or "information display," contains the following elements:

Each 2-page spread focuses on a single skill.

Concise text that introduces the basic principles discussed in the lesson. Procedures are easier to learn when concepts fit into a framework.

Creating New Colors

Illustrator 9.0

Illustrator comes with 36 process colors from which you can choose. Process colors are colors that are created using one or more of the following four colors: Cyan, Magenta, Yellow, and Black (also referred to as CMYK). You can change an existing Illustrator color by changing the amount of any of the CMYK colors used to create it. You can also create new colors by mixing any combination of Cyan, Magenta, Yellow and Black. You can add new colors to the Swatches palette and give them unique names. You can also easily remove colors from the Swatches palette. ▬▬ Bill creates two new colors and adds them to the Swatches palette.

Steps

QuickTip
Clicking the Fill icon or the Stroke icon opens the Color palette.

1. Click **Window** on the menu bar, then click **Show Color**, if necessary
   The White color chip is still selected on the Swatches palette because the last item that was selected was the rectangle, which has a White fill. The Color palette displays the CMYK percentages for White (0% C, 0% M, 0% Y, and 0% B) as shown in Figure C-7. You may need to click the Show Options arrow ▣, then click CMYK if you do not see the Cyan, Magenta, Yellow, and Black sliders.

2. Drag the **C (Cyan) slider** on the Color palette to **100%**

3. Drag the **Y (Yellow) slider** on the Color palette to **50%**
   Notice the new color in the Fill icon on the toolbox and on the Color palette.

QuickTip
To delete colors click a swatch in the Swatches palette, then click the Delete Swatch icon ▣ on the Swatches palette.

4. Drag the **Fill icon** on the Color palette on top of the Swatches palette until you see ▯, as shown in Figure C-8, then release the mouse button to add the new color to the Swatches palette
   The new color appears wherever your pointer is positioned on the Swatches palette when you release the mouse button.

5. Double-click the **new swatch** on the Swatches palette
   The Swatch Options dialog box opens.

6. Name the swatch **Dark Green** in the Swatch Options dialog box, then click **OK**

QuickTip
When you create new colors, in Illustrator documents they are available only in the document in which they were created.

7. Create another color using **0%C, 0%M, 0%Y, and 15%K**, then drag the new color swatch to the Swatches palette

8. Double-click the **new color** on the Swatches palette, then name it **Light Gray** and click **OK**

9. Press and hold **[Shift]**, then click **each rectangle** to select all five rectangles

10. Click **Dark Green** on the Swatches palette to fill the rectangles with the new color as shown in Figure C-9, then save your work
    The five rectangles are filled with the new Dark Green color.

▶ ILLUSTRATOR C-8 POSITIONING AND ARRANGING ILLUSTRATOR OBJECTS

QuickTips as well as troubleshooting advice right where you need it – next to the step itself.

Clear step-by-step directions, with what students are to type in green. When students follow the numbered steps, they quickly learn how each procedure is performed and what the results will be.

Every lesson features large-size, full-color representations of what the students' screen should look like after completing the numbered steps.

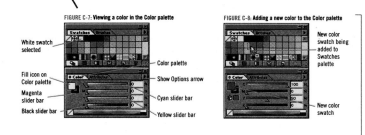

FIGURE C-7: Viewing a color in the Color palette

White swatch selected

Fill icon on Color palette

Magenta slider bar

Black slider bar

Color palette

Show Options arrow

Cyan slider bar

Yellow slider bar

FIGURE C-8: Adding a new color to the Color palette

New color swatch being added to Swatches palette

New color swatch

FIGURE C-9: Five rectangles filled with Dark Green

Dark Green swatch

Light Gray swatch

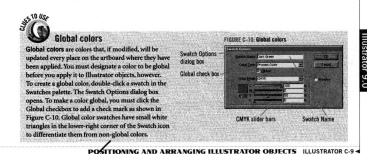

Global colors

Global colors are colors that, if modified, will be updated every place on the artboard where they have been applied. You must designate a color to be global before you apply it to Illustrator objects, however. To create a global color, double-click a swatch in the Swatches palette. The Swatch Options dialog box opens. To make a color global, you must click the Global checkbox to add a check mark as shown in Figure C-10. Global color swatches have small white triangles in the lower-right corner of the Swatch icon to differentiate them from non-global colors.

FIGURE C-10: Global colors

Swatch Options dialog box

Global check box

CMYK slider bars

Swatch Name

Illustrator 9.0

Clues to Use boxes provide concise information that either expands on one component of the major lesson skill or describes an independent task that is in some way related to the major lesson skill.

Additional Features

The two-page lesson format featured in this book provides the new user with a powerful learning experience. Additionally, this book contains the following features:

► **Tryout Software**
At the back of this book, you will find a CD containing Tryout versions of Adobe Illustrator 9.0 for both the Macintosh and Windows operating systems. Students can use this software to work through most of the exercises in this book. Note: The Tryout version does not enable you to save, export, or print artwork. For installation instruction, please see the Read This Before You Begin page.

► **Dual Platform**
The units in this book can be completed either on a Macintosh or on a Windows platform. The steps are written for both operating systems; however, the images throughout the book display the screens as they would appear in Windows.

► **Real-World Case**
The case study used throughout the textbook, a fictitious company called Zenith Design, is designed to be "real-world" in nature and introduces the kinds of activities that students will encounter when working with Illustrator. With a real-world case, the process of solving problems will be more meaningful to students.

► **End-of-Unit Material**
Each unit concludes with a Concepts Review that tests students' understanding of what they learned in the unit. The Concepts Review is followed by a Skills Review, which provides students with additional hands-on practice of the skills. The Skills Review is followed by Independent Challenges, which pose case problems for students to solve. At least one Independent Challenge in each unit asks students to use the World Wide Web to solve the problem as indicated by a Web Work icon. The Visual Workshops that follow the Independent Challenges help students develop critical thinking skills. Students are shown completed Web pages or screens and are asked to recreate them from scratch.

Instructor's Resource Kit

The Instructor's Resource Kit is Course Technology's way of putting the resources and information needed to teach and learn effectively into your hands. With an integrated array of teaching and learning tools that offers you and your students a broad range of technology-based instructional options, we believe this kit represents the highest quality and most cutting edge resources available to instructors today. Many of these resources are available at www.course.com. The resources available with this book are:

Course Test Manager Designed by Course Technology, this Windows-based software helps you design, administer, and print tests and pre-tests. A full-featured program, Course Test Manager also has an online testing component that allows students to take tests at the computer and have their exams automatically graded.

Instructor's Manual Available as an electronic file, the Instructor's Manual is quality-assurance tested and includes unit overviews, detailed lecture topics for each unit with teaching tips, an Upgrader's Guide, solutions to all lessons and end-of-unit material, and extra Independent Challenges. The Instructor's Manual is available on the Instructor's Resource Kit CD-ROM or you can download it from www.course.com.

Course Faculty Online Companion You can browse this textbook's password-protected site to obtain the Instructor's Manual, Solution Files, Project Files, and any updates to the text. Contact your Customer Service Representative for the site address and password.

Project Files Project Files contain all of the data that students will use to complete the lessons and end-of-unit material. A Readme file includes instructions for using the files. Adopters of this text are granted the right to install the Project Files on any standalone computer or network. The Project Files are available on the Instructor's Resource Kit CD-ROM, the Review Pack, and can also be downloaded from www.course.com.

Solution Files Solution Files contain every file students are asked to create or modify in the lessons and end-of-unit material. A Help file on the Instructor's Resource Kit includes information for using the Solution Files.

Figure Files The figures in the text are provided on the Instructor's Resource Kit CD to help you illustrate key topics or concepts. You can create traditional overhead transparencies by printing the figure files. Or you can create electronic slide shows by using the figures in a presentation program such as PowerPoint.

Student Online Companion This book features its own Online Companion where students can go to access Web sites that will help them complete the Webwork Independent Challenges. Because the Web is constantly changing, the Student Online Companion will provide the reader with current updates regarding links referenced in the book.

WebCT WebCT is a tool used to create Web-based educational environments and also uses WWW browsers as the interface for the course-building environment. The site is hosted on your school campus, allowing complete control over the information. WebCT has its own internal communication system, offering internal e-mail, a Bulletin Board, and a Chat room.

Course Technology offers pre-existing supplemental information to help in your WebCT class creation, such as a suggested Syllabus, Lecture Notes, Student Downloads, and Test Banks in which you can schedule an exam, create reports, and more.

Brief Contents

Contents

Illustrator 9.0

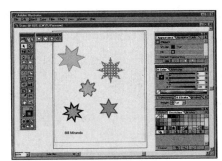

Contents

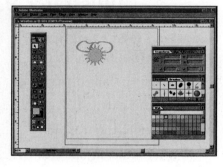

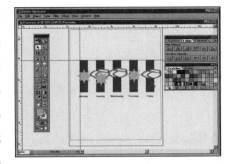

Drawing with the Pen Tool   ILLUSTRATOR D-1

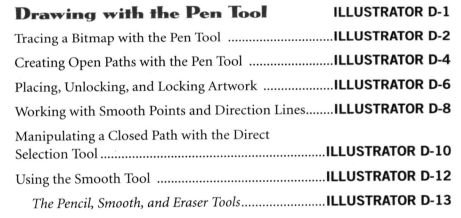

Contents

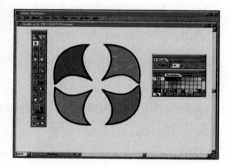

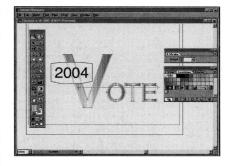

Contents

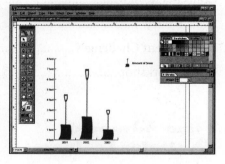

Read This Before You Begin

Project Files
To complete the lessons and end-of-unit material in this book, students need to obtain the necessary project files. Please refer to the instructions on the back inside cover for various methods of getting these files. Once obtained, the user selects where to store the files, such as to the hard disk, network server, or Zip disk.

Free Software Tryout
Included on a CD with this book is the Adobe Illustrator 9.0 Tryout software. This same software is available as a free download from the Adobe Corporation Web site (*http://www.adobe.com*).
Installation instructions for the included CD-ROM are as follows:

- **Windows**: Insert the CD in the CD-ROM drive, open Windows Explorer, select the CD-ROM drive, double-click Setup.exe file in the right pane of Windows Explorer Illustrator 9.0 Tryout folder, then follow the on-screen instructions to complete the installation.

- **Macintosh**: Insert the CD in the CD-ROM drive, double-click the CD icon, double-click the Install Adobe Illustrator Tryout icon, then follow the on-screen instructions to complete the installation.

If you are using the Adobe Illustrator 9.0 Tryout software, you cannot save, export, or print out of the program. The Tryout application also does not include third-party color libraries, spelling and hyphenation dictionaries, Photoshop filters, sample art, fonts, clip art, action sets, tutorials, and movies.
To print screen results, students can use Print Screen, and then copy or move the image into any graphics capable program.

To Use Print Screen:

- **Windows**: Click [Print Screen], and then paste the image into a graphics capable program.

- **Macintosh**: Press and hold [Shift] [Command] [3] to create a graphics file on the hard drive, and then open the file in a graphics capable program.

Getting
Started with Illustrator 9.0

Objectives

▶ **Define illustration software**
▶ **Start Illustrator**
▶ **View the Illustrator window**
▶ **Create basic shapes and enter text**
▶ **Modify objects**
▶ **Save an Illustrator document**
▶ **Use Illustrator Help**
▶ **Print your document and exit Illustrator**

Adobe Illustrator is a professional illustration software program used to create graphics for page layout, multimedia, and the Web. Illustrator includes many tools for creating and modifying illustrations. It also allows you to export your illustrations in a variety of file formats so that they can be used in other software programs.  Bill Miranda is a recent college graduate with a bachelor's degree in communications. His knowledge of computers and interest in design have helped him land a position at a local TV station, WHJY as the new junior computer graphics artist. He'll work with a team of designers who create computer graphics for the evening news and the station's Web site. Bill will use Illustrator to create these graphics.

Defining Illustration Software

Illustrator is a software program used to create **vector graphics** for print, multimedia, and the Web. **Vector graphics** are mathematically calculated objects that are composed of anchor points and straight or curved line segments. Another type of computer-generated graphics is **bitmap graphics** that are composed of **pixels**, small squares used to display a digital image on the rectangular grid of a computer screen. Examples of a vector graphic and a bitmap graphic are shown in Figures A-1 and A-2, respectively. One drawback of using bitmap graphics is that they are **resolution-dependent**, meaning that they cannot be resized without losing image quality. Vector graphics are **resolution-independent**, meaning that you can reduce or enlarge them without any loss of quality. Vector graphics produce smooth lines, known as **paths**, and are considered ideal for type, logos, and line art. Figure A-3 is an example of a picture created using Illustrator.

Today is Bill's first day at WHJY. His supervisor gives him some examples of Illustrator documents that have been created at WHJY so that he can see the kind of work he will be doing. With Illustrator, Bill will be able to:

Details

Create objects using the Shape, Pen, Pencil, and Paintbrush tools
You can create a variety of shapes using the premade shape tools. The Pencil and Paintbrush tools allow you to draw smooth lines in varying thicknesses and styles. The Pen Tool is used for drawing new objects or tracing part of a bitmap graphic.

Apply color, pattern, and gradient fills to objects
Illustrator comes with a variety of colors, patterns, and gradients that you can apply to objects. You can also create and name your own colors, patterns, and gradients. **Gradients** are multicolor fills used to fill the inside of a closed path.

Change the appearance of an object using Styles, Effects, and Filters
Appearance attributes are a list of formatting attributes that have been applied to an object, such as an object's fill color, stroke color, stroke weight, transparency amount, or any special effects. Appearance attributes are listed in the Appearance palette as they are applied to an object. A **Style** is a saved set of appearance attributes that you can apply to other objects in your illustration. **Effects** and **Filters** include many ways to manipulate an object's appearance including twirling an object or applying a drop shadow to an object. Effects can be removed from an object if desired, whereas Filters cannot; they permanently change the object's appearance.

Create text
You can create and format text in Illustrator just as you can in other software programs. In addition, Illustrator allows you to type along a straight or curved path, fill shapes with text, and import and export text from and to a word-processing program. For example, text selected in Illustrator can be exported back to Microsoft Word or WordPerfect.

Control the arrangement of objects using layers, grouping, and alignment
You can align and distribute objects, group them together, and place them on specific layers. Objects can be temporarily locked so that they cannot be selected or grouped to something else by mistake. You can also hide and show objects as a way of viewing different versions of your illustration.

Create graphs and use custom designs for graphs
Illustrator has a graphing feature for creating basic bar and pie graphs. Graphs can be edited with colors and fonts, just like other Illustrator objects. You can also create your own custom designs to apply to columns and markers on a graph.

FIGURE A-1: Example of a vector graphic

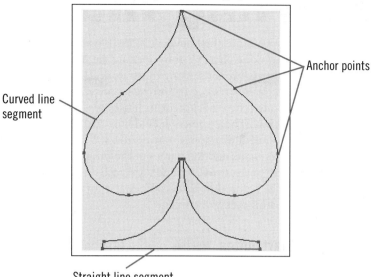

Anchor points

Curved line segment

Straight line segment

FIGURE A-2: Example of a bitmap graphic

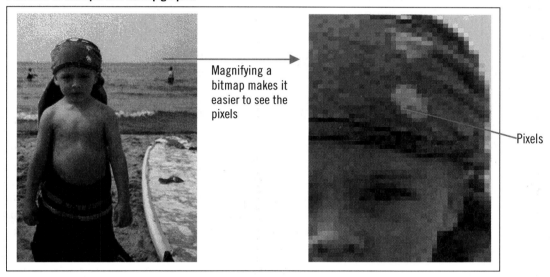

Magnifying a bitmap makes it easier to see the pixels

Pixels

FIGURE A-3: Example of an illustration

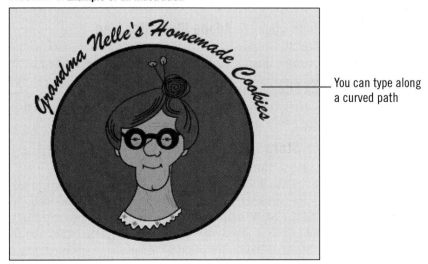

You can type along a curved path

Starting Illustrator

Illustrator 9.0

To start Illustrator, you must first navigate to the Illustrator software application by clicking the Start button if you are working on a PC, or by opening the Adobe Illustrator folder if you are working on a Macintosh. Your procedure for starting Illustrator may differ from the steps below if your computer system is set up differently. See your instructor or technical support person if you need assistance. Each time you create a new document in Illustrator, you will be able to make choices in the New Document dialog box. These choices include the Artboard Size, the Color Mode, and the name of your document. While Illustrator is starting you will see a **splash screen**—a window that displays details about the software, and the names of the programmers who created it. ✎ Bill receives his first assignment: to create five unique stars; each one different from the others. His supervisor will then choose one to be used in a special news report about constellations. Bill begins by starting Illustrator and creating a new document.

WIN

1. Click the Start button 🏁 **Start** **on the taskbar, then point to Programs**

The Programs menu opens, displaying all of the available software programs installed on your computer. The programs on your computer may differ from those in Figure A-4.

Trouble?

If you have trouble locating Illustrator under the Programs menu, see your instructor or technical support person for help.

2. Click Adobe Illustrator 9.0 as shown in Figure A-4

When Illustrator is finished loading, a gray background, the menu bar containing the Illustrator menus, and some floating windows called palettes appear.

3. Click File on the menu bar, then click New

The New Document dialog box opens, prompting you to choose a Name, Artboard Size, and Color Mode, as shown in Figure A-5.

4. Type Stars in the Name field, do not change the Color Mode and Artboard Size settings, then click OK

The Artboard Size is 8.5 x 11 inches; however, it is currently displayed in **points**, a unit of type size equal to 0.01384 inches, or approximately 1/72 of an inch. The Color Mode can be either CMYK or RGB. CMYK stands for Cyan, Magenta, Yellow, and Black–the color mode used for printed materials. RGB stands for Red, Green, and Blue–the color mode used for graphics that will only be shown on a monitor or projector, and never printed. The new document opens displaying the document name and the color mode in the title bar as shown in Figure A-6.

MAC

1. Double-click your Macintosh hard drive icon as shown in Figure A-4

Trouble?

If you have trouble locating Illustrator, see your instructor or technical support person.

2. Double-click your Adobe Illustrator 9.0 folder

3. Double-click the Adobe Illustrator icon

When Illustrator is finished loading, a gray background, the menu bar containing the Illustrator menus, and some floating windows called palettes appear.

4. Click File on the menu bar, then click New

The New Document dialog box opens, prompting you to choose a Name, Artboard Size, and Color Mode, as shown in Figure A-5.

5. Type Stars in the Name field; do not change the Color Mode and Artboard Size settings, then click OK

The Artboard Size is 8.5 x 11 inches; however, it is currently displayed in **points**, a unit of type size equal to 0.01384 inches, or approximately 1/72 of an inch. The Color Mode can be either CMYK or RGB. CMYK stands for Cyan, Magenta, Yellow, and Black—the color mode used for printed materials. RGB stands for Red, Green, and Blue—the color mode used for graphics that will only be shown on a monitor or projector and never printed. The new document opens displaying the document name and the color mode in the title bar as shown in Figure A-6.

FIGURE A-4: Starting Adobe Illustrator on a Windows and a Macintosh computer

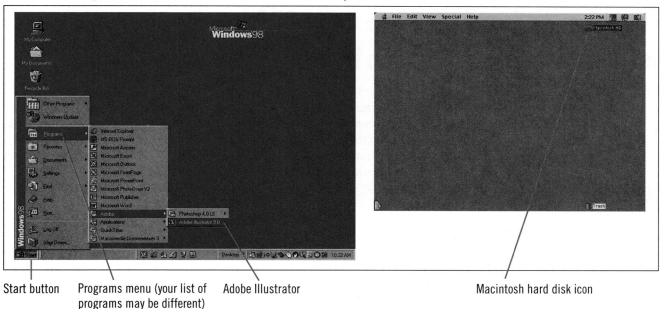

Start button   Programs menu (your list of   Adobe Illustrator   Macintosh hard disk icon
                programs may be different)

FIGURE A-5: The New Document dialog box on a Windows and a Macintosh computer

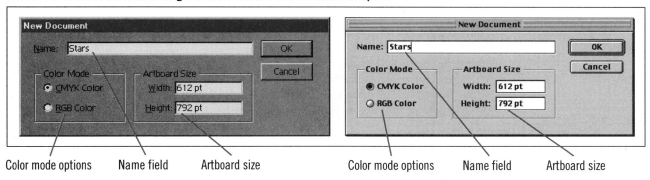

Color mode options   Name field   Artboard size   Color mode options   Name field   Artboard size

FIGURE A-6: The Illustrator window on a Windows and a Macintosh computer

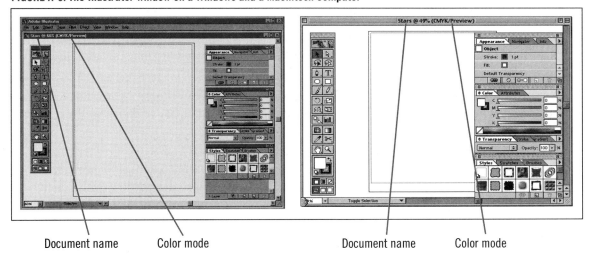

Document name   Color mode   Document name   Color mode

Illustrator 9.0

Viewing the Illustrator Window

The Illustrator window includes the artboard, scratch area, toolbox, and palettes—all of which are described below. Refer to Figure A-7 as you locate these elements. If you have a really large or small monitor, or if previous users have opened or closed specific palettes, your window may look a little different than the one in the figure. The palettes shown in the figure are the default palettes displayed when you start Illustrator for the first time. ✎ Bill takes some time to familiarize himself with the Illustrator window elements before he begins his project.

Details

 Title bar
A bar that contains the name of your document, magnification level, and color mode; also contains the Minimize, Maximize, and Close buttons.

 Menu bar
A bar that includes all of the Illustrator menus, which you click to display submenus; commands that are not currently available are grayed out, while commands that require additional input are followed by an ellipsis.

 Artboard
The area, bounded by a solid line, in which you create your artwork; the size of the artboard can be set as large as 227" × 227".

 Imageable area
The area inside the dotted line on the artboard representing the portion of the page that your default printer can print; objects placed in the **nonimageable area** of the page (the area between the dotted line and the solid bounding line) will not print because your printer needs to "grab" this area of the page to pull the paper through.

 Scratch area
The area outside the artboard where you can store objects before placing them on the artboard; objects on the scratch area will not print.

 Toolbox
A box containing tools that let you create, select, and manipulate objects in Illustrator.

 Zoom text box
A box in the lower-left corner of the Illustrator window that displays the current magnification level. To the right of the Zoom text box is the Zoom menu which you access by clicking the small black triangle. The Zoom menu lets you choose another magnification level to work in.

 Status bar
A bar that contains a list arrow menu from which you can choose a status line with information about the current tool, the date and time, the amount of free memory, or the number of undo operations.

 Scroll bars
Bars that run along the bottom and right sides of the window; dragging the scroll boxes, clicking in a scroll bar, or clicking the scroll arrows changes the portion of the document that is viewable in the Illustrator window.

 Palettes
Windows containing features for modifying and manipulating Illustrator objects.

FIGURE A-7: **The Illustrator window**

Menu bar ——

Title bar ——

Toolbox ——

Scratch area ——

Artboard ——

Imageable area ——

Zoom menu ——

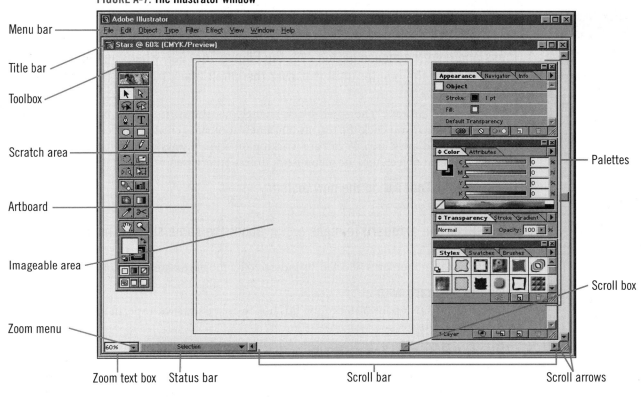

Palettes

Scroll box

Zoom text box   Status bar   Scroll bar   Scroll arrows

 CLUES TO USE

Using Illustrator default settings

When you create a new Illustrator document for the first time, you will see the Illustrator window's default settings. Default settings include the arrangement of window elements, colors in the toolbox, open and closed palettes, and shown or hidden rulers. When you begin interacting with the software, you will probably want to change some of these settings, such as opening or closing certain palettes. If you make significant changes to the default settings, and you want to return to the original default settings, exit Illustrator. In Windows Explorer or My Computer, open the Illustrator 9.0 folder, which is located in the Adobe subfolder of the Program Files folder. Delete the AIprefs file by placing it in the Recycle Bin, then start Illustrator again. You will see the default window settings. If you are working on a Macintosh computer, quit Illustrator, then delete the Adobe Illustrator 9.0 Prefs file. This file is located in the Preferences folder, which is found in the System folder on the hard drive.

Illustrator 9.0

Illustrator 9.0

Creating Basic Shapes and Entering Text

The toolbox contains six shape tools: Ellipse, Polygon, Star, Spiral, Rectangle, and Rounded Rectangle. Only the Ellipse Tool and the Rectangle Tool appear on the toolbox—the other shape tools are hidden underneath them. Tools that have other tools underneath them have black triangles in their lower-right corners. In addition to creating basic shapes, you can create text in Illustrator using the Type Tool, or import text from a word-processing software program. ✒ Bill locates the Star Tool and uses it to make several stars, then enters his name on the artboard.

Steps

QuickTip

Place your pointer over a tool and wait a moment to display a Tool Tip that shows the name of the tool and its shortcut key.

QuickTip

Before releasing the mouse button, you can increase or decrease the number of points on your star by pressing ↑ or ↓.

Trouble?

If you want to delete the star and start over, while the star is still selected, press [Delete] (Win) or [delete] (Mac) on your keyboard.

1. Press and hold the mouse button over the **Ellipse Tool** 🔘, when the hidden toolbar **appears**, drag the pointer until it is over the small black triangle, then release the mouse button

   A new toolbar appears. The small black triangle, as shown in Figure A-8, is called the **tearoff tab**. When you click the tearoff tab, a new toolbar is created that can be positioned anywhere on the work area. If you are working on a PC, always use the left mouse button when clicking an object, tool, or menu item, unless otherwise instructed.

2. Click the **Star Tool** ⭐ on the new toolbar

   Your pointer becomes ┼ .

3. Drag ┼ on the **artboard** to make a star about the same size as the one shown in Figure A-9

   A star appears and remains selected, as indicated by the blue outline around it.

4. Click the **artboard** with ┼

   The Star dialog box opens. You can use this box to create stars with specific dimensions and number of points.

5. Click the **Points spin box up arrow** until you see 7, then click **OK**

   A star with seven points appears on the page.

6. Click the **Selection Tool** 🔺, click the **five-point star** you created if neccessary, then press **[Delete]** (Win) or **[delete]** (Mac)

   To delete an object, you must first select it.

7. Create four more stars using either the Star Tool or the Star dialog box

8. Click the **Selection Tool** 🔺, drag each star to a new location on the artboard so that it does not overlap with any other star

9. Click the **Type Tool** 🅣 on the toolbox

   Your pointer turns into ⊺.

10. Click **Type** on the menu bar, point to **Size**, then click **24 pt**

11. Click the lower-left corner of the artboard, then type your **first** and **last name** as Bill has done in Figure A-10

    The Fill icon changes to Black and the Stroke icon changes to None.

12. Click the **Selection Tool** 🔺, then click the **artboard** to deselect the text object

    You can also deselect objects by clicking Edit on the menu bar, then clicking Deselect All.

FIGURE A-8: Showing hidden tools

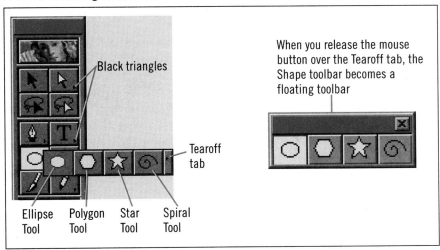

Black triangles

When you release the mouse button over the Tearoff tab, the Shape toolbar becomes a floating toolbar

Tearoff tab

Ellipse Tool

Polygon Tool

Star Tool

Spiral Tool

FIGURE A-9: Creating a star

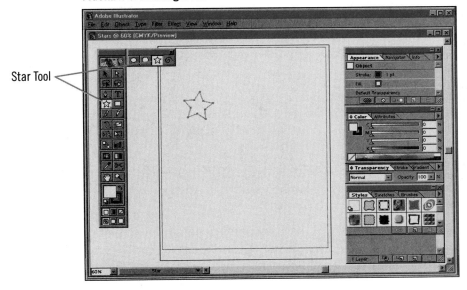

Star Tool

FIGURE A-10: Entering text on the artboard

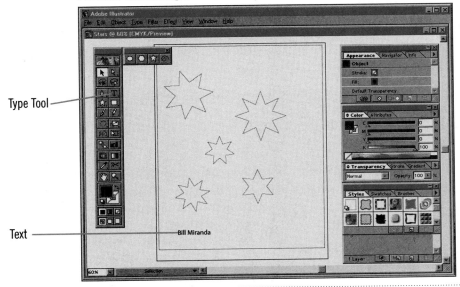

Type Tool

Text

Bill Miranda

Illustrator 9.0

Modify Objects

When you start a new Illustrator document for the first time, the default colors displayed in the toolbox are White and Black. That is why the stars that you just created have a fill color of White and a stroke color of Black. The **fill** is the inside area of an object and the **stroke** is the border or frame of an object. Illustrator objects can be filled with solid colors, gradients, or patterns. In addition, they can be stroked with solid colors, patterns, and brush styles. **Styles**, which are sets of appearance attributes that have been saved with unique names, can also be applied to objects. Bill looks over the choices on the Swatches and the Styles palettes, then applies new fill colors, stroke colors, and styles to his five stars.

Steps 1234

1. Click the **Swatches tab** next to the Styles tab on Styles palettes to display the Swatches palette

   Each palette shares space with two or more palettes. Clicking a palette tab activates its palette. The Swatches palette, as shown in Figure A-11 contains 36 colors including None and Registration, six gradient fills, and six pattern fills.

2. With the Selection Tool ▮, click a **star** on the artboard, then click **Yellow** on the Swatches palette

   Each color is named and has four variations, for example, Yellow, 75% Yellow, 50% Yellow, and 25% Yellow. Place your pointer over a color swatch on the Swatches palette to display the color's name.

QuickTip

Click the Swap Fill and Stroke icon ⇄ on the toolbox to swap the fill and stroke colors.

3. Press **[X]** on your keyboard

   The shortcut for toggling the Fill and Stroke icons on the toolbox is **[X]**. To change the stroke color, the Stroke icon must be in front of the Fill icon. To change the fill color, the Fill icon must be in front of the Stroke icon.

QuickTip

If you want to apply the fill and stroke colors or styles from one object to another, click the object that you want to change, click the Eyedropper Tool 🖊, then click the object that has the desired fill and stroke colors or styles.

4. Click the **75% Green swatch** on the Swatches palette

   A green stroke is placed on the yellow star. The stroke is set to 1 point wide unless you increase it using the Stroke palette.

5. Click the **Stroke tab** on the Transparency palette to activate the Stroke palette

   If you do not see the Stroke tab or the Stroke palette, click Window on the menu bar, then click Show Stroke. The Stroke palette is used to change the thickness of an object's stroke.

6. Click the **Weight list arrow** on the Stroke palette, then click **4 pt**

   You can also increase or decrease the stroke weight using the up and down arrows to the left of the stroke field.

7. With the Selection Tool, click another **star** on the artboard, press **[X]** to activate the Fill icon on the toolbox, then click the **Azure Rings pattern** on the Swatches palette as shown in Figure A-12

8. Click the **Styles tab** on the Swatches palette to activate the Styles palette

9. Click another **star** on the artboard, then click the **Rounded Edges** style on the Styles palette

10. Apply fill and stroke colors to the two remaining stars as shown in Figure A-12

    You can change the Stroke weight on each of the remaining stars if you wish to using the Stroke palette. If you make a mistake, you can undo your last step by pressing [Ctrl] [Z] (Win) or [Command] [Z] (Mac) on your keyboard.

FIGURE A-11: **The Fill and Stroke icons in the toolbox and the Swatches palette**

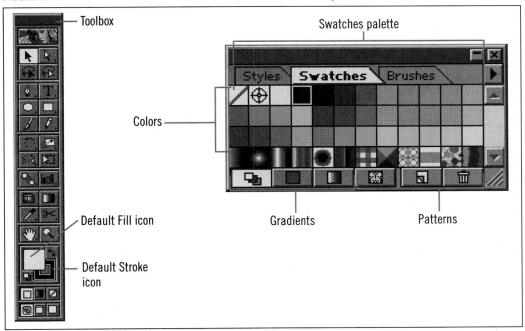

FIGURE A-12: **Five stars with new colors, patterns, and styles**

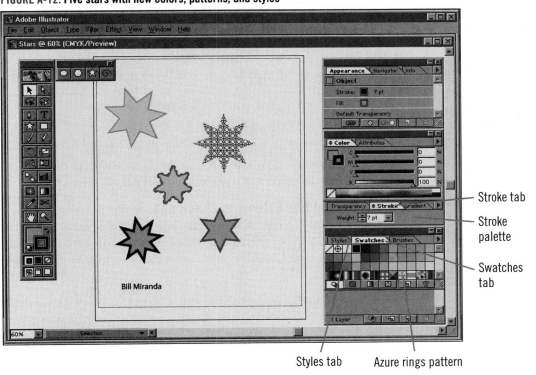

CLUES TO USE

Multiple Undo Levels

It is possible to undo your last 200 steps in Illustrator. To change the number of undo levels, click the File menu, point to Preferences, then click Units and Undo. Type in the desired number of Minimum Undo Levels. Most users set this number anywhere between 12 and 20. Setting the number of undo levels too high can interfere with the amount of computer memory available while using Illustrator. Click OK to return to your document.

Illustrator 9.0

Saving an Illustrator Document

It is important to save your work early and often as you work on an illustration because Illustrator does not have an automatic save feature. The first time you save your Illustrator document, you will be prompted to store it somewhere on your computer. Each time you save after that, Illustrator will save the changes that you have made since your last save. Illustrator files are saved in Adobe Illustrator AI format. They can also be saved as Adobe PDF files and Illustrator EPS files, or exported in other file formats. Bill saves the Stars document and stores it on his computer.

WIN

1. Click File on the menu bar, then click Save

The Save dialog box opens, as shown in Figure A-13. The .ai extension is added to the filename (Stars.ai).

2. Click the Save in list arrow, then click the drive containing your Project Disk

This book assumes your Project Disk is in Drive A. Substitute the correct drive if this is not the case. See your instructor or technical support person for assistance.

QuickTip

Printing, saving, and exporting are disabled in the Illustrator Tryout! software. To learn more about the Tryout! software that accompanies this book, see the Read This Before You Begin page.

3. Click Save

The Save dialog box closes and the Illustrator Native Format Options dialog box opens. This dialog box allows you to save your Illustrator document in another version of Illustrator using the Compatibility list arrow. For the remainder of this book, save your documents in Illustrator 9.0 format.

4. Click OK

The Stars document remains open displaying the new name Stars.ai in the title bar.

MAC

1. Click File on the menu bar, then click Save

The Save dialog box opens, as shown in Figure A-13.

2. Navigate to the drive where you store your project files

This book assumes your Project Disk is in Drive A. Substitute the correct drive if this is not the case. See your instructor or technical support person for assistance.

QuickTip

If you plan on opening a Macintosh Illustrator file on a Windows computer, you will need to add the .ai or .AI file extension to the filename in order for Illustrator for Windows to open it.

3. Click the Append File Extension check box as shown in Figure A-13

Macintosh computers do not automatically add the file extension to the filename as Windows computers do. When you click Append File Extension, .AI will be added to the filename. You can also click the Lower Case check box so that the file extension will be lower case (.ai).

4. Click Save

The Save dialog box closes and the Illustrator Native Format Options dialog box opens. This dialog box allows you to save your Illustrator document in another version of Illustrator using the Compatibility list arrow. For the remainder of this book, save your documents in Illustrator 9.0 format.

5. Click OK

The Stars document remains open displaying the new name Stars.AI in the title bar.

Drawing tips

If you press and hold down [Shift] while drawing with the Ellipse Tool, you can create a perfect circle. If you press and hold down [Shift] while drawing with the Rectangle Tool, you can create a perfect square. If you press and hold down [Alt] (Win) or [Option] (Mac) while you are drawing an object, the object will grow from its center point instead of from the point of the mouse click on the artboard. You can duplicate any Illustrator object by pressing and holding [Alt] (Win) or [Option] (Mac) while dragging the object.

Save dialog box

Save in list arrow

Filename

Save button

Save dialog box

Project Disk

Filename

Save button

Append File Extension check box

Lower case check box

Format list arrow

CLUES TO USE

Saving your document for use in an older version of Illustrator

You can save your Illustrator document for use in an older version of Adobe Illustrator so that you or someone else can open and work with the document on another computer that has the earlier version of Illustrator on it. When saving an Illustrator document for the first time, you can click the Save button in the Save dialog box, the Illustrator Native Format Options dialog box will open. You can click the Compatibility list arrow and choose another version. If you already saved the document, you must use the Save As option to access the Illustrator Native Format Option dialog box. Keep in mind when saving your documents in older versions of Adobe Illustrator that features that are new to version 9.0 will not be available.

Using Illustrator Help

Illustrator has an extensive Help menu from which you can get information on Illustrator topics and features and through which you can download top technical issues and corporate news. The Help menu offers links to Illustrator-specific Web sites such as Tips and Techniques, Online Services, and Plugins and links to other Adobe Web sites, (the company that manufactures Illustrator), including the Adobe home page, Store Specials, and Free Tryouts. To take advantage of these features and receive help about Illustrator, you need to have an Internet connection established and a Web browser, such as Microsoft Internet Explorer or Netscape Navigator, available on your computer. ✎⟶ Bill wonders what ⊕ means on the Swatches palette. He finds out the name of it using Tool Tips, and then finds out more information about it using the Help menu.

Steps

1. Place your mouse over ⊕ on the Swatches palette until you see the Registration Tool Tip appear

   If you do not see the Swatches palette, click Window on the menu bar, then click Show Swatches. If you see the Swatches tab but not the Swatches palette, click the Swatches tab to activate the Swatches palette.

Trouble?

If you do not have access to the Internet or a Web browser installed on your computer, see your instructor or technical support person for assistance.

2. Click **Help** on the menu bar, then click **Illustrator Help**

   The Adobe Help Web site opens. There are four buttons on the left including How to use Help, Contents, Index, and Search as shown in Figure A-14. The Contents list appears by default in the Adobe Help window.

3. Click the **Index button**

   The alphabet appears. Whenever you click one of the letters, topics that begin with that letter appear.

4. Click **R**, then using the bottom scroll arrow, scroll down until you see Registration color 1 as shown in Part A of Figure A-15

5. Click **1** after Registration color

   Information about swatch types appears in the right pane of the window.

6. Click the down scroll arrow on the right until you see information about Registration as shown in Part B of Figure A-15

7. Click **File** on the menu bar, then click **Close** or **Quit**, depending on your browser.

FIGURE A-14: The Adobe Help Web site

Index

Contents

How to use
Help

Contents list

Search

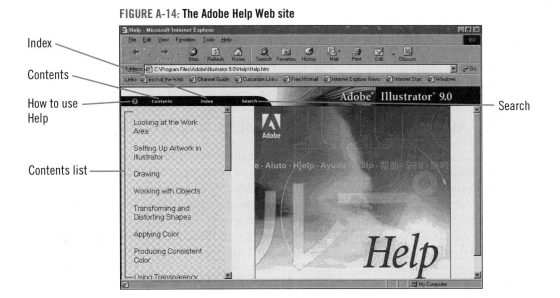

FIGURE A-15: Using the Index button to find Registration

Part A

Part B

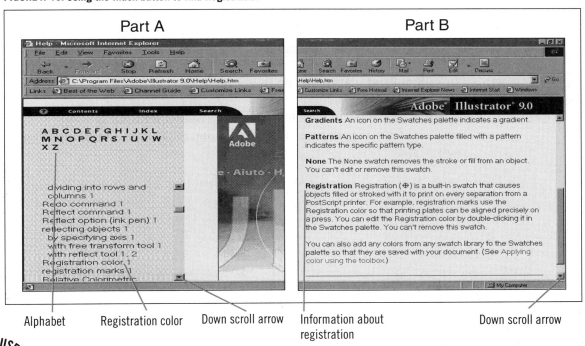

Alphabet   Registration color   Down scroll arrow   Information about registration   Down scroll arrow

Shortcuts

When you click any tool in the toolbox, the pointer remains in that tool mode until you click a new tool. If you press [Ctrl] (Win) or [Command] (Mac) on the keyboard, the current tool turns into the Selection Tool. Once you release [Ctrl] (Win) or [Command] (Mac), your pointer will return to the tool mode in which you were previously working. For example, if you want to make a rectangle, move it to the bottom of the page, and then make another rectangle, follow these steps: make the first rectangle, and then, while pressing and holding down [Ctrl] (Win) or [Command] (Mac), drag the rectangle to the desired location. When you have finished moving the rectangle, release [Ctrl] (Win) or [Command] (Mac). The mouse pointer becomes the Rectangle Tool again, and you can make your next rectangle. Pressing and holding down the [Spacebar] will temporarily convert the pointer into the Hand Tool. The Hand Tool moves the artboard around in the Illustrator window.

Illustrator 9.0

Printing Your Document and Exiting Illustrator

Though you will most likely incorporate your illustrations into documents you are working on in other programs, you may occasionally want to print them directly from Illustrator. When you are finished working on a document, you will want to save it one last time, and then close it. You can close a document without exiting Illustrator by clicking the Close button on the document window, but if you are through with your Illustrator session, you can save and close your document, and exit Illustrator all in one step. ✒ Bill checks his work one last time as shown in Figure A-16, prints one copy of it, then exits Illustrator.

Steps 1 2 3 4

1. Click **File** on the menu bar, then click **Print**
   The Print dialog box opens, as shown in Figure A-17.

2. Make sure **1** is selected in the **Copies text box** or the **Number of Copies spin box**, depending on your Print dialog box

Trouble?

If you have trouble printing your document, see your instructor or technical support person for help.

3. Click **OK** or **Print**, depending on your Print dialog box

4. Click **File** on the menu bar, then click **Exit** (Win) or **Quit** (Mac)
   Bill walks over to the printer, collects his printout, and delivers it to his supervisor. He is now ready to start a new project.

CLUES TO USE

Printing in color and in black and white

Printers are capable of printing in black and white, in color, or both. If you have a color printer, you can choose whether you would like to print your document in color or black and white using a setting in the Print dialog box. If you are printing a first draft of a document, you may want to print it in black and white first to save the color toner or inks that your printer uses. If you have a black and white printer, your colored objects will be printed in shades of gray.

FIGURE A-16: **The final project**

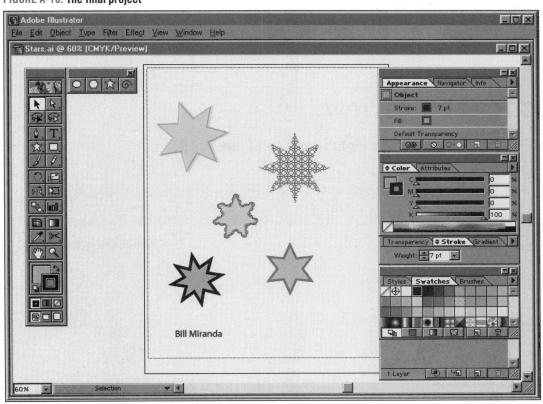

FIGURE A-17: **Print dialog box**

Your Print dialog box
may look different

Default printer

Number of
copies

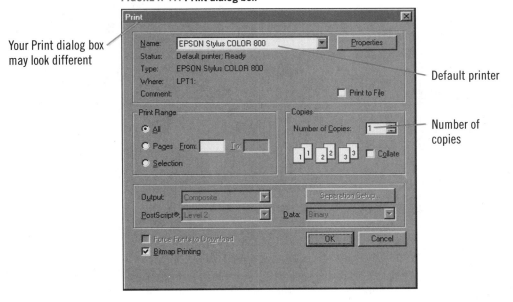

Practice

▶ Concepts Review

Label the Illustrator window elements shown in Figure A-18.

FIGURE A-18

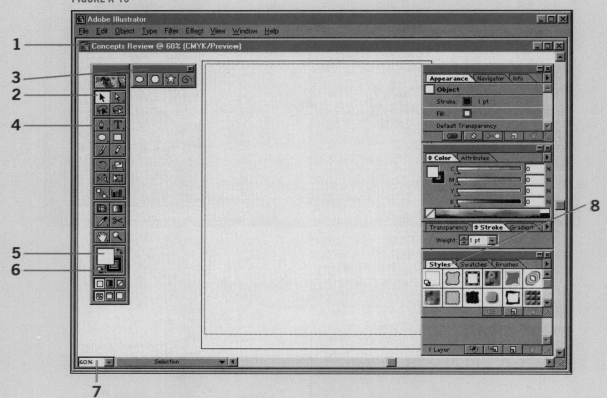

Match each term with the statement that describes it.

9. **Palettes**
10. **Artboard**
11. **Vector graphics**
12. **Bitmap graphics**
13. **Scratch area**

a. The area outside the artboard where you can store objects before placing them on the artboard

b. Graphics that are composed of pixels, small squares used to display a digital image on the rectangular grid of a computer screen

c. Windows that contain features for modifying and manipulating Illustrator objects

d. Mathematically calculated objects that are composed of anchor points and straight or curved line segments

e. The area surrounded by a solid line in the work area, where you create your work

14. Which palette contains patterns and gradients?
- **a.** Toolbox
- **b.** Swatches
- **c.** Fill box
- **d.** Color

15. What do you click to create a floating toolbar?
- **a.** The title bar
- **b.** A palette
- **c.** A tearoff tab
- **d.** The toolbox

16. Which key toggles the Fill and Stroke icons on the toolbox?
- **a.** [F]
- **b.** [T]
- **c.** [X]
- **d.** [S]

17. You need to have your illustration completely inside of the _____ for it to print.
- **a.** work area
- **b.** artboard
- **c.** imageable area
- **d.** scratch area

▶ Skills Review

1. Start Illustrator and view the Illustrator window.
- **a.** Start Illustrator using the Start menu (Win) or by double-clicking the Adobe Illustrator icon (Mac).
- **b.** Click File on the menu bar, then click New.
- **c.** Name the file *Shapes* in the New Document dialog box.
- **d.** Click OK.
- **e.** If you do not see the Swatches palette, click Window on the menu bar, then click Show Swatches.
- **f.** If you do not see the Stroke palette, click Window on the menu bar, then click Show Stroke.
- **g.** Locate the artboard, the scratch area, and the imageable area.
- **h.** Click Edit on the menu bar, point to Preferences, then click Units & Undo.
- **i.** Change the Minimum Undo Levels to **15**, then click OK.
- **j.** Click the status bar, then click Date and Time.
- **k.** Press and hold the mouse button over the Ellipse Tool. When the hidden toolbar appears, drag the pointer over the tearoff tab, then release the mouse button to tear off a Shape toolbar.
- **l.** Create a shape toolbar from the Rectangle Tool.
- **m.** Drag the two new toolbars to the top of the artboard.
- **n.** Make sure that the Fill icon is activated (on top of the Stroke icon) by pressing [X], if necessary.
- **o.** Choose a new fill color on the Swatches palette.

2. Create basic shapes and enter text.
- **a.** Create a circle by pressing and holding [Shift] as you draw with the Ellipse Tool. (Since you will need room on your page for more shapes, don't make the circle too large.)

b. Create an ellipse by drawing with the Ellipse Tool, without holding [Shift].

c. Create a square by holding down [Shift] as you draw with the Rectangle Tool.

d. Press [Ctrl] (Win) or [Command] (Mac) to switch to the Selection Tool.

e. While in the Selection Tool mode, move all of the shapes to the top of the artboard so that they are next to each other in a horizontal row.

f. Release [Ctrl] (Win) or [Command] (Mac). Your pointer will return to the Rectangle Tool mode.

g. Create a star with five points, and move it to a new row underneath the first row of shapes. Leave about 1" between the two rows of shapes.

h. Create a spiral, and place it next to the star.

i. Create a triangle by clicking the Polygon Tool, then clicking the artboard to change the number of sides to 3 in the Polygon dialog box.

j. Place the triangle next to the spiral.

k. Click Type on the menu bar, point to Size, then click 24 pt.

l. Click the Type Tool on the toolbox.

m. Create a text label that says circle, then use the Selection Tool to drag it underneath the circle.

n. Create a text label that says ellipse, then use the Selection Tool to drag it underneath the ellipse.

o. Create a text label that says square, then use the Selection Tool to drag it underneath the square.

p. Create a text label that says star, then use the Selection Tool to drag it underneath the star.

q. Create a text label that says spiral, then use the Selection Tool to drag it underneath the spiral.

r. Create a text label that says triangle, then use the Selection Tool to drag it underneath the triangle.

s. Create a text label with your first and last name, then use the Selection Tool to drag it to the lower-left corner of the artboard.

3. Apply colors, patterns, and styles to objects.

a. Click the Selection Tool on the toolbox, then click the circle.

b. Make sure that the Fill icon is in front of the Stroke icon on the toolbox, then click Red on the Swatches palette.

c. Press [X], then click Black on the Swatches palette to change the stroke to Black.

d. Increase the stroke weight to 3 pt on the Stroke palette.

e. Click the ellipse, then fill the ellipse with Azure and apply a 4 pt, Black stroke to it.

f. Click the square, press [X], then click the Red Tablecloth pattern on the Swatches palette.

g. Apply a 5 pt, 60% Black stroke to the square.

h. Click the star, click the Styles tab to activate the Styles palette, then click the Bizzaro style. Style names can be seen if you place your pointer on top of each style in the Styles palette.

i. Click the spiral, click the Eyedropper Tool, then click the circle to apply the same formatting to the spiral.

j. Click the Selection Tool.

k. Click the triangle, click the Eyedropper Tool, then click the star to apply the same formatting to the triangle.

4. Save the Shapes document.

a. Click File on the menu bar, then click Save.

b. Navigate to the drive where you store your project files. This book assumes your Project Disk is in Drive A. Substitute the correct drive if this is not the case. See your instructor or technical support person for assistance

c. Click Save.
The Illustrator Native Format Options dialog box opens.

d. Save your document in Illustrator 9.0.format.

e. Click OK.

5. Use Illustrator Help.
   a. Click Help on the menu bar, then click Illustrator Help.
   b. Click the Index button.
   c. Click the letter S.
   d. Scroll down through the list of topics until you see styles 1, 2.
   e. Click the 2.
   f. Read about Using styles.
   g. Click File on the menu bar, then click Close or Quit.

6. Print your document and exit Illustrator.
   a. Click File on the menu bar, then click Print.
   b. Make sure 1 is selected in the Copies text box or the Number of Copies spin box, depending on your Print dialog box.
   c. Click OK or Print, depending on your Print dialog box.
   d. Click File on the menu bar, then click Exit (Win) or Quit (Mac).

▶ Independent Challenges

1. You work at a local library as the software librarian. Your job is to learn everything you can about software so that you can make recommendations to patrons who use the computer resource room. Today you are going to find out about Illustrator. You have been asked whether it can be used to create graphics for the Web.
   To complete this independent challenge:

   a. Start Illustrator.
   b. Click Help on the menu bar, then click Illustrator Help.
   c. Click Looking at the Work Area in the Contents list.
   d. Click Toolbox Overview (1 of 5).
   e. Read through the featured tools.
   f. Click Looking at the Work Area again to return to the list of topics.
   g. Click the remaining Toolbox Overview items (2 of 5, 3 of 5, etc.).
   h. Click File on the menu bar, then click Close or Quit.

2. You are a designer for a large clock manufacturer. You have been asked to design a contemporary clock face for a child's room clock.
   To complete this independent challenge:

FIGURE A-19

   a. Start Illustrator.
   b. Click File on the menu bar, then click New.
   c. Name the file *Clock*, then click OK.
   d. Click the Fill icon on the toolbox, then click None on the Swatches palette.
   e. Click the Stroke icon on the toolbox, then click Black on the Swatches palette.
   f. Click the Ellipse Tool.
   g. Press and hold [Shift] while you drag the Ellipse Tool to create a perfect circle.
   h. Increase the stroke weight of the circle to 20 pt.
   i. Click the Selection Tool, and then click the artboard to deselect the circle.
   j. Change the Fill icon to Black and the Stroke icon to None on the toolbox.
   k. Create a text object that says **12**.
   l. Click the Selection Tool to select the text object.
   m. Choose a typeface that you like for the number 12.

Illustrator 9.0

n. Change the type size to 21 pt.

o. Choose a new fill color for the number 12; make sure the Fill icon is in the front of the Stroke icon.

p. Drag 12 on top of the clock face.

q. Create text objects for each hour (1, 2, 3, 4, 5, 6, 7, 8, 9, 10, and 11). After you create a number, drag it to its approximate position on the clock.

r. Using the Rectangle Tool, create a thin rectangle for the minute hand of the clock. Make it point to 12:00.

s. Using the Rectangle Tool again, create a thin rectangle for the hour hand of the clock. Make it point to 3:00.

t. Fill the two thin rectangles with new colors.

u. Create a text object with your first and last names, then place it in the lower-left corner of the artboard.

v. Save the clock document on the drive where you store your project files.

w. Print one copy of the Clock document.

x. Exit (Win) or Quit (Mac) Illustrator.

3. You work as a graphic designer specializing in symbols and icons. The highway department in your area has contacted you for some help with designing a new highway sign that reads, "School Zone." It wants the sign to be very simple and to have bold type.

To complete this independent challenge:

FIGURE A-20

a. Start Illustrator.

b. Click File on the menu bar, then click New.

c. Name the file *Sign*, then click OK.

d. Right-click (Win) or [Control] click (Mac) the Zoom text box, then click 100%.

e. Create a tearoff toolbar from the Ellipse Tool.

f. Click the Polygon Tool, then click the artboard.

g. Click the spin box up arrow until you see 7.

h. Click OK.

i. Fill the polygon with Yellow.

j. Choose a 10-pt Black stroke for the polygon.

k. Create a text object with the typeface of your choice. Choose a bold typeface.

l. Type **School**, press [Enter] (Win) or [Return] (Mac), then type **Zone**.

m. Change the type size to 14 pt.

n. Change the text color to Black. Make sure that the text does not have a stroke.

o. Place the text object on top of the polygon.

p. Select the text object with the Selection Tool.

q. Click the Type menu, then click Paragraph. Click the second icon (Align Center) on the Paragraph palette to center the text. You may need to move the text into place again.

r. Create a text object with your first and last names, then place it in the lower-left corner of the artboard.

s. Save the Sign document on the drive where you store your Project files.

t. Exit (Win) or Quit (Mac) Illustrator.

4. You work for a large bookstore chain as a graphic designer. Your boss has asked you to make some simple changes to the company's Web site. She does not like the detailed and ornate style of the current buttons. She would like you to change the buttons into regular or rounded rectangles containing text labels.

To complete this independent challenge:

a. Connect to the Internet and go to http://www.course.com
b. Navigate to the page for this book, then click the link for the Student Online Companion.
c. Click the links for this unit.
d. Notice the types of buttons that these sites use for Books, Bestsellers, Videos, Music, Electronics and Software, and other categories. Some are rectangles, and some are rounded rectangles that look like traditional folder tabs.
e. Exit (Win) or Quit (Mac) your browser.
f. Start Illustrator.
g. Click File on the menu bar, then click New.
h. Name the file *Buttons,* then click OK.
i. Create a rectangle for your first button.
j. Choose a fill and stroke color for the rectangle.
k. Press and hold down [Alt] (Win) or [Option] (Mac) while dragging the rectangle to the right to duplicate it. Repeat this step until you have three rectangles.
l. Move the rectangles next to one another so that they appear in a horizontal row.
m. Create three text labels that say **Books**, **CDs**, and **Videos** to be placed inside each rectangle as shown in Figure A-21. You may have to increase or decrease the type size, depending on the size of your rectangles.
n. Choose a fill color for the text labels.
o. Click the Type Tool, then type your name in the lower-left corner of the artboard.
p. Save the Buttons document on the drive where you store your project files.
q. Print one copy of Buttons and Exit (Win) or Quit (Mac) Illustrator.

FIGURE A-21

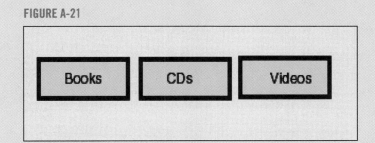

► Visual Workshop

Use the Type Tool, the Rounded Rectangle Tool, and the Star Tool to create three buttons that look like those in Figure A-22. Save your document as *Bookstore*, print one copy of it, then Exit (Win) or Quit (Mac) Illustrator.

FIGURE A-22

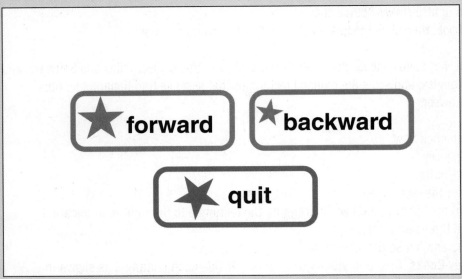

Creating
an Illustration

Objectives

► **Plan your illustration**
► **Work with palettes**
► **Draw with the Paintbrush Tool**
► **Scale objects**
► **Distort an object**
► **Choose colors from the Web Swatch library**
► **Use the Transform palette**
► **Use the Save for Web feature**

The vast array of options that Illustrator tools, palettes, and preferences provide enables you to create illustrations exactly as you envision them. For example, not only can you choose from a wide variety of paintbrush styles, but you can also edit the brush styles so that their strokes appear exactly as desired. If you can't find a color that you need in the Swatches palette, you can make your own colors or choose from several other Swatch libraries. Objects can be scaled, rotated, and even distorted using specific measurements. Finally, when you are finished with your illustration, you can export it in many different file formats for use in other software applications. ✐ Bill has been asked to create a sun and some clouds that will be used as a weather update logo on the station's Web site. He has looked at some other weather graphics on the Internet and is ready to start his project.

Illustrator 9.0

Planning Your Illustration

All projects—whether created on a computer or by hand—will benefit from a little planning. Planning steps, such as creating a list of needed materials, drawing a timeline for your project, or sketching your ideas on paper first, can help you identify potential issues that can be avoided or resolved before you get too far into your work. Figure B-1 is an example of an illustration that was first sketched on paper, then re-created in Illustrator. Before working in Illustrator, you should take a few moments to check preference settings, make sure you can see the rulers and the palettes you will need, and think about colors and fonts that you want to use for your document. ▰▰▰ Bill thinks about his project and puts some notes down on paper. He also takes time to adjust his Illustrator window and to change a few preference settings.

1. Start Illustrator, if necessary

2. Click **Edit** on the menu bar, point to **Preferences**, then click **Units and Undo**
   The General list arrow displays the current unit of measure that is used for Illustrator rulers, dialog boxes, and palettes. You can choose from points, picas, inches, millimeters, centimeters or pixels.

3. Click the **General list arrow**, then click **Inches**

QuickTip

The maximum number of undo levels is 200; however, setting this preference too high may use up computer memory allocated to run Illustrator.

4. Double-click the number in the **Minimum Undo Levels** field to highlight it, enter **20**, then click **OK**
   You are now able to undo your last 20 actions performed in Illustrator.

5. Click **File** on the menu bar, then click **New**

6. Name the document **Weather**, then click **OK**
   Notice the artboard measurements are displayed in inches.

7. Click **View** on the menu bar, then click **Show Rulers**
   Notice the rulers placed at the top and the left side of the Illustrator window.

8. Click **View** on the menu bar, then click **Hide Bounding Box**
   If this menu item says "Show Bounding Box", do not select it. The bounding box is useful for resizing objects but it can also be distracting. Read more about the bounding box in the Clues to Use in this lesson.

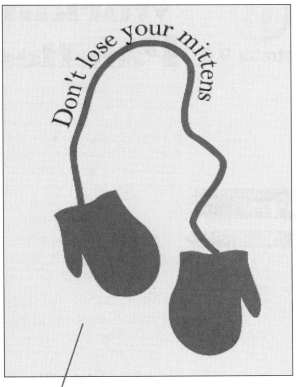

Sketch drawn on
paper

Illustration created
in Illustrator

CLUES TO USE

The bounding box

The **bounding box** is a box that surrounds an object when it is selected. The bounding box contains eight small white squares called selection handles. **Selection handles**, which are found on all four corners of the box and at the horizontal and vertical centers of the box's sides, can be dragged to resize the object. Because the bounding box may sometimes cover up anchor points or just be distracting, and because Illustrator offers many other ways to resize objects, you may sometimes want to turn the feature off. You can do so using the View menu.

Working with Palettes

Illustrator includes 22 palettes that contain features for modifying and manipulating Illustrator objects. Palettes are used for many tasks, including mixing new colors, choosing brush styles, and resizing objects. Palettes are usually grouped with one or two other palettes, as shown in Figure B-2, but they can easily be separated and displayed as single palettes as well. All palettes have tabs that display their names. Palettes also have option menus, which are displayed when you click the Show Options arrow ▶ as shown in Figure B-2, which offer additional options. ✎ Bill takes a few minutes to organize the palettes he will need to start his project.

Steps

Trouble?

If you do not see the Styles palette, click Window on the menu bar, then click Show Styles.

1. **Locate the Styles palette on the artboard**
   The Styles palette is grouped with the Swatches and Brushes palettes, unless previous users have separated them.

2. **While pressing and holding the mouse button on the Styles tab, drag it to a new location, as shown in Figure B-3**
   You will not have to perform this step if your Styles palette is already separated. You can also drag a palette on top of another palette window to group the two palettes together.

3. **Click the Close button ✖ (Win) or ▣ (Mac) on all palettes except the Swatches and Brushes palettes**

QuickTip

Press [Tab] to temporarily hide all of the palettes that are currently open. Press [Tab] again to show all of the palettes that are currently open. Press [Shift] [Tab] to hide and show all of the palettes that are currently open, without hiding the toolbox.

4. **Click Window on the menu bar, then click Show Transform**

5. **Drag the Transform palette to the right side of the Illustrator window**
   Your screen should look like Figure B-4

6. **Click the Brushes tab, then click the Swatches tab**
   When you click a palette tab, that palette becomes active.

7. **Click the Minimize button ▣ in the upper-right corner of the Transform palette to collapse the palette, then click the Maximize button ▣ to expand it**

8. **Click the Show Options arrow ▶ on the Transform palette to view its menu, then release the mouse button**

9. **Close any floating toolbars that may have been created from the toolbox in an earlier lesson**

FIGURE B-2: Palettes

The Styles, Swatches, and Brushes name tabs

Show Options arrow

Palette menu

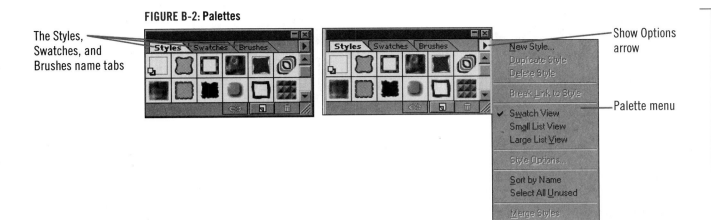

FIGURE B-3: Separating palettes

The Styles palette separated from the Swatches and Brushes palettes

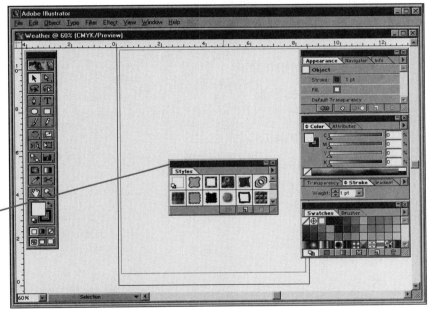

FIGURE B-4: Palettes arranged in the Illustrator window

Swatches tab

Brushes tab

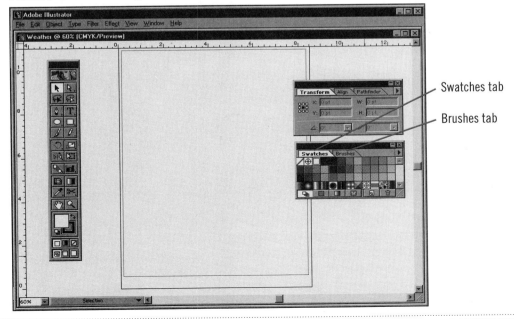

Drawing with the Paintbrush Tool

Illustrator has four paintbrush categories: Calligraphic, Scatter, Art, and Pattern. Each category includes several styles. For example, the Scatter brushes include handprints, pushpins, and grape leaves, whereas the Calligraphic brushes have unique angles, roundnesses, and diameters. Additional brush libraries exist for each category. Brush libraries consist of eight more palettes from which you can choose brush styles. You can import additional brush libraries from the Illustrator Extras folder, found on the Illustrator 9.0 installation CD. Bill uses Calligraphic brushes to create some puffy clouds.

1. Click the **Default fill and stroke icon** ⬛ to make sure that the fill is set to **White** and the stroke is set to **Black**, if necessary
   Each time you click the Fill or Stroke icon, the Color palette opens.

2. Click the **Paintbrush Tool** 🖌 on the toolbox

3. Click the **Brushes tab** on the Swatches palette to view the brush styles
   When your pointer is over the artboard or the scratch area, it turns into 🖌ₓ.

4. Click the **third brush style** in the first row of the Brushes palette called **12 pt Oval**
   See Figure B-5. The first row of brushes consists of the Calligraphic brushes, which draw like traditional calligraphy pens.

5. Position the cursor over the artboard. Press and hold the mouse button, then drag 🖌ₓ to create a cloud as shown in Figure B-6
   If you do not like your cloud, press [Ctrl] [Z] (Win) or [Command] [Z] (Mac) to undo your last step. You can also press [Delete] (Win) or [delete] (Mac) on the keyboard to delete the selected object.

6. Create another cloud underneath the first cloud, as shown in Figure B-7

7. Click the **Swatches tab** on the Swatches palette to make it the active palette
   You will not have to perform this step if your Swatches palette and Brushes palette are already separated.

8. Click **File** on the Menu bar, then click **Save**

9. Navigate to the drive where you store your project files, then click **Save**
   An Illustrator Format Options box will appear.

10. Click **OK** to accept default options.

QuickTip

When you create a brush stroke with the Paintbrush Tool, and draw a second brush stroke that touches the first brush stroke, the original one conforms to the direction of the second one, leaving you with just one stroke. To turn this feature off, double-click the Paintbrush Tool, then click Edit Selected Paths to remove the check mark.

Trouble?

Printing, saving, and exporting are disabled in the Illustrator Tryout! software. To learn more about the Tryout! software that accompanies this book, see the Read This Before You Begin page.

Brush Libraries

Illustrator has seven additional brush libraries including Animal, Arrow, Artistic, Border, Calligraphic, Flower, and Object samples. Brush Libraries are available under the Window menu and look very much like the default Brushes palette. Each time you use a brush style from one of the brush libraries, that style is added to the default Brushes palette. The Artistic brush samples include styles that imitate traditional mediums for painting and drawing such as watercolor, chalk, charcoal, and ink.

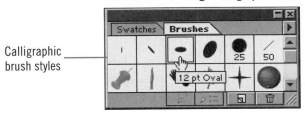

FIGURE B-5: Choosing a Calligraphic brush style

Calligraphic brush styles

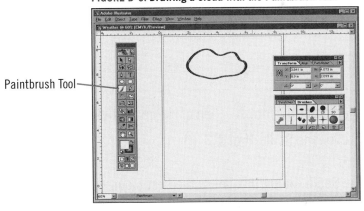

FIGURE B-6: Drawing a cloud with the Paintbrush Tool

Paintbrush Tool

FIGURE B-7: Two clouds

CLUES TO USE

Setting Calligraphic brush options

Calligraphic brushes have three settings: the angle, the roundness, and the diameter. To change any or all of these settings, double-click the brush style that you want to change on the Brushes palette. The Brush Options dialog box opens. You can modify the angle of a calligraphy brush by dragging the picture in the Brush Shape Editor window. You can change the percentage of roundness of the brush by dragging one of the black circles in the Brush Shape Editor window. Drag the Diameter width slider to alter the diameter of the brush. Each setting can be either fixed or random. Random settings allow you to choose a variation. For example, a random roundness of 50% with a 10% variation will make brush strokes with a minimum of 40% roundness and a maximum of 60% roundness.

FIGURE B-8: Setting Calligraphic brush options

Brush name

Preview of new brush style

Brush shape editor window

Preview of variations of new brush style

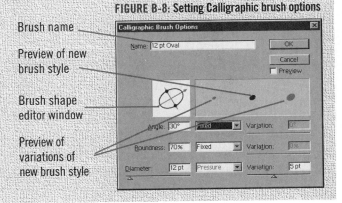

Scaling Objects

Illustrator 9.0

When you create an Illustrator object, it does not matter where the image appears on the artboard or how large or small it is, because you can adjust the object to your liking using the transformation tools. The transformation tools include the Move, Scale, Rotate, Reflect, Shear, and Free Rotate Tools. You can transform an object by using the transformation tools on the toolbox, the Transform palette, or the Transform menu. ![brush] Bill scales the clouds so that they are a bit smaller, then moves them next to each other on the artboard.

Steps

1. Click the **Selection Tool** ![arrow], then click the **first cloud** to select it

QuickTip

Whenever you scale an object using the Scale dialog box, the object is scaled from its center point.

2. Double-click the **Scale Tool** ![icon]
   The Scale dialog box opens.

3. Drag the **Scale dialog box** below the first cloud by dragging the blue title area (Win) or the gray title bar (Mac) of the Scale dialog box, so that it is positioned as shown in Figure B-9

4. Click the **Preview check box** on the Scale dialog box to select it, as shown in Figure B-9

5. Type **75** in the **Scale field**, then press **[Tab]**
   Pressing [Tab] moves the cursor to the next available field and registers the number you entered. Notice that the Scale dialog box also gives you the option of scaling the thickness (weight) of the stroke to the same percentage as used with the scaled object. The Scale dialog box also gives you the option of copying the item that you are scaling. For example, if you scale a circle 50% and copy it simultaneously, you will end up with two circles: the original and a copy of it that is 50% smaller.

Trouble?

If you do not see the cloud become smaller, the cursor is still in the Scale text field. Press [Tab] to move the cursor to the next available text field and to register the number you entered.

6. Click **OK** to close the Scale dialog box
   Notice that your pointer is still in the Scale tool mode ┼ . Objects can be scaled manually using ┼ . To manually scale objects proportionately, however, you must press and hold [Shift] while you drag ┼ .

7. Click ![arrow], click the **second cloud** to select it, then scale it **75%**

8. Move the two clouds next to each other using ![arrow] as shown in Figure B-10, then save your work

Using the Transform Again command

When you transform an object using any of the five transformation tools, you can repeat the last transformation command by using the Transform Again command. For example, you can scale an object 50% and then scale it 50% again by pressing [Ctrl] [D] (Win) or [Command] [D] (Mac). Each time you press [Ctrl] [D] (Win) or [Command] [D] (Mac), you will scale the object down another 50%. This command is useful when you are unsure how much you want to transform an object. For example, if you want to rotate an object slightly, you can start by rotating it 1°, then use the Transform Again command so that you can observe its change in increments, stopping when you are satisfied with the object's appearance.

FIGURE B-9: Scaling an object using the Scale dialog box

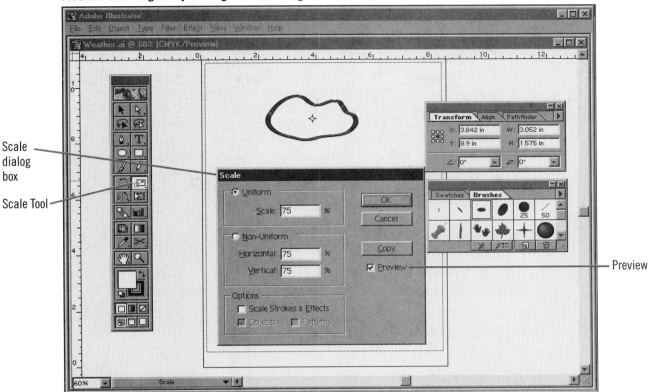

Scale dialog box

Scale Tool

Preview

FIGURE B-10: Two clouds

Illustrator 9.0

Distorting an Object

Illustrator filters are special features that are used to alter the appearance of Illustrator objects. For example, filters can blend the colors of two or more objects, distort objects, or apply drop shadows to objects. Illustrator objects consist of line segments, or paths, and anchor points. A path can be opened or closed. The first and last points of an open path are called endpoints. Anchor points are tiny squares that represent the points of a line segment in a vector object. The **Distort filters** are a category of Illustrator filters that move the original location of an object's anchor points to new locations, thereby distorting the object. The results that are possible when using filters would be very difficult to achieve using only the drawing tools. Indeed, filters can dramatically change the appearance of simple objects and add sophistication to your illustration. Bill adds new anchor points to a circle and then uses the Punk & Bloat Distort feature to convert it to a sun with many rays.

Steps

1. Click the **Ellipse Tool** ⬭ on the toolbox
   Your pointer becomes ⊹ .

2. Press and hold [**Shift**] while you drag ⊹ to create a perfect circle, as shown in Figure B-11
   The circle has the same paintbrush style as the clouds.

3. Click the **Show Options arrow** ▶ on the Brushes palette, then click **Remove Brush Stroke**
   The stroke on the circle changes to a 1 point Black stroke

QuickTip

Without adding extra anchor points to the circle, the sunburst would have had only four rays.

4. Click **Object** on the menu bar, point to **Path**, then click **Add Anchor Points**
   New anchor points are placed on the circle in between the four original anchor points.

5. Repeat Step 4 to add eight more anchor points to the circle
   Your screen should resemble Figure B-12.

Trouble?

If all of your options are unavailable, then you selected the second Distort menu item instead of the first. The second Distort menu item is used with bitmap images.

6. Click **Filter** on the menu bar, point to the first **Distort command** on the menu, then click **Punk & Bloat**
   The Punk & Bloat dialog box opens. Drag the Punk & Bloat dialog box up or down to see more of your circle, if necessary.

7. Drag the **triangle slider** to the left until you reach **−35**, then click the **Preview button** on the Punk & Bloat dialog box, as shown in Figure B-13
   You can also type -35 in the Punk & Bloat dialog box if you have trouble dragging the triangle slider to exactly -35.

8. Click **OK** to close the Punk & Bloat dialog box and save your work

FIGURE B-11: Creating a perfect circle

FIGURE B-12: Adding anchor points to the circle

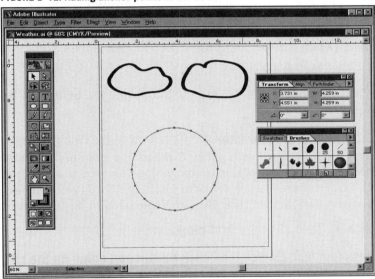

FIGURE B-13: Distorting an object using the Punk & Bloat filter

Punk & Bloat
dialog box

Preview

Circle with −35%
punk applied

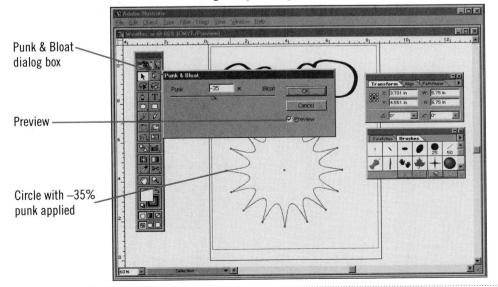

Choosing Colors from the Web Swatch Library

In addition to the colors found on the Swatches palette, Illustrator has 20 Swatch libraries from which you can choose. Most of the Swatch libraries contain colors created by manufacturers with which you may be familiar, such as Pantone, Trumatch, and Focoltone. These colors are specifically used for printed materials. If you plan to design an illustration for the Web, however, you would probably want to use a color from the Web Swatch library, which is a palette of 216 colors that will look the same in your illustrations whether they are being viewed in a browser on a Macintosh or Windows computer. Bill chooses two colors from the Web swatches and applies them to the clouds and the sunburst.

Steps

1. Click **Window** on the menu bar, point to **Swatch Libraries**, then click **Web**; when the Web palette appears, drag it to the right if it is hiding part of the sunburst

2. Press **[X]** on the keyboard until the Fill icon appears in front of the Stroke icon on the toolbox, if necessary

3. Select the **sunburst**, if necessary, by clicking the **Selection Tool** , then clicking the sunburst

4. Click the **fourth color chip** in the first row of the Web palette, as shown in Figure B-14
   The sunburst is filled with yellow. If the sunburst did not fill with yellow, it may be that the Stroke icon is the active icon on the toolbox, and you made the stroke yellow instead of the fill. Change the stroke color back to Black, click the Fill icon to bring it in front of the Stroke icon or press [X], then click the fourth color chip in the first row of the Web palette.

5. Click , then click the **first cloud** on the left

6. Press and hold **[Shift]**, then click the **second cloud on the right** to select both clouds

7. Press **[X]** on the keyboard to bring the Stroke icon in front of the Fill icon on the toolbox

8. Scroll through the **Web palette** and choose any light blue swatch, as shown in Figure B-15

9. Save your work

Trouble?

If you click the sunburst with the Ellipse Tool, the Ellipse dialog box will appear. Click Cancel, click , then click the sunburst again.

FIGURE B-14: Choosing a Web swatch

Web palette

Web color applied
to sunburst

FIGURE B-15: Applying a stroke color to the clouds

Web color applied
to stroke of clouds

Web palette

Illustrator 9.0

Illustrator 9.0

Using the Transform Palette

The Transform palette displays the location, width, height, rotation angle, and shear angle of a selected object. You can change any of an object's features by changing the numbers in the Transform palette. To make a shape with a specific width and height, for example, you might first create the shape, then change the width and height fields in the Transform palette. Bill has been asked to make the weather graphics fairly small because they will be placed on a Web page with many other news topics. He uses the Transform palette to reduce the size of his graphics.

Steps

1. Click the artboard to deselect the clouds

2. Click one of the clouds with the **Selection Tool**

3. Click once in the **X field** on the Transform palette to place the cursor inside Transform palette
   The Transform palette is shown in Figure B-16.

> **Trouble?**
>
> If the Transform palette is displaying measurements in points (pt) instead of inches (in), click File on the menu bar, point to Preferences, then click Units and Undo. Click the General list arrow, then click Inches. Click OK and repeat Step 3.

4. Press **[Tab]** twice to highlight the **Width (W) field**, then type **2 in**

5. Press **[Tab]** once to highlight the **Height (H) field**, then type **1 in**
   Once your cursor is placed in a palette, pressing [Tab] will move the cursor to the next available field that can be changed. Pressing [Shift] [Tab] will move the cursor backward through all of the available fields.

6. Press **[Enter]** (Win) or **[Return]** (Mac) to register the new width and height

7. Select the other cloud and change its width to **2 in** and its height to **1 in**
   The final numbers in the Transform palette may be slightly off—for example, 1.994 instead of 2 inches as shown in Figure B-16.

8. Select the **sunburst** and change both its width and height to **2 in**, then save your work

ILLUSTRATOR B-14 CREATING AN ILLUSTRATION

FIGURE B-16: Changing the width and height of an object

Transform palette

Width field

Height field

X coordinate

Y coordinate

Reference points

X and Y Coordinates

The **X and Y coordinates** of an object indicate the object's horizontal (X) and vertical (Y) locations on the artboard. These numbers, which appear in the Transform palette, represent the horizontal and vertical distance from the bottom-left corner of the artboard. The current X and Y coordinates also depend on the specified reference point. Nine reference points are listed to the left of the X and Y fields on the Transform palette. **Reference points** are those points of a selected object that represent the four corners of the object's bounding box, the horizontal and vertical centers of the bounding box, and the center point of the bounding box. (You do not need to have the bounding box option turned on to view any of the reference point coordinates.) In Figure B-16, the X and Y coordinates displayed refer to the center reference point of the selected cloud. To see other reference points for the selected cloud, you can simply click a

new reference point on the Transform palette. You can use these reference points to determine the exact location of an object. For example, if you want to know the location of the rectangle's upper-right corner (relative to the lower-left corner of the artboard,) you would select the rectangle, click the upper-right reference point on the Transform palette, and the X and Y fields would give you the horizontal and vertical location of the rectangle's upper-right corner. X and Y coordinates are also useful for placing objects on the artboard with accuracy. For example, if you want to position the center of a square on the center of an 8.5" by 11" artboard, you can select the square, make sure the center reference point is selected on the Transform palette, and type 4.25 in the X field and 5.5 in the Y field. When you press Enter (Win) or Return (Mac), the object will move to the new location.

Using the Save for Web Feature

Illustrations are often placed in other software programs and media such as the Web, multimedia presentations, and animated sequences. The Save for Web feature saves your illustration as a GIF file, which is a special format required by Web design software programs and HTML code. Although there are other file formats that Web browsers recognize, such as PNG and JPEG, the GIF format is the best choice for vector art and flat areas of color. It uses a lossy compression system, meaning that some information in the file is eliminated to ensure faster download times from Web sites. The Save for Web dialog box contains options that offer tradeoffs between image quality and download time. Bill positions the sun and clouds on the artboard, and then uses the Save for Web feature to prepare his file for the Web Design Department.

Steps

1. Drag the **second cloud** so that it overlaps the first cloud

2. Drag the **sunburst** so that it slightly overlaps both clouds, as shown in Figure B-17

3. Click **File** on the menu bar, then click **Save for Web**
   The Save for Web dialog box opens as shown in Figure B-18.

4. Click the **Optimized** tab, if necessary
   You will see a preview of your illustration, information about your file below it, and various setting on the right side of the window. You have been told by the Web Design department to leave the default settings alone in this dialog box.

5. Click **OK**
   The Save Optimized As dialog box opens. Notice the .gif file extension has been added to the filename.

6. Navigate to the drive and folder where you store your project files, then click **Save**
   Your original Illustrator document remains open.

7. Click **File** on the menu bar, then click **Exit** (Win) or **Quit** (Mac) Illustrator, saving changes to the Weather document

FIGURE B-17: Finished illustration

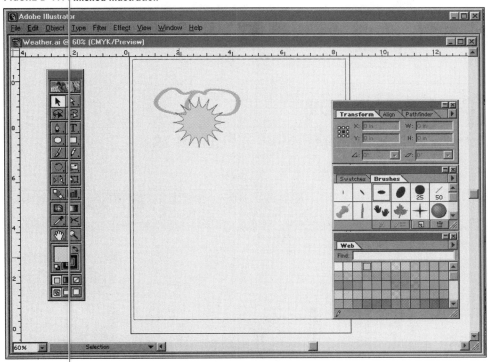

FIGURE B-18: Save for Web dialog box

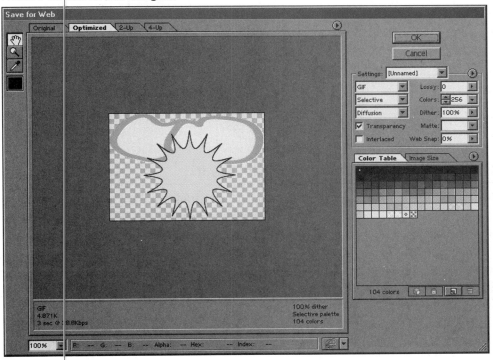

Practice

▶ Concepts Review

Label the Illustrator window elements shown in Figure B-19.

FIGURE B-19

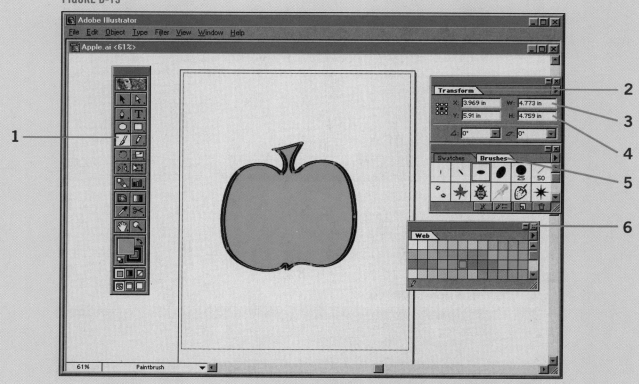

Match each term with the statement that describes it.

7. **Distort filter**
8. **Transformation tools**
9. **Web colors**
10. **Bounding box**
11. **X and Y coordinates**
12. **Calligraphic brushes**

a. Brushes that draw like traditional calligraphy pens
b. Colors that display correctly on both Macintosh and Windows computers
c. The horizontal and vertical location of an object on the artboard
d. A filter that moves the original location of an object's anchor points
e. The Move, Scale, Rotate, Reflect, Shear, and Free Rotate Tools
f. A box containing eight selection handles that surround a selected object

Select the best answer from the list of choices.

13. You can have a maximum of _____ undo levels in Illustrator.
  a. 100
  b. 50
  c. 200
  d. 300

14. Pressing _____ will temporarily hide and show all open palettes.
  a. [Ctrl]
  b. [Shift]
  c. [Tab]
  d. [Esc]

15. Punk & Bloat is an example of a:
  a. Distort palette.
  b. file format.
  c. Distort filter.
  d. transformation tool.

▶ Skills Review

Make sure that you have extra blank floppy disks on hand so that if you run out of room on your Project Disks while completing the Skills Review or Independent Challenges, you will have a place to save your file.

1. Plan your illustration.
  a. Start Illustrator.
  b. Click File on the menu bar, then click New.
  c. Name the file *Flower*, then click OK.
  d. Click View on the menu bar, then click Show Rulers.
  e. Click Edit on the menu bar, point to Preferences, then click Units & Undo.
  f. Make sure the General Unit of measure is set to Inches.
  g. Set the Minimum Undo Levels to 20, if necessary.
  h. Click OK to close the Preferences dialog box.
  i. Click View on the menu bar, then click Hide Bounding Box. (If the menu item reads "Show Bounding Box," do not select it.)

2. Set your palettes.
  a. Show the Transform palette, if necessary.
  b. Show the Swatches palette.
  c. Separate the Swatches palette from the Brushes palette, and the Styles palette, if necessary.
  d. Close any other palettes you may have open, keeping the Swatches, Brushes and Transform palettes, and the toolbox open.

3. **Draw with the Paintbrush Tool.**
   a. Change the Fill icon on the toolbox to None.
   b. Change the Stroke icon on the toolbox to 75% Violet.
   c. Click the Paintbrush Tool on the toolbox.
   d. Click the fourth brush style called 20 pt. Oval, in the first row of the Brushes palette.
   e. Draw a circle with the paintbrush (it does not have to be perfect).
   f. Click the Selection Tool ⬉, then click the artboard to deselect the circle.
   g. Click the 75% Green swatch on the Swatches palette to change the stroke color to green.
   h. Click the Paintbrush Tool.
   i. Draw a line underneath the circle as if the circle were a flower and the green line were the flower's stem.
   j. Save your work.

4. **Scale objects.**
   a. Click ⬉, then click the edge of the purple circle to select it.
   b. Press and hold down [Shift] while clicking the green line to select it.
   c. Double-click the Scale Tool.
   d. Check the Preview check box.
   e. Scale the objects by 75%.
   f. Click OK.
   g. Click ⬉, then click the artboard to deselect the objects.
   h. Save your work.

5. **Distort an object.**
   a. Click the edge of the purple circle to select it.
   b. Click Object on the menu bar, point to Path, then click Add Anchor Points.
   c. Click Filter on the menu bar, point to Distort, then click Punk & Bloat.
   d. Drag the Punk & Bloat dialog box to a new location if it is blocking the purple circle.
   e. Check the Preview check box.
   f. Drag the triangle slider to approximately 35, then 45, then 55 to see the changes to the new flower.
   g. Keep the Bloat amount at 55%.
   h. Click OK.
   i. Click the flower stem to select it.
   j. Click Filter on the menu bar, point to Distort, then click Twirl.
   k. Type 10 in the Angle field.
   l. Click OK.
   m. Save your work.

6. **Choose colors from the Web Swatch library.**
   a. Click Window on the menu bar, point to Swatch Libraries, then click Web.
   b. Click the flower, (not the stem) to select it.
   c. Click one of the purple colors in the Web palette.
   d. Click the stem to select it.
   e. Click one of the green colors in the Web palette. You may have to scroll through the palette to see the greens.
   f. Save your work.

7. Use the Transform palette.

   a. Click the flower (not the stem) to select it.
   b. Increase the flower width amount in the Transform palette by 1". For example, if the width is currently 2.654, change it to 3.654.
   c. Place your name in the lower-left corner of the artboard.
   d. Save your work.
   e. Print one copy of *Flower*.

8. Use the Save for Web feature.

   a. Click File on the menu bar, then click Save for Web.
   b. Click the Optimized tab, if necessary.
   c. Click OK.
   d. Navigate to the place where you store your project files.
   e. Click Save.
   f. Click File on the menu bar, then Exit (Win) or Quit (Mac) Illustrator.

▶ Independent Challenges

1. You are a Web designer for an advertising agency. Your client, Rainbow Rugs, makes rugs for children's rooms using the colors of the rainbow. They are creating a new Web site and would like you to create a color palette containing the closest possible matches to traditional rainbow colors: red, orange, yellow, green, blue, and violet. They will use this palette each time they create new artwork for their Web site. You tell the client that you will make a color palette for them in Illustrator, and that you will use colors that will display correctly on all computer platforms.

To complete this independent challenge:

a. Start Illustrator.
b. Click File on the menu bar, then click New.
c. Name the file *Rainbow*, then click OK.
d. Click Window on the menu bar, point to Swatch Libraries, then click Web.
e. Click the Show Options arrow ▶ on the Web palette, then click Name View to view the Web colors in their name view.
f. Create six rectangles and fill them with six different colors from the Web palette. The colors should be the closest possible matches to the traditional rainbow colors: red, orange, yellow, green, blue, and violet.
g. Create text labels underneath each rectangle that display the rectangle color name. For example, FFFF00.
h. Place your name in the lower-left corner of the artboard.
i. Save the Rainbow file on the drive and folder where you store your project files.
j. Print one copy of Rainbow.
k. Click File on the menu bar, then click Exit (Win) or Quit (Mac) Illustrator.

Illustrator 9.0

2. You are a wedding cake decorator and plan to advertise in some upcoming issues of bridal magazines. You need to provide an illustration of one of your wedding cake designs.
  To complete this independent challenge:

a. Start Illustrator.

b. Click File on the menu bar, then click New.

c. Name the file *Cake*, then click OK.

d. Create three rounded rectangles in varying sizes, using the Rounded Rectangle Tool . (*Hint:* The Rounded Rectangle Tool is hidden underneath the Rectangle Tool.)

e. Stack the three rectangles as shown in Figure B-20. They represent three tiers of a wedding cake.

f. Use a combination of tools and palettes, such as the Ellipse Tool, the Paintbrush Tool, and the Scale Tool, the Swatches palette, and the Transform palette to create flowers, swirls, shapes, and decorations to be placed on the cake.

g. Keep in mind that you can use the artboard area to create your designs and scale them to be smaller if necessary.

h. Duplicate objects by pressing and holding [Alt] (Win) or [Option] (Mac) while dragging them.

i. Create a table for the cake to sit on using the Rectangle Tool.

j. Place your name in the lower-left corner of the artboard, then print one copy of Cake.

k. Save the Cake file on the drive and folder where you store your project files.

l. Exit (Win) or Quit (Mac) Illustrator, saving your changes.

FIGURE B-20

3. You work for the Human Resources Department of a large company. This department has been asked to coordinate fun learning activities for interested employees. The events will take place after work hours and will range from yoga to watercolor classes. A flyer is being created, and you have been assigned to create a graphic for the dart-throwing classes.
  To complete this independent challenge:

a. Start Illustrator.

b. Click File on the menu bar, then click New.

c. Name the file *Dartboard*, then click OK.

d. Create a large perfect circle by pressing and holding [Shift] as you draw the circle. The circle should be at least 6" wide. (*Hint:* Use the Transform palette if you need to adjust the size of the circle.)

e. The circle should have a 1-pt stroke of black, but the fill color can be any color you choose. (*Hint:* You can choose colors from any of the Swatch libraries, if you want.)

f. Double-click the Scale Tool. Scale the circle by 75% and copy it simultaneously. Make sure to press the Copy button instead of the OK button in the Scale dialog box.

g. Change the fill color of the second circle.

h. Press [Ctrl] [D] (Win) or [Command] [D] (Mac) to transform the image again. You will now have three circles. Change the fill color of the third circle.

i. Press [Ctrl] [D] (Win) or [Command] [D] (Mac) three more times, changing the fill colors each time. The last circle should have a black fill.

j. Place your name in the lower-left corner of the artboard.

k. Save the Dartboard file on the drive and folder where you store your project files.

l. Print one copy of Dartboard, then Exit (Win) or Quit (Mac) Illustrator, saving your changes.

4. You are an artist who has always used charcoal and paint on paper. You have a new computer and are interested in using your talent with illustration software. First, you decide to see if other artists are using illustration software for their art. Then you'll experiment with Illustrator.

To complete this independent challenge:

a. Connect to the Internet and go to http://www.course.com
b. Navigate to the page for this book, then click the link for the Student Online Companion.
c. Click the links for this unit.
d. Look at as many examples of artwork as possible. Think about the tools and palettes available in Illustrator that might provide similar results (Paintbrush Tool, Brush Libraries, Styles Palette).
e. Exit (Win) or Quit (Mac) your Web browser.
f. Start Illustrator, if necessary.
g. Click File on the menu bar, then click New.
h. Name the file *Art*, then click OK.
i. Double-click the Paintbrush Tool, then make sure Edit Selected Paths is not checked.
j. Click Window on the menu bar, point to Brush Libraries, then click Artistic Sample.
k. Thinking about the illustrations you just saw on the Internet, create a simple illustration of anything that inspires you. If you need an idea, try drawing a tree, a house, or a sailboat.
l. Use a variety of tools and brush libraries.
m. Place your name in the lower-left corner of the artboard.
n. Save the Art document on the drive and folder where you store your project files.
o. Print one copy of Art.
p. Exit (Win) or Quit (Mac) Illustrator.

Illustrator 9.0

► **Visual Workshop**

Use the tools and features that you have learned about in Illustrator to recreate the picture in Figure B-21. You may use different colors than the ones shown in the picture here. Place your name in the lower-left corner of the artboard. Save your document as *Garden*, print one copy of Garden, then Exit (Win) or Quit (Mac) Illustrator.

FIGURE B-21

Positioning
and Arranging Illustrator Objects

Objectives

- ► **Open and save an Illustrator document**
- ► **Create guides and snap objects to them**
- ► **Use the Move command**
- ► **Create new colors**
- ► **Align, distribute, and group objects**
- ► **Arrange the stacking order of objects**
- ► **Use the Zoom command**
- ► **Select part of a grouped object**

Illustrator offers many features that enable you to work with precision and accuracy. For example, you can set guides at specific points on the artboard, and then snap objects to them. You can move objects or copies of them using a specific horizontal and/or vertical measurements. You can align and group objects to ensure that they stay intact, and even edit one or more parts of a grouped object without ungrouping it. Illustrator also has a zoom feature that helps you to see and edit small objects. ✎ Bill's next project is to work on a five-day forecast graphic for the evening news. Some of the text and graphics have already been created for him. Bill's job is to finish the illustration. The final illustration will be imported into WHJY's video editing software program, then shown on the evening news.

Illustrator 9.0

Opening and Saving an Illustrator Document

If you plan to work on an Illustrator document that has already been created, you have the option of opening the existing file and making changes to it, or opening the file, saving it with a new name using the Save As command, and then making your changes to the new file. When you save a document with a new name, you are duplicating the original document, and changes that you make to the newly named document will not affect the original. Saving an existing document with a new name before making changes to it ensures that you will always be able to go back to the original document and start over if you do not like what you have done to the copy. Bill starts his work by opening the document that has been supplied to him and then saves it with a new name.

Steps

WIN

1. Start Illustrator, then insert your Project Disk in the appropriate drive
2. Click **File** on the menu bar, then click **Open**
   The Open dialog box opens, as shown in Figure C-1.
3. Click the **Look in list arrow**, then click the drive and folder where you store your project files
4. Click **AI C-1** in the Open dialog box, then click **Open**
   The AI C-1 document opens.
5. Click **File** on the menu bar, then click **Save As**
   The Save dialog box opens.

Trouble?

Some features are disabled in the Illustrator Tryout! software. See the Read This Before You Begin page for additional information.

6. Navigate to the drive or folder where you store your project files (if necessary), type **Forecast** in the File name text box, then click **Save**
   The first time you click Save, the .ai extension is added to your filename.
7. Click **Save**, and then click OK in the Illustrator Native Format Options dialog box.
   The original document closes and the Forecast.ai file appears in the Illustrator window. Note the new name of the document in the title bar.

MAC

1. Start Illustrator, then insert your Project Disk in the appropriate drive
2. Click **File** on the menu bar, then click **Open**
   The Open dialog box opens, as shown in Figure C-1.
3. Click the **Desktop button** if you do not already see your Project Disk, then double-click your Project Disk to open it
4. Click **AI C-1**, then click **Open**
   The AI C-1 document opens.
5. Click **File** on the menu bar, then click **Save As**
   The Save dialog box opens.
6. Navigate to the drive or folder where you store your project files (if necessary), type **Forecast** in the File name text box
7. Click the **Append File Extension checkbox** to add the .AI extension to the file name
8. Click **Save**, and then click OK in the Illustrator Native Format Options dialog box
   The original document closes and the Forecast.ai file appears in the Illustrator window. Note the new name of the document in the title bar.

FIGURE C-1: Opening a document using a Windows and a Macintosh computer

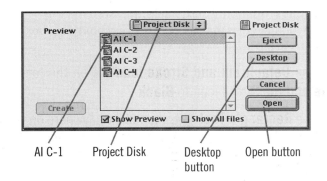

AIC-1

Look in list
arrow

Open button

AI C-1

Project Disk

Desktop
button

Open button

Illustrator 9.0

Creating Guides and Snapping Objects to Them

Illustrator guides are useful for arranging objects on the artboard. Guides are locked into place when you first create them but they can be unlocked if you need to delete them or move them to a new location. Guides can be temporarily hidden when they are distracting, and then easily shown again when needed. By snapping objects to guides, you can position objects precisely on the artboard. ✎ Bill creates a horizontal and a vertical guide, then creates the first of five rectangles, on top of which he will later place graphics and text for a five-day weather forecast. Bill snaps the top of the first rectangle to the intersection of the horizontal and vertical guides.

Steps

QuickTip

To access the General Preferences dialog box, press [Ctrl] [K] (Win) or [Command] [K] (Mac)

1. Click **View** on the menu bar, then click **Show Rulers**
   If your rulers do not display inches, click Edit on the menu bar, point to Preferences, then click Units & Undo. Click the General list arrow, click Inches, then click OK.

2. Position the pointer on the horizontal ruler as shown in Figure C-2, then drag the pointer toward the artboard, stopping at the **8"** mark on the vertical ruler as shown in Figure C-3
   If you need to move a guide after you create it, click View on the menu bar, point to Guides, then select Lock Guides to remove the check mark in front of it, then move the guide to the new location.

3. Drag a guide from the vertical ruler to the **1"** mark on the horizontal ruler as shown in Figure C-3

4. Click the **View** menu, then click **Hide Bounding Box**, if necessary. If the menu item reads "Show Bounding Box," skip this step
   The selection handles that are part of every bounding box may hide the anchor points that you are trying to select.

QuickTip

You can also press [D] on your keyboard to activate the Default Fill and Stroke colors.

5. Click the **Default Fill and Stroke icon** 🔲 on the toolbox to change the Fill icon to **White** and the Stroke icon to **Black**

6. Click the **Rectangle Tool** 🔲, then click anywhere on the artboard
   The Rectangle dialog box opens, showing measurements from the last rectangle that was created. You can create a rectangle with a specific width and height using the Rectangle dialog box.

7. Type **.75** in the Width field, press **[Tab]**, type **3** in the Height field, then click **OK**
   The 0.75" x 3" rectangle appears on the page and remains selected.

Trouble?

If you do not see the anchor points because the bounding box is on top of them, click View on the menu bar, then click Hide Bounding Box.

8. Click the **Selection Tool** 🔲, then place your pointer directly over the **upper-left anchor point** so that your pointer changes to ▶₀ as shown in Part A of Figure C-4

9. With ▶₀ still placed over the anchor point, drag the rectangle to the intersection of the horizontal and vertical guides until your pointer becomes ▶ as shown in Part B of Figure C-4

10. Release the mouse button and save your work
    Your rectangle is snapped to the guides.

FIGURE C-2: Placing pointer in ruler to create a new guide

Pointer placed on horizontal ruler

Horizontal ruler

Vertical ruler

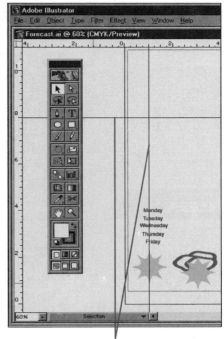

FIGURE C-3: Horizontal and vertical guides

Horizontal and vertical guides positioned on the artboard

Part A

Part B

FIGURE C-4: Snapping a point on an object to a guide

Rectangle Tool

Default Fill and Stroke colors

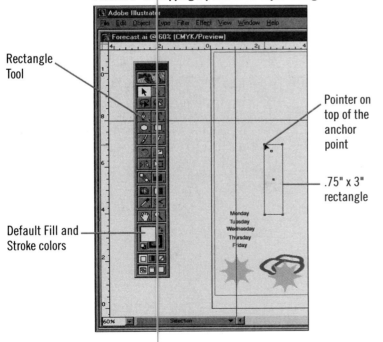

Pointer on top of the anchor point

.75" x 3" rectangle

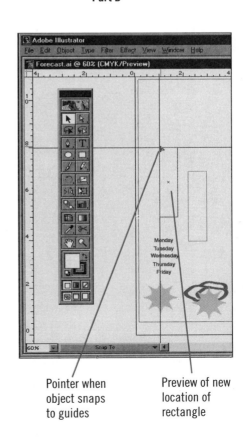

Pointer when object snaps to guides

Preview of new location of rectangle

Using the Move Command

The Move command allows you to move an object or move and copy an object with more accuracy than when you simply move an object with the mouse. The Move command is useful if you want to duplicate an object and give the copy a specific horizontal or vertical offset from the original object. Because moving is a transformation feature, you can repeat the same move amount by pressing [Ctrl] [D] (Win) or [Command] [D] (Mac). Bill makes four duplicates of the rectangle, spaced 0.75" apart.

Steps

1. Click the **rectangle** to select it, if necessary

2. Click **Object** on the menu bar, point to **Transform**, then click **Move**

   The Move dialog box opens.

QuickTip

If you are not sure of the width of an object, select the object, then read the width value in the Transform palette.

3. Type **1.5** in the Horizontal field

   The amount that an object is moved is measured from the upper-left point of the selected object. In this case, the object is 0.75" wide, and Bill wants a duplicate 0.75" away from the first rectangle, so he adds the width of the object plus the desired space between the object and the duplicate to get 1.5".

QuickTip

When you move or copy an object to the right or above the selected object, you enter a positive number in the Move fields. When you move or copy an object to the left or below the selected object, you enter a negative number in the Move fields.

4. Press **[Tab]**, then type **0** (zero, not the letter O) in the Vertical field

   If you do not want an object or a duplicate of the object to move vertically, you enter 0 in the Vertical text field, meaning no change in the vertical location.

5. Press **[Tab]** again to automatically update the new distance amount in the Distance text field as shown in Figure C-5

6. Click the **Copy** button in the Move dialog box

   A duplicate rectangle appears 0.75" away from the original rectangle.

7. Press **[Ctrl] [D]** (Win) or **[Command] [D]** (Mac) three times to create three more rectangles 0.75" away from the others as shown in Figure C-6

8. Click the **artboard** to deselect the fifth rectangle, then save your work

The keyboard increment

The keyboard increment is equal to 0.014" or 1 point. A **point** is a unit of type size equal to 0.01384", or approximately 1/72 of an inch. The keyboard increment setting is the amount that a selected object moves when you press one of the arrow keys once on your keyboard. If you are using an extended keyboard, the arrow keys are located in the lower-right corner of the keyboard to the left of the number pad. When the keyboard increment amount is too much for what you need to do, simply modify the keyboard increment amount by going to the General Preferences dialog box and changing the number in the keyboard increment text field. Changing the keyboard increment amount to .25 pt will give you much more control when moving objects using the arrow keys. If you enter a unit of measure other than inches, such as points or picas, Illustrator will convert this number to inches if you are working with inches as your General unit of measure.

FIGURE C-5: Move dialog box

Move dialog box

Horizontal field

Vertical field

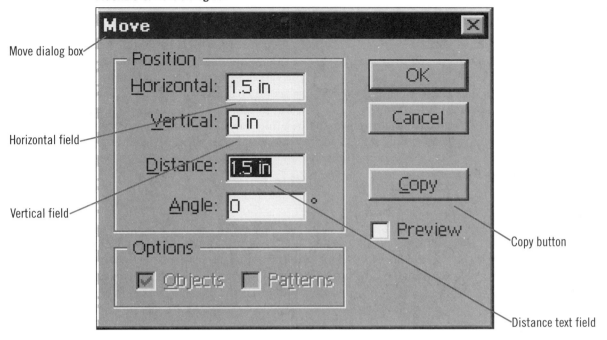

Copy button

Distance text field

FIGURE C-6: Five rectangles equidistant from each other

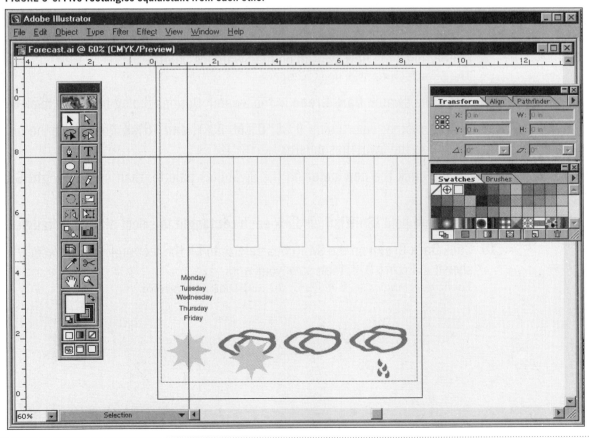

Creating New Colors

Illustrator comes with 36 process colors from which you can choose. **Process colors** are colors that are created using one or more of the following four colors: Cyan, Magenta, Yellow, and Black (also referred to as CMYK). You can change an existing Illustrator color by changing the amount of any of the CMYK colors used to create it. You can also create new colors by mixing any combination of Cyan, Magenta, Yellow and Black. You can add new colors to the Swatches palette and give them unique names. You can also easily remove colors from the Swatches palette. ✎ Bill creates two new colors and adds them to the Swatches palette.

Steps

1. Click **Window** on the menu bar, then click **Show Color**, if necessary
   The White color chip is still selected on the Swatches palette because the last item that was selected was the rectangle, which has a White fill. The Color palette displays the CMYK percentages for White (0% C, 0% M, 0% Y, and 0% B) as shown in Figure C-7. You may need to click the Show Options arrow ▶, then click CMYK if you do not see the Cyan, Magenta, Yellow, and Black sliders.

2. Drag the **C (Cyan) slider** on the Color palette to **100%**

3. Drag the **Y (Yellow) slider** on the Color palette to **50%**
   Notice the new color in the Fill icon on the toolbox and on the Color palette.

4. Drag the **Fill icon** on the Color palette on top of the Swatches palette until you see 🖐 as shown in Figure C-8, then release the mouse button to add the new color to the Swatches palette
   The new color appears wherever your pointer is positioned on the Swatches palette when you release the mouse button.

5. Double-click the **new swatch** on the Swatches palette
   The Swatch Options dialog box opens.

6. Name the swatch **Dark Green** in the Swatch Options dialog box, then click **OK**

7. Create another color using **0%C, 0%M, 0%Y, and 15%K**, then drag the new color swatch to the Swatches palette

8. Double-click the **new color** on the Swatches palette, then name it **Light Gray** and click **OK**

9. Press and hold [Shift], then click **each rectangle** to select all five rectangles

10. Click **Dark Green** on the Swatches palette to fill the rectangles with the new color as shown in Figure C-9, then save your work
    The five rectangles are filled with the new Dark Green color.

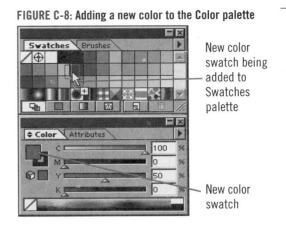

FIGURE C-7: Viewing a color in the Color palette

FIGURE C-8: Adding a new color to the Color palette

White swatch selected

Fill icon on Color palette

Magenta slider bar

Black slider bar

Color palette

Show Options arrow

Cyan slider bar

Yellow slider bar

New color swatch being added to Swatches palette

New color swatch

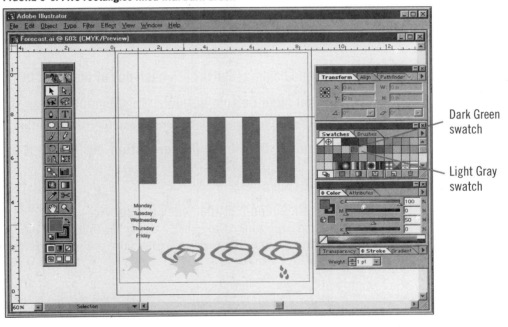

FIGURE C-9: Five rectangles filled with Dark Green

Dark Green swatch

Light Gray swatch

Global colors

Global colors are colors that, if modified, will be updated every place on the artboard where they have been applied. You must designate a color to be global before you apply it to Illustrator objects, however. To create a global color, double-click a swatch in the Swatches palette. The Swatch Options dialog box opens. To make a color global, you must click the Global checkbox to add a check mark as shown in Figure C-10. Global color swatches have small white triangles in the lower-right corner of the Swatch icon to differentiate them from non-global colors.

FIGURE C-10: Global colors

Swatch Options dialog box

Global check box

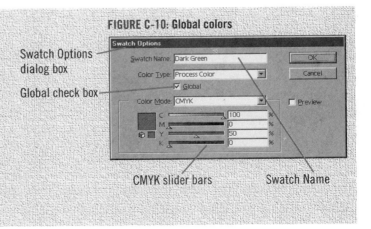

CMYK slider bars

Swatch Name

Illustrator 9.0

Aligning, Distributing, and Grouping Objects

Illustrator 9.0

Aligning is arranging objects by their tops, bottoms, left or right sides, or centers. For example, if you have an illustration of three cubes and you want their tops to be located at the same vertical location on the artboard, you would align them by their tops. **Distributing** is evenly spacing the tops, bottoms, centers, left or right sides of objects on the artboard. Once you have aligned and distributed objects, it is helpful to group them together, so that they will then be treated as one object. **Grouping** objects ensures that the alignment and distribution of the individual objects stays intact. Bill positions the text labels, aligns them, distributes them, and groups them together.

Steps

1. Close the Color palette and open the **Align palette** by clicking **Window** on the menu bar, then clicking **Show Align**

2. Drag **each text label**, beginning with "Monday", underneath the five rectangles as shown in Figure C-11

3. While pressing and holding **[Shift]**, click **each day of the week** to select all of them

4. Click the **Vertical Align Bottom button** on the Align palette as shown in Figure C-11
   The bottoms of the text labels are placed on the same vertical location.

5. Click the **Horizontal Distribute Center button** on the Align palette as shown in Figure C-12
   The text labels are evenly distributed.

6. Click **Object** on the menu bar, then click **Group**
   The five text labels are grouped together. Remember that when objects are grouped, their appearances do not change. The easiest way to figure out whether an object is grouped is to deselect it, then click it again.

7. Save your work

CLUES TO USE

Ungrouping objects

Just as you can group two or more objects together, you can ungroup grouped objects. To ungroup a grouped object, click the group to select it, click Object on the Menu bar, then click Ungroup. The individual objects that made up the original group will all be selected. You must click a blank space on the artboard to deselect all of the objects, then select one at a time to manipulate it. You can also press [Ctrl] [Shift] [A] (Win) or [Command] [Shift] [A] (Mac) to deselect all selected objects.

FIGURE C-11: **Vertically aligning objects**

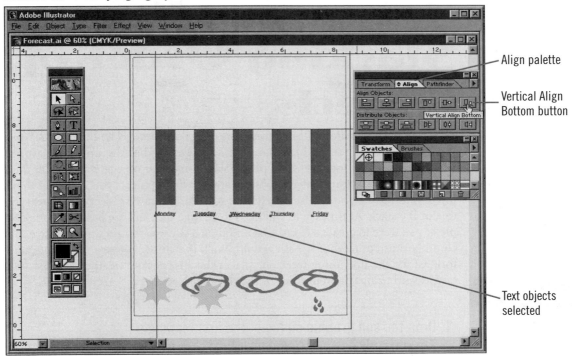

Align palette

Vertical Align
Bottom button

Text objects
selected

FIGURE C-12: **Horizontally distributing objects**

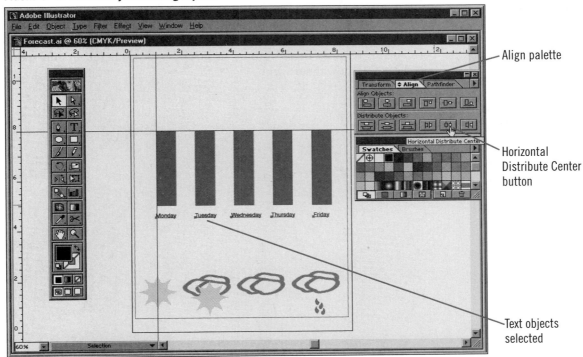

Align palette

Horizontal
Distribute Center
button

Text objects
selected

Arranging the Stacking Order of Objects

Each object you create in Illustrator exists on its own level. The first object you create exists on the lowest level, the second exists on the next level, and so on, up to the last object you create, which exists on the top level. This property of Illustrator objects is known as the **stacking order** of objects. The stacking order of objects affects which objects you see when they are dragged on top of one another, or in a "stack"; the most recently created object will appear in the front, or on top, of the stack. At times, you will need to change the stacking order of your objects. For example, if you were to create a cloud first and then a sky, you would want to place the sky behind the cloud because otherwise the sky would block the cloud. ✏️ Bill has received the five-day forecast for the upcoming week. He places the appropriate weather graphics on top of the rectangles and brings them in front of the rectangles.

Steps

1. Drag the **sun graphic** on top of the first rectangle
   The sun is behind the first rectangle because it was created before Bill created the rectangles.

2. Click **Object** on the menu bar, point to **Arrange**, then click **Bring to Front**
   The sun is now in front of the rectangle as shown in Figure C-13.

3. Refer to Figure C-14 to position the weather graphics on the remaining bars, bringing each weather graphic in front of each rectangle; don't worry that you're short one sun, you'll duplicate it in the next step

4. Duplicate the sun to be placed on the Thursday rectangle by pressing **[Alt]** (Win) or **[Option]** (Mac) while dragging the sun

5. Click **View** on the menu bar, point to **Guides**, then click **Hide Guides**
   When you no longer need guides on the page, you can clear or hide them. Clearing guides permanently removes them from the artboard, while hiding them only removes them until you choose to show them again.

6. Save your work

> **Trouble?**
> If you do not create a duplicate sun after following Step 4, you probably let go of the [Alt] (Win) or [Option] (Mac) too early. While pressing the key combination, drag the sun, then release the mouse button first and [Alt] (Win) or [Option] (Mac) last.

FIGURE C-13: Sun in front of the rectangle

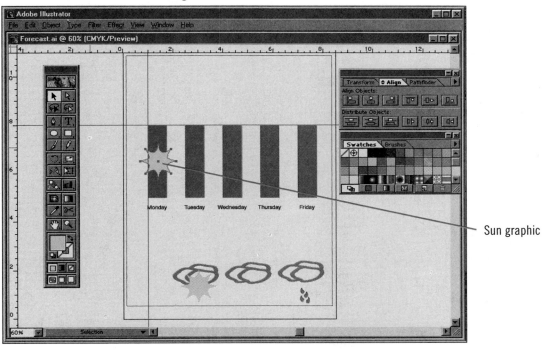

Sun graphic

FIGURE C-14: Completed five-day forecast

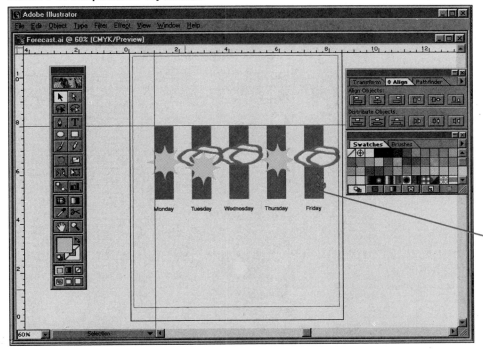

Weather graphics
stacked on top of
rectangles

Using the Zoom Command

You can increase your viewing area in Illustrator by as much as 6400%. This feature is helpful if you are trying to manipulate a small or detailed object on the artboard. There are many ways to enlarge areas on the artboard, including using the View menu, the Zoom Tool, and the Zoom menu. The Zoom Tool offers a unique way of zooming in on a specific area; you can drag this tool on top of the area you would like to zoom in on. As you drag, a **marquee**, or dotted rectangle, appears, encompassing the area over which you've dragged the Zoom Tool. When you stop dragging, everything inside the marquee fills the Illustrator window. Regardless of how much you increase the zoom level, you can return to the original full artboard view by using the Fit In Window command. ✒ Bill experiments with Illustrator's zoom features.

Steps

1. Click the **Zoom menu** in the lower-left corner of the Illustrator window as shown in Figure C-15, then click **100%**
   Notice that the zoom level also appears in the title bar.

QuickTip
You can zoom out on the artboard by pressing and holding down [Alt] (Win) or [Option] (Mac) while clicking with the Zoom Tool.

2. Click the **Zoom Tool** 🔍, then click the **sun** and **clouds graphic** twice
   Your pointer becomes ⊕. Notice that the zoom level increases by 50% each time you click ⊕.

3. Press and hold the **Spacebar** on your keyboard
   The pointer becomes the Hand Tool ✋. When you press the Spacebar, whichever pointer is current becomes the Hand Tool.

4. While pressing the Spacebar, drag ✋ to move the artboard in different directions, exposing different areas of your artwork

QuickTip
You can also use the Fit In Window menu item under the View menu to return to a full view of the Illustrator window.

5. Double-click the **Hand Tool** ✋ on the toolbox to return to a full view of the Illustrator window

6. Click the **Zoom Tool** 🔍, then place it to the left of the topmost raindrop on the Friday rectangle

7. Drag ⊕ to create a **marquee** about the same size as the one shown in Figure C-16
   When you release the mouse button, the raindrops area of the illustration fills the window.

FIGURE C-15: Changing the zoom level with the zoom menu

Current zoom level

Maximum zoom level

100%

Zoom menu

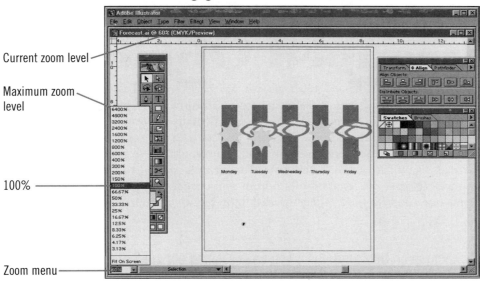

FIGURE C-16: Dragging the Zoom Tool to create a marquee

Hand Tool

Zoom Tool

Marquee

Dragging Zoom Tool

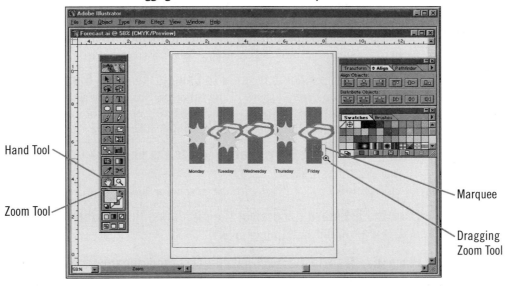

CLUES TO USE

The Navigator palette

The Navigator palette, found on the Window menu and shown in Figure C-17, provides you with another way to zoom in on areas of the artboard. The Navigator palette has a Zoom slider, which you can drag to the right to increase the zoom level and drag to the left to decrease it. The red rectangle inside the Navigator palette is called the Proxy Preview Area. You can drag the red rectangle around inside the Navigator palette to define the area of the artboard you wish to zoom in on.

FIGURE C-17: Navigator palette

Navigator palette

Proxy Preview Area

Current zoom level

Zoom slider

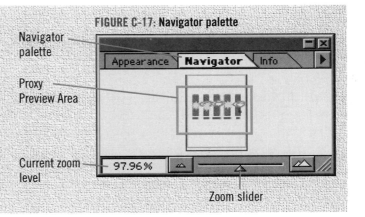

Illustrator 9.0

Illustrator 9.0

Selecting Part of a Grouped Object

You may need to edit an object after it has been grouped with other objects. The Direct Selection Tool allows you to select part of a group without having to ungroup it first. This approach eliminates the possibility of you accidentally moving or deleting ungrouped objects. The Select menu options find and select objects with the same fill colors, stroke colors, and other properties. These options are useful if you would like to select each item on the artboard that has been filled with a certain color, for example, so that you can change all of those items at once. ✎ Bill selects the raindrops and changes their fill color to Light Gray. He then prints out a copy of the five-day forecast to present to his supervisor.

Steps 1 2 3 4

1. Zoom in on the raindrops if you have zoomed out since the last lesson

2. Click the **Selection Tool** ▶, then click **one of the raindrops**
   Notice that the four raindrops have already been grouped together.

3. Click the **artboard** to deselect the group of raindrops

Trouble?

If you cannot select only one of the raindrops with the Direct Selection Tool, then the group of raindrops is probably still selected. The Direct Selection Tool works only when the grouped object is deselected first. Click the artboard to deselect the group of raindrops, then repeat Step 4.

4. Click the **Direct Selection Tool** ▶ on the toolbox, then click **one of the raindrops**
   Notice that only that raindrop is selected, as shown in Figure C-18.

5. Click **Edit** on the menu bar, point to **Select**, then click **Same Fill Color**
   All four raindrops are selected. If any other objects on the artboard had the same Blue fill, they would also be selected. If you click Select Inverse, all objects on the artboard with a fill that is different than the fill of the selected object(s) will be selected.

6. Click the **new Light Gray swatch** next to the new Dark Green swatch that you made on the Swatches palette
   The four raindrops are filled with the new color, as shown in Figure C-19.

7. Click the **artboard** to deselect the raindrops, then double-click the **Hand Tool** 🖑 to go back to the Fit In Window view

8. Place your name in the lower-left corner of the artboard, then print **one copy of Forecast**
   Your screen should resemble Figure C-20.

9. Exit (Win) or Quit (Mac) Illustrator, saving your changes to **Forecast**

CLUES TO USE

Selecting objects using a marquee

As with the Zoom Tool, you can use the Selection Tool to drag a marquee around objects that you want to select. To place a marquee around objects, place the Selection Tool slightly above the first object that you plan to select. Click and drag the artboard, and pull in the direction of the objects you need to select. Make sure that the Selection Tool is not on top of any object, but rather on a blank area of the artboard before you begin to drag it. A dotted rectangle appears as you drag the Selection Tool. Everything inside the marquee will be selected when you stop dragging the Selection Tool. The tool can select an entire object even if only part of the object lies within the marquee boundaries. Be careful not to have an object selected before you begin dragging the Selection Tool—you will end up moving that object instead of creating a marquee selection.

Direct
selection
Tool

One raindrop
selected with
the Direct
Selection Tool

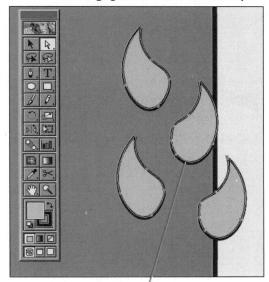

Raindrops
filled with
Light Gray

FIGURE C-20: **The finished illustration**

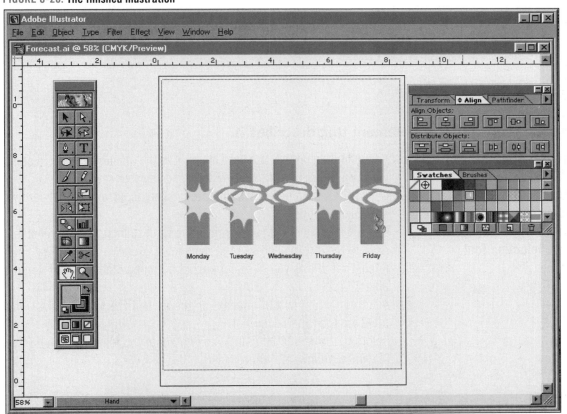

Illustrator 9.0

Practice

▶ Concepts Review

Label the Illustrator window elements shown in Figure C-21.

FIGURE C-21

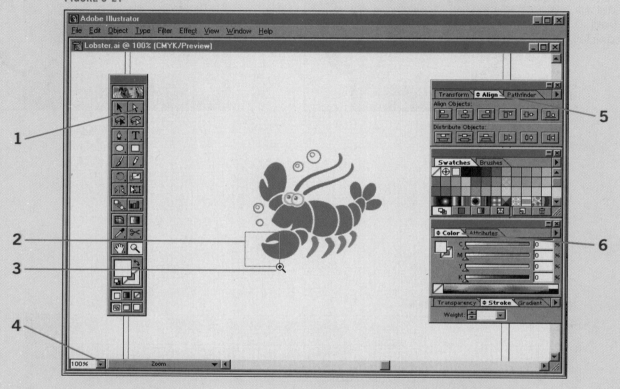

Match each term with the statement that describes it.

7. **Marquee**
8. **Keyboard increment**
9. **Process colors**
10. **Global colors**
11. **Navigator palette**
12. **Direct Selection Tool**

a. An amount equal to 0.014" or 1 point; it is the amount a selected object moves when you press one of the arrow keys once on your keyboard

b. Colors that, if modified, will update in every place on the artboard where they have been applied

c. Has a Zoom slider that you drag to the right to increase the zoom level and drag to the left to decrease the zoom level

d. A tool that allows you to select part of a group without having to ungroup the object first

e. A dotted rectangle that appears on the area of the artboard over which you have dragged the Zoom Tool

f. Colors that are created using one or more of the following colors: Cyan, Magenta, Yellow, and Black

13. **What is the maximum zoom amount in Illustrator?**
    a. 500%
    b. 600%
    c. 6400%
    d. 1000%

14. **Which palette do you use to make new colors?**
    a. Swatches
    b. Global
    c. Color
    d. CMYK

15. **What is arranging objects by their tops, bottoms, left sides, right sides, or centers called?**
    a. Distributing
    b. Aligning
    c. Grouping
    d. Layering

Make sure that you have extra blank floppy disks on hand so that if you run out of room on your Project Disks while completing the Skill Review or Independent Challenges, you will have a place to save the files you create.

 ## Skills Review

1. Open and save an Illustrator document.
  a. Start Illustrator.
  b. Insert your Project Disk into the appropriate drive.
  c. Click File on the menu bar, then click Open.
  d. Locate your Project Disk, then open AI C-2 from the drive and folder where you store your project files.
  e. Click File on the menu bar, then click Save As.
  f. Save AI C-2 as *Blocks*.

2. Create guides and snap objects to them.
  a. Show the rulers using the View menu.
  b. Make sure the rulers are displaying inches; change the ruler units to inches, if necessary.
  c. Drag a guide from the horizontal ruler to the 8" mark on the vertical ruler.
  d. Drag a guide from the vertical ruler and line it up with the 1" mark on the horizontal ruler.
  e. Press [X] until the Fill icon appears in front of the Stroke icon, then click the Red swatch on the Swatches palette.
  f. Press [X] to bring the Stroke icon in front of the Fill icon, then click the None swatch on the Swatch palette.
  g. Click the Rectangle Tool, then click the artboard.
  h. Enter **2** in the Width field and **2** in the Height field.
  i. Click OK.
  j. Position the Selection Tool on top of the square's upper-left anchor point. If you do not see the anchor points, click View on the menu bar, then click Hide Bounding Box.
  k. Drag the anchor point to the intersection of the horizontal and vertical rulers until it snaps into place.
  l. Save your work.

3. Use the Move command.

a. Make sure that the red square is selected.

b. Click Object on the menu bar, point to Transform, then click Move.

c. Enter 2 in the Horizontal field, press [Tab], then enter 0 (zero) in the Vertical field.

d. Click Copy.

e. Press [X] to bring the Fill icon in front of the Stroke icon on the toolbox.

f. Change the fill color of the second square to Yellow.

g. While the yellow square is still selected, press [Shift], then click the red square to select both squares.

h. Click Object on the menu bar, point to Transform, then click Move.

i. Enter 0 (zero) in the Horizontal field, press [Tab], then enter –2 in the Vertical field.

j. Click Copy.

k. Click the artboard to deselect the two new squares.

l. Click the first square in the second row, then click the Yellow swatch on the Swatches palette.

m. Click the second square in the second row, then click the Red swatch on the Swatches palette.

n. Click the artboard to deselect the red square.

o. Save your work.

4. Create new colors.

a. Show the Color palette, if necessary.

b. Drag the Cyan slider to 10%. You can also enter values manually, if necessary.

c. Drag the Magenta slider to 60%.

d. Drag the Yellow slider to 25%.

e. Drag the new swatch to the Swatches palette.

f. Double-click the new swatch, then name it *Berry*.

g. Click OK.

5. Align, change the stacking order of, and group objects.

a. Click one of the squares with the Selection Tool.

b. While pressing and holding [Shift], click the three remaining squares.

c. Click Object on the menu bar, then click Group.

d. Click the black diamond to select it.

e. Drag the black diamond to the center of the four squares. When you release the mouse, the black diamond falls behind the four squares

f. Click the group of four squares to select it.

g. Click Object on the menu bar, point to Arrange, then click Send to Back. The black diamond appears on top of the four squares.

h. Group the black diamond and the four squares together.

i. Make sure the new group is still selected, then, while pressing and holding [Shift], click the word Blocks to select both objects using the Selection Tool.

j. Click Window on the menu bar, then click Show Align, if necessary.

k. Click the Horizontal Align Center button to center the text above the group.

6. Use the Zoom command.

a. Click the Zoom Tool, then drag a marquee around the grouped object so that it fills the artboard. Notice how perfectly the four squares are aligned.

b. Double-click the Hand Tool to return to the Fit In Window view.

c. Click the Zoom Tool on the center of the four squares until the zoom level is 100%.

7. Select part of a grouped object.

a. Click the Direct Selection Tool, then click one of the red squares.

b. Click Edit on the menu bar, point to Select, then click Same Fill Color.

c. Click the berry swatch on the Swatches palette.

d. Keeping the berry squares selected, click Edit on the menu bar, point to Select, then click Inverse.

e. Click a blue swatch on the Swatches palette to fill the other two squares, the diamond and the word Blocks with blue, then click the artboard to deselect them.

f. Click the diamond with the Direct Selection Tool, then change its fill color to Black again.

g. Place your name in the lower-left corner of the artboard.

h. Print one copy of *Blocks*.

i. Save *Blocks*, then Exit (Win) or Quit (Mac) Illustrator.

▶ Independent Challenges

1. You are a textile designer who is updating pattern samples for a new catalog. You wish to change the colors in your fabric samples.

To complete this independent challenge:

a. Start Illustrator.

b. Open AI C-3 from the drive and folder where you store your project files.

c. Save AI C-3 as *Fabric*.

d. Create two new colors for the fabric sample, then add them to the Swatches palette.

e. Double-click the two new colors, then give them new names.

f. Click one of the colors in the fabric sample with the Direct Selection Tool.

g. Click Edit on the menu bar, point to Select, then click Same Fill Color.

h. Change the color to one of your new colors.

i. Click Edit on the menu bar, point to Select, then click Inverse.

j. Change the color of the second color to your other new color.

k. Place your name in the lower-left corner of the artboard.

l. Print one copy of *Fabric*, then Exit (Win) or Quit (Mac) Illustrator, saving changes to your document.

2. You are a designer for a tile store. You have been asked to create a display of tiles using one wall in the tile store. You have been asked to use different size tiles and two different colors. You decide to design the tiled wall in Illustrator first so you will have a reference to use when you place the tiles on the wall.

To complete this independent challenge:

a. Start Illustrator, if necessary.

b. Click File on the menu bar, then click New.

c. Name the file *Tiles*, then click OK.

d. Refer to Figure C-22 for ideas during this exercise.

e. Create two new colors and add them to the Swatches palette

f. Double-click each new color on the Swatches palette and give them new names.

g. Click the Rectangle Tool, then create a rectangle of any width and height.

FIGURE C-22

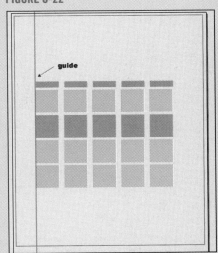

h. Keeping the rectangle selected, use the Move command to copy and move the rectangle to the right. Leave a little space between the two rectangles to represent where the grout will be placed. For example, if your rectangle is 1" wide, enter 1.125 inches in the Move dialog box to place .125" between the two rectangles.

i. Press [Ctrl] [D] (Win) or [Command] [D] (Mac) to transform the rectangle again.

j. Repeat Step 8 until you have as many rectangles as you want in your first row.

k. Continue to use the Move dialog box to move and copy the rectangles vertically.

l. Create a guide that snaps to the left side of the rectangles as shown in Figure C-22.

m. Create another smaller rectangle that will be used for the top row of tile as shown in Figure C-22.

n. Snap the new rectangle to the guide so that it is aligned with the larger rectangles as shown in Figure C-22.

o. Move and copy the new rectangle as needed to complete the wall design.

p. Apply the two new colors on the Swatches palette to the rectangles.

q. Place your name in the lower-left corner of the artboard.

r. Print one copy of *Tiles*.

s. Exit (Win) or Quit (Mac) Illustrator, saving changes to your document.

3. Your friend is opening a restaurant and working on some advertising for his new venture. He knows only the basics of Illustrator and has started an ad that he would like you to help clean up.

To complete this independent challenge:

a. Start Illustrator.

b. Open AI C-4 from the drive and folder where you store your project files.

c. Save AI C-4 as *Pizza*.

d. Show the Align palette, if necessary.

e. Using the Selection Tool, drag a marquee around all of the blue squares.

f. Align the squares by their tops vertically.

g. Distribute the squares by their centers horizontally.

h. Group the squares together.

i. Select the group of squares and the two text objects.

j. Align the three items by their left sides horizontally.

k. Group the three objects together.

l. Place your name in the lower-left corner of the artboard.

m. Print one copy of *Pizza*.

n. Exit (Win) or Quit (Mac) Illustrator, saving changes to your document.

WEB WORK

4. You are a recent college graduate who is hoping to start a career in graphic design. Your interest lies in typography (the art of designing text) and creating logos. You believe that logos should be simple and not too detailed. You decide to take a look at logos and text from other companies to get some ideas.
To complete this Independent Challenge:

a. Connect to the Internet and go to *http://www.course.com*.
b. Navigate to the page for this book, then click the link for the Student Online Companion.
c. Click the links for this unit to look at logos from different companies. Notice that the logos are made up of both graphics and text. The logos on these pages are colorful, creative, and descriptive of the company's products or services.
d. Exit (Win) or Quit (Mac) your browser.
e. Start Illustrator.
f. Click File on the menu bar, then click New.
g. Name the file *Logo*, then click OK.
h. Create a simple logo using the Text Tool, the Shape tools, and the Paintbrush tools. Use any of the transformation tools, the Align palette, the Transform palette, and the Swatch libraries. Create new colors, if necessary. If you need ideas for your logo, consider creating a logo for a jewelry store, tire shop, astrology shop, book store, restaurant, or ice cream store. You can also recreate a logo with which you are already familiar, a company logo that you like, or a friend's or family's company logo. Remember to keep it very simple. The goal here is to practice using Illustrator.
i. Place your name in the lower-left corner of the artboard.
j. Print one copy of *Logo*.
k. Exit (Win) or Quit (Mac) Illustrator, saving changes to your document.

Illustrator 9.0

► Visual Workshop

To recreate Figure C-23, you will need to create two new colors and then add them to the Swatches palette. The first color should be made with 20% C, 50% M, 0% Y, and 0% K. The second color should be made with 90% C, 30% M, 0% Y, and 0% K. Place your name in the lower-left corner of the artboard, save the document as *Pattern*, print one copy, then Exit (Win) or Quit (Mac) Illustrator.

FIGURE C-23

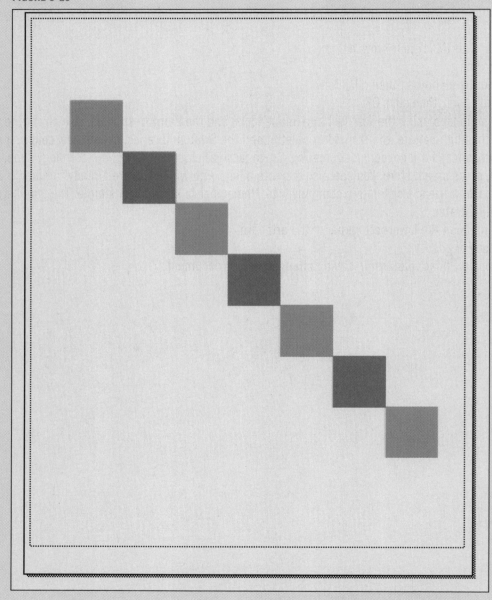

Drawing
with the Pen Tool

Objectives

- ► Trace a bitmap with the Pen Tool
- ► Create open paths with the Pen Tool
- ► Place, unlock, and lock artwork
- ► Work with smooth points and direction lines
- ► Manipulate a closed path with the Direct Selection Tool
- ► Use the Smooth Tool
- ► Create a gradient and add it to the Swatches palette
- ► Apply a gradient and use the Gradient Tool

In addition to using the shape tools and the Paintbrush Tool, you can create objects by drawing with the Pen Tool. You can draw objects from scratch or trace the outline of a digital image that you have placed into an Illustrator document. For example, if you need a picture of a key, but are unable to draw one yourself, you can place a digital image of a key into an Illustrator document, trace the edge of the key, then delete the digital image, thereby leaving the outline of it in your document. WHJY is producing a special news report on nutrition, focusing on the categories of the food pyramid. Bill needs to create an illustration of the food pyramid. To get started, he downloaded a royalty-free image of the food pyramid from the Internet. He will trace the food pyramid in Illustrator using the Pen Tool, then turn his finished document over to the video department.

Illustrator 9.0

Tracing a Bitmap with the Pen Tool

When you trace an object or draw a new object using the Pen Tool, you are creating **vector graphics**—mathematically calculated objects referred to as paths. **Paths** are composed of a series of points, called **anchor points** that can be smooth, straight corner, curved corner, or combination corner points as shown in Part A of Figure D-1. Using the Pen Tool you can create **open paths**, straight or curved lines that do not connect, like a piece of string; and **closed paths**, like an orange or an egg shape, that are joined as one continuous line without any **endpoints**—the two points at the ends of an open path. See Part B of Figure D-1 for an example of an open path, a closed path, and endpoints. ◢ Bill has already placed the food pyramid image into his Illustrator document. He begins tracing it, using the Pen Tool.

Steps 1 2 3 4

1. Start Illustrator

Trouble?

Printing, saving, and exporting are disabled in the Illustrator Tryout! Software. To learn more about the Tryout! Software that accompanies this book, see the Read This Before You Begin page.

2. Open **AI D-1** from the drive and folder where you store your project files and save it as **Pyramid**

3. Click the **Pen Tool** 🖋
   Your pointer becomes 🖋ₓ.

4. Change the fill color to **None** and the stroke color to **Red** as shown in Figure D-2
   It's much easier to see your path as you trace with the Pen Tool if there is no fill color.

5. Click the **top point of the pyramid** as shown in Part A of Figure D-3
   A corner anchor point appears, represented by a small blue square. Corner points are created when you click once with the Pen Tool.

6. Click the **lower-left point of the pyramid** as shown in Part B of Figure D-3
   When you add a second corner point, a line segment is automatically drawn between the two anchor points. The line segment is straight.

QuickTip

If you press and hold [Shift] when creating diagonal lines with the Pen Tool, you will create line segments with 45-degree angles.

7. Press and hold **[Shift]** while you click the **lower-right point of the pyramid** as shown in Part C of Figure D-3
   Holding [Shift] while you drop corner points with the Pen Tool will constrain the segment to 45-degree angle increments and keep it straight.

8. Place 🖋 directly on top of the first anchor point until your pointer becomes 🖋ₒ as shown in Part D of Figure D-3, then click the first anchor point
   The small circle that appeared to the left of the pointer in 🖋ₒ indicates that you are about to close a path.

9. Click the **Selection Tool** ▶, click the **artboard** to deselect the path, then save your work
   It is a good idea to switch back to the Selection Tool when you have finished using the Pen Tool. Otherwise, you may attach unwanted segments, or click the artboard accidentally with the Pen Tool, leaving stray points on the artboard.

FIGURE D-1: Examples of open and closed paths, corner points, and line segments

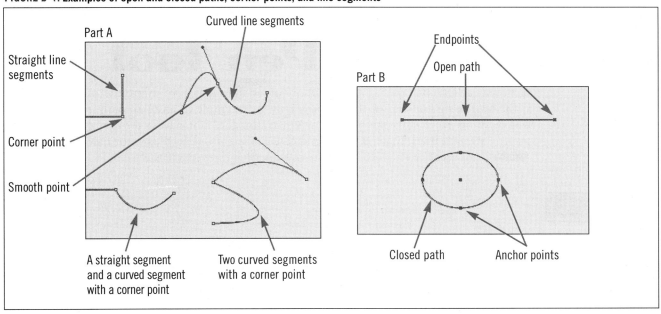

Part A

Curved line segments

Straight line segments

Corner point

Smooth point

A straight segment and a curved segment with a corner point

Two curved segments with a corner point

Part B

Endpoints

Open path

Closed path

Anchor points

FIGURE D-2: Getting ready to use the Pen Tool

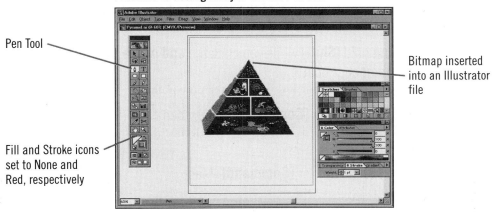

Pen Tool

Fill and Stroke icons set to None and Red, respectively

Bitmap inserted into an Illustrator file

FIGURE D-3: Creating a closed path with the Pen Tool

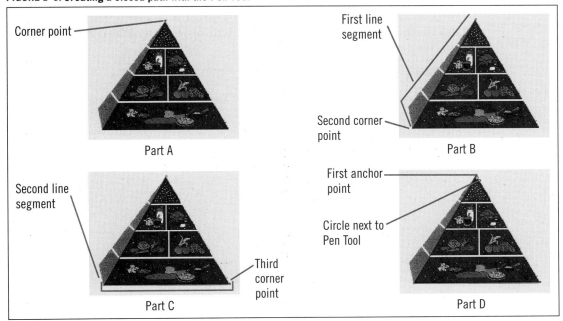

Corner point

Part A

First line segment

Second corner point

Part B

Second line segment

Third corner point

Part C

First anchor point

Circle next to Pen Tool

Part D

Creating Open Paths with the Pen Tool

As noted earlier, open paths are straight or curved lines that have endpoints, or anchor points, at the beginning and end of the line segment. An example of an open path is a straight line. Unlike some other software programs, Illustrator does not have a tool used exclusively for making straight lines. Instead, you can create a straight line in Illustrator using the Pen Tool. Bill uses the Pen Tool to create five dividing lines inside the triangle.

Steps

1. Make sure that the Fill icon is still set to **None** and that your Stroke icon is still set to **Red**

2. Drag a **marquee** around the **four middle food groups** using the **Zoom Tool** 🔍 so that the amount of the pyramid that is visible is similar to the amount visible in Figure D-4

Trouble?

If you zoom in too much, double-click the Hand Tool 🖑 to zoom out to the Fit In Window view, then repeat Step 2.

3. Select the **Pen Tool** ✒️.

4. Click ✒️× at the **beginning of the top white horizontal line** as shown in Figure D-4
You have added a corner anchor point.

5. Press and hold **[Shift]** while you click the **end of the top white horizontal line**, to add a second anchor point
A straight-line segment is drawn between the points.

QuickTip

Pressing [Ctrl] (Win) or [Command] (Mac) temporarily changes the pointer into the Selection Tool or the Direct Selection Tool depending on which one you used last. Clicking the artboard with ▶ or ▷ deselects the new path, allowing you to continue to use the Pen Tool without connecting new line segments to the last line segment.

6. Press **[Ctrl]** (Win) or **[Command]** (Mac), then click the **artboard**
Your pointer temporarily changes to the Selection Tool and the new line segment is deselected when you click the artboard.

7. Release **[Ctrl]** (Win) or **[Command]** (Mac)
The pointer returns to ✒️×.

8. Repeat Steps 4 through 7 to create two more horizontal lines and two more vertical lines, using Figure D-5 as a guide for their locations
You may have to zoom out if the palettes obstruct your view of the horizontal lines. You can also use the 🖑 to move the artboard around, or you can collapse the palettes temporarily if they block your view.

9. Save your work

FIGURE D-4: **Creating open paths**

Blue anchor point

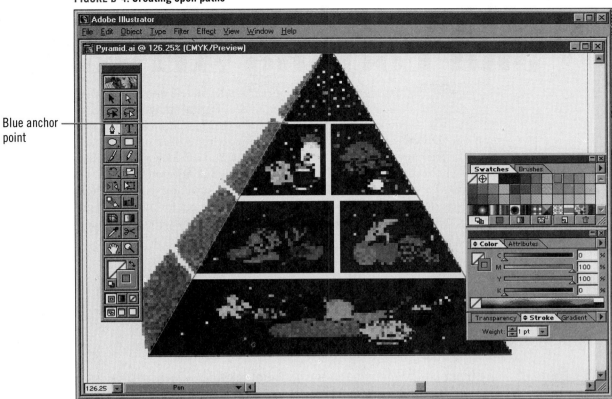

FIGURE D-5: **Horizontal and vertical line segments**

New paths

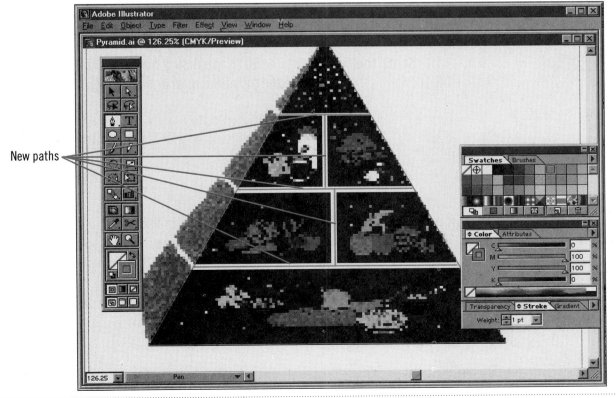

DRAWING WITH THE PEN TOOL ILLUSTRATOR D-5 ◀

Placing, Unlocking, and Locking Artwork

The Place command in Illustrator is used to import artwork and text into an Illustrator document. This artwork may include digital images or vector objects. **Digital images**, also known as bitmap images or bitmaps, can be illustrations or photographs that have been scanned, or pictures that have been taken with a digital camera. It is common practice to place a bitmap in an Illustrator document for the purpose of tracing it with the Pen Tool. You can **lock** a placed image before you trace it. Locking holds the image in place so that you do not accidentally move it. Locked objects can be unlocked whenever needed. ✎ The pyramid structure is now complete. Now Bill needs to draw an example of each food group, starting with an egg for the protein group. In order to continue, he needs to remove the digital image of the food pyramid and place a new digital image of an egg into his document.

Steps

1. Double-click the Hand Tool 🖐 to return to the Fit In Window view

2. Click the **Selection Tool** ▶

3. Click **Object** on the menu bar, then click **Unlock All**
   The picture of the food pyramid becomes unlocked and is selected, as shown in Figure D-6.

> **QuickTip**
>
> If you have locked more than one object on the artboard, all of the locked objects will become unlocked when you choose the Unlock All command.

4. Press **[Delete]** (Win) or **[delete]** (Mac) on the keyboard to remove the food pyramid picture
   The food pyramid picture is no longer needed. The illustration of the food pyramid remains on the artboard.

5. Click **Edit** on the menu bar, then click **Select All**
   The new pyramid is selected.

6. Click **Object** on the menu bar, then click **Group**
   The illustration of the food pyramid is grouped together and remains selected.

> **Trouble?**
>
> If you have trouble dragging the pyramid, place the Selection Tool on the blue border of the pyramid and drag the image again. You cannot select or move an object without a fill color if you place the Selection Tool inside the transparent areas. If you accidentally drag with the Scale Tool still selected, click Undo on the Edit menu, then use the ▶ to drag the pyramid.

7. Double-click the **Scale Tool** 🔲 and enter **50** in the dialog box to scale the pyramid 50%, click **OK**, then drag the pyramid to the top of the artboard using ▶, as shown in Figure D-7
   Make sure that the Uniform option button is checked in the Scale dialog box when you scale the pyramid. "Uniform" means that the selected object will be scaled horizontally and vertically in the same amount.

8. Click **File** on the menu bar, then click **Place**
   The Place dialog box opens as shown in Figure D-8.

9. If you are working on a Windows Computer, click the **Look in list arrow**, click the drive containing your Project Disk, click **AI D-2.tif**, then click **Place**; if you are working on a Macintosh, click **Desktop button** if you do not already see the Project Disk, click **Project Disk**, click **Open**, click **AI D-2**, then click **Open** again
   A picture of three eggs appears on the artboard and is selected.

10. Click **Object** on the menu bar, click **Lock**, then save your work

FIGURE D-6: Unlocking and deleting a bitmap graphic

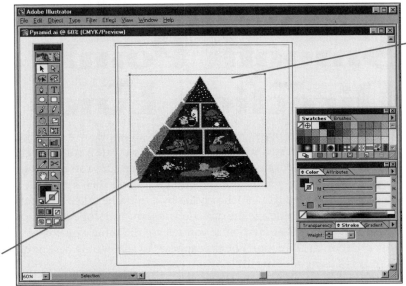

Unlocked and selected bitmap graphic

New vector graphic on top of bitmap graphic

FIGURE D-7: Scaling and moving a grouped object

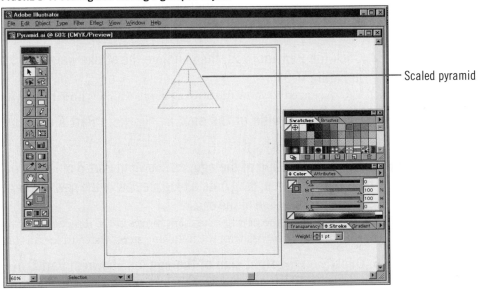

Scaled pyramid

FIGURE D-8: Placing artwork in Illustrator using a Windows computer and a Macintosh

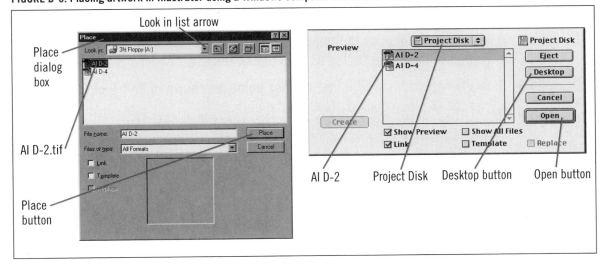

Look in list arrow

Place dialog box

AI D-2.tif

Place button

AI D-2

Project Disk

Desktop button

Open button

Working with Smooth Points and Direction Lines

When you trace an object with curves, like an apple or a pumpkin, you need to use smooth anchor points to create the curved segments. To create a curved segment, instead of clicking and releasing the Pen Tool as you do when you are creating a straight segment, you click and drag the Pen Tool. Direction points and direction lines will then appear. A **direction point** is a round, black dot connected to an anchor point by a thin line called a **direction line**. By dragging direction points, you can define the direction, length, and slope of the actual line segments that enter and exit the anchor point. Before you release the mouse button, you can manipulate the direction point on the direction line that appears to achieve the desired angle. Bill traces one of the eggs using the Pen Tool.

Steps 1 2 3 4

1. Drag a **marquee** with the **Zoom Tool** 🔍 around the **picture of the eggs** so that it fills the window as shown in Figure D-9

2. Make sure the Stroke icon is set to **Red** on the toolbox

3. Click the **Pen Tool** ✒, then change the stroke weight to **1 pt**, if necessary as shown in Figure D-9
   You may need to show the Stroke palette which is under the Window menu.

4. Click the **left side of the egg**, as shown in Part A of Figure D-10, to place the first anchor point

Trouble?

If you do not achieve the same result as shown in Part B of Figure D-10, you may have clicked with the Pen Tool and released the mouse button before you dragged it. To create a curved line segment, you must click and drag immediately without stopping in between. Undo your last step and try again.

5. Click ✒ on the **top of the egg**, as shown in Part B of Figure D-10, and, without releasing the mouse button, drag until a blue preview of the new line segment is curved to the same degree as the edge of the egg
   The preview of the new line segment moves in the direction that you are dragging the direction point. As you proceed with the following steps, watch to see this happen.

6. Click ✒ on the **right side of the egg**, as shown in Part C of Figure D-10, and, without releasing the mouse button, drag until a blue preview of the new line segment is curved to the same degree as the edge of the egg

7. Click ✒ **the bottom of the egg**, as shown in Part D of Figure D-10, and, without releasing the mouse button, drag until a blue preview of the new line segment is curved to the same degree as the edge of the egg

Trouble?

Don't worry if your lines are jagged or not curved properly—just do your best. This task can be very difficult; like anything, it takes practice.

8. Position ✒ on top of the first **anchor point**, as shown in Part E of Figure D-10, until you see ✒₀, then click ✒₀ to close the path
   If your last line segment is not perfectly aligned with the edge of the egg, the angle of the last direction line is the problem. Notice how in Part F of Figure D-10, the direction line is pointing straight to the left, forcing the last line segment to point to the left as well. You will learn how to fix such issues using the Direct Selection Tool shortly.

9. Save your work

FIGURE D-9: Zooming in on egg picture

Stroke weight

FIGURE D-10: Tracing a bitmap using smooth points

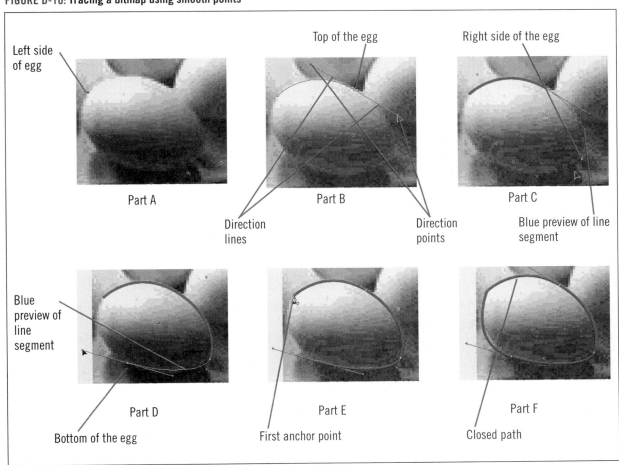

Left side of egg

Top of the egg

Right side of the egg

Part A

Part B

Part C

Direction lines

Direction points

Blue preview of line segment

Blue preview of line segment

Part D

Part E

Part F

Bottom of the egg

First anchor point

Closed path

Manipulating a Closed Path with the Direct Selection Tool

You can manipulate open and closed paths by using the Direct Selection Tool. If you click a path with the Direct Selection Tool, all anchor points along the path will become white or hollow instead of their normal solid blue color. When anchor points are white, they can be dragged to a new location using the Direct Selection Tool. Like anchor points, line segments and direction lines can be selected and moved using the Direct Selection Tool. You can think of the two direction lines attached to a smooth anchor point as a pair of handles. Moving one direction line automatically moves the other. It is also possible to move one direction line independently, thereby changing one line segment but not the other. Direction lines have direction points at their tops. To move a direction line, you must click the direction point and then drag. One direction line controls the segment coming into the anchor point, and the other direction line controls the segment coming out of the anchor point. ✒️ Bill fixes the last line segment of the egg using the Direct Selection Tool.

Steps

Trouble?

If the bounding box is showing, click View on the menu bar, then click Hide Bounding Box.

1. Click the **Selection Tool** ▶, then click anywhere along the edge of **the closed path** that traces the edge of the egg
   When you click an open or closed path with the Selection Tool, the anchor points appear solid blue and are all selected. When the anchor points are solid Blue, they cannot be manipulated.

2. Click the **artboard** to deselect the path

3. Click the **Direct Selection Tool** ▶, then click the **closed path** that traces the edge of the egg
   The anchor points are now white, and one of the direction lines appears for whichever line segment you clicked.

4. If you didn't click the **last line segment** of the closed path in Step 3, click it now with ▶ as shown in Figure D-11

5. Place your pointer on the **direction point** shown in Part A of Figure D-12, then drag slowly to the right as shown
   As the direction lines move, both line segments associated with them change shape, as you can see in the blue preview lines.

6. Click **[Ctrl] [Z]** (Win) or **[Command] [Z]** (Mac) to undo the last step

QuickTip

To see both direction lines, click the anchor point instead of the line segment.

7. Press and hold **[Alt]** (Win) or **[Option]** (Mac), then position the pointer over the **direction point** again
   Your pointer becomes ▶+, as shown in Part B of Figure D-12.

Trouble?

If you press and hold [Alt] (Win) or [Option] (Mac) after you click the direction point, you will duplicate the line segment instead of moving one direction point independently of the other. Undo your last step and try again.

8. Drag ▶+ slightly to the right until you see the last line segment move closer to the side of the egg, as shown in Part C of Figure D-12
   Pressing and holding [Alt] (Win) or [Option] (Mac) while you drag the direction point moves only one direction line, so as not to affect both line segments.

9. Save your work
   Part D of Figure D-12 shows that the last line segment has been adjusted to eliminate the gap.

FIGURE D-11: Manipulating a closed path with the Direct Selection Tool

Direct Selection Tool

Last line segment

Direct Selection pointer

Direction point

Direction line

White anchor points

FIGURE D-12: Moving direction lines

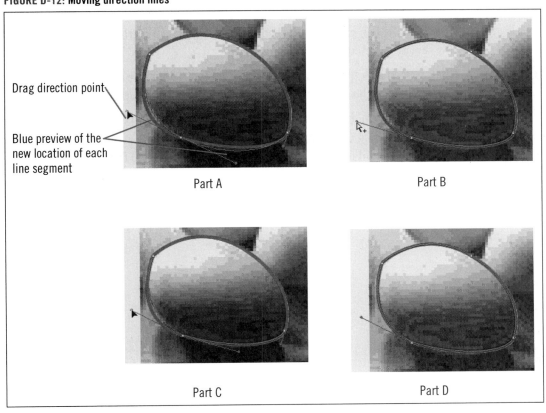

Drag direction point

Blue preview of the new location of each line segment

Part A

Part B

Part C

Part D

Illustrator 9.0

Using the Smooth Tool

The Smooth Tool is used to smooth out sharp or bumpy areas of line segments. It enables you to fix problem areas on paths easily—a welcome feature when you are just beginning to use the Pen Tool. Bill notices two places on the egg path that he considers to be slightly pointed. He uses the Smooth Tool to soften them.

Steps 1234

1. Click the **artboard** to deselect the path

2. Notice the two pointed areas shown in Figure D-13 that need to be smoother

3. Click the **path** with the **Selection Tool**
   The anchor points should be solid blue.

4. Click the **Pencil Tool** and, without releasing the mouse button, position the pointer over the tearoff tab, then release the mouse button to tear off a Pencil toolbar

5. Click the **Smooth Tool** on the new toolbar, then drag over the **first pointed area of the egg path** as shown in Part A of Figure D-14
   The first pointed area becomes smoother. The pointed areas on your egg may differ from the ones in Part A of Figure D-14. Use the Smooth Tool wherever your egg needs it.

6. Drag over the **second pointed area** as shown in Part A of Figure D-14
   The second pointed area becomes smoother.

Trouble?

It may take some time for you to become accustomed to working with the Smooth Tool. If you are not happy with your results after using it, undo your last couple of steps, then try again.

7. Click , then click the **artboard** to deselect the egg path
   Notice how much smoother the egg path is, as shown in Part A of Figure D-14.

8. Click **Object** on the menu bar, click **Unlock All**, press **[Delete]** (Win) or **[delete]** (Mac), then save your work
   You unlocked and deleted the picture of three eggs because it is no longer needed. Compare your screen to Part B of Figure D-14.

FIGURE D-13: **Looking for problem areas**

Two pointed areas
that could be
smoother

FIGURE D-14: **Using the Smooth Tool**

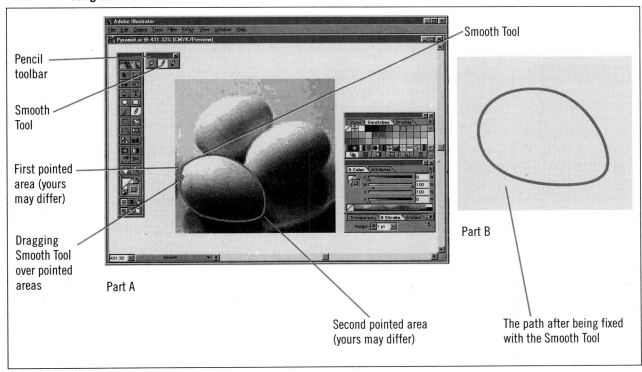

Smooth Tool

Pencil
toolbar

Smooth
Tool

First pointed
area (yours
may differ)

Dragging
Smooth Tool
over pointed
areas

Part A

Part B

Second pointed area
(yours may differ)

The path after being fixed
with the Smooth Tool

CLUES TO USE

The Pencil, Smooth, and Eraser Tools

The Pencil, Smooth, and Eraser tools are grouped together on the toolbox. You can draw freehand paths with the Pencil Tool and then manipulate them using the Direct Selection Tool, the Smooth Tool, and the Eraser Tool. The Smooth Tool is used to smooth over line segments that are too bumpy or too sharp. The Eraser Tool looks and acts just like an eraser found at the end of a traditional pencil; dragging it over a line segment erases part of the segment from the artboard.

Creating a Gradient and Adding it to the Swatches Palette

Gradients are multicolor fills used to fill the inside of a closed path. Illustrator includes six gradient swatches on the Swatches palette: **White, Black**; **Black, White Radial**; **Steel Bar II**; **Rainbow, Emerald Eye**; and **Sunset**. You can create new gradients from one of these preset gradients, then add your customized gradients to the Swatches palette much like you did when you created new colors. Gradients are either linear or radial. **Linear gradients** consist of gradually blending lines of colors. **Radial gradients** consist of gradually blending circles of color and are usually used to fill circles and ovals. Bill creates a radial gradient and drags it to the Swatches palette.

Steps

1. Show the Gradient, Color, and Swatches palette, then separate the Gradient palette so that it is not grouped to any other palettes, as shown in Figure D-15

2. Click the **Show Options arrow** ▶ on the right of the Gradient palette, then click **Show Options**

   The Gradient palette expands, displaying the Gradient slider, as shown in Figure D-15. The Gradient palette shows the gradient swatch that was used last in the Swatches palette.

3. Click the **White, Black gradient** on the Swatches palette as shown in Figure D-15

   Two small squares that look like little houses appear at the beginning and end of the Gradient slider. These squares, called **stops**, indicate where a new color starts in the gradient. A diamond appears at the top of the Gradient slider, indicating the midpoint of the gradient.

4. Click the **last stop** (rightmost color stop that represents the color black) to select it on the gradient bar

   When you click a color stop, the top of it (a small gray triangle) turns black. This indicates that the color stop is selected, and the color that it represents may be edited on the Color palette.

5. Drag the **K slider** (Black) on the Color palette to **0%**, drag the **C slider** (Cyan) to **10%**, the **M slider** (Magenta) to **15%**, and the **Y slider** (Yellow) to **30%**, as shown in Figure D-16

   You have created a new color that resembles the color of an egg. Notice the new gradient on the Gradient palette.

6. Click the **Type list arrow** on the Gradient palette, then click **Radial** as shown in Figure D-16

7. Click the **Gradient Fill icon** on the Gradient palette and drag it to the Swatches palette as shown in Figure D-17, then release the mouse button

   Your pointer becomes 🔲 when you drag a gradient to the Swatches palette.

8. Save your work

FIGURE D-15: The Gradient palette

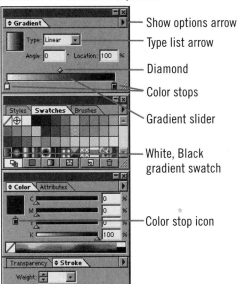

— Show options arrow
— Type list arrow
— Diamond
— Color stops
— Gradient slider
— White, Black gradient swatch
— Color stop icon

FIGURE D-16: Creating a Radial gradient

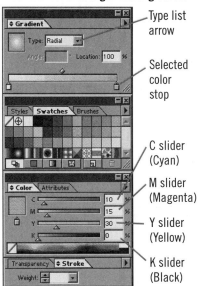

— Type list arrow
— Selected color stop
— C slider (Cyan)
— M slider (Magenta)
— Y slider (Yellow)
— K slider (Black)

FIGURE D-17 Adding a new gradient to the Swatches palette

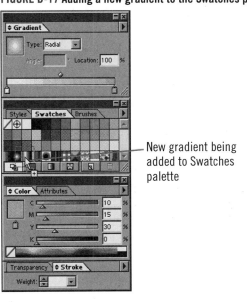

— New gradient being added to Swatches palette

The Swatches palette

The Swatches palette contains 36 colors (including Registration and None), four gradients, and four patterns. You can change the viewable contents in the Swatches palette by clicking the appropriate buttons at the bottom of the palette. You click the first button to show all swatches, and the second button to show only the colors. You can click the third and fourth buttons to show only the gradients and only the patterns, respectively. Clicking the fifth button will create a new swatch, and clicking the last button will delete a selected swatch.

FIGURE D-18: The Swatches palette

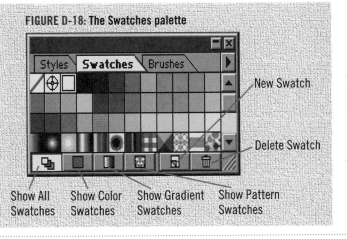

— New Swatch
— Delete Swatch

Show All Swatches   Show Color Swatches   Show Gradient Swatches   Show Pattern Swatches

Illustrator 9.0

Applying a Gradient and Using the Gradient Tool

Once you have added a customized gradient to the Swatches palette you can give it a unique name. After applying a gradient to an object, you can change the angle of the gradient fill using the Gradient palette. You can also change the length, direction, or center point of a gradient fill using the Gradient Tool. Bill names his new gradient Eggshell, and applies it to the egg. He then adjusts the center point on the egg using the Gradient Tool. Eventually he will fill all of the sections on the food pyramid with new illustrations.

Steps 1234

1. Double-click the **new gradient swatch** on the Swatches palette as shown in Figure D-19, name it **Eggshell**, then click OK

2. Click the **egg path** with the **Selection Tool** to select it

3. Make sure that the Fill icon is in front of the Stroke icon, then click the **Eggshell gradient** on the Gradient palette
   The egg is filled with the Eggshell gradient.

4. Press **[X]** to bring the Stroke icon forward, then click **None** on the Swatches palette to remove the stroke color from the egg path

5. Click the **Gradient Tool** on the toolbox
   Your pointer becomes -⌿- .

6. Click -⌿- on the egg where indicated in Figure D-19
   The center point moves to the area where you clicked, thereby changing the highlight point.

7. Double-click the **Hand Tool** to return to the Fit In Window view, switch to ▶, then drag the egg to the location on the food pyramid indicated in Figure D-20
   If your egg is too big, make it smaller using the Scale Tool.

8. Place your **name** on the artboard, print **one copy** of **Pyramid**, then **Exit** (Win) or **Quit** (Mac) Illustrator, saving the changes to your document
   Bill will continue working on this project tomorrow.

FIGURE D-19: Using the Gradient Tool

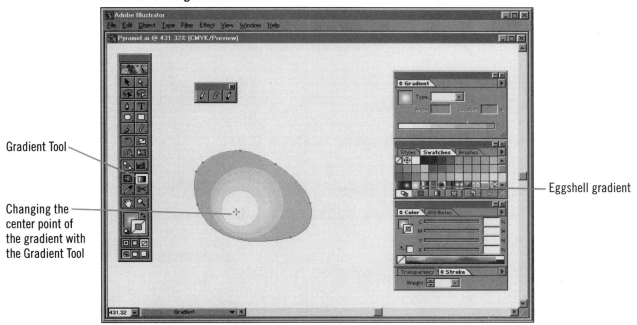

Gradient Tool

Changing the center point of the gradient with the Gradient Tool

Eggshell gradient

FIGURE D-20: The finished project

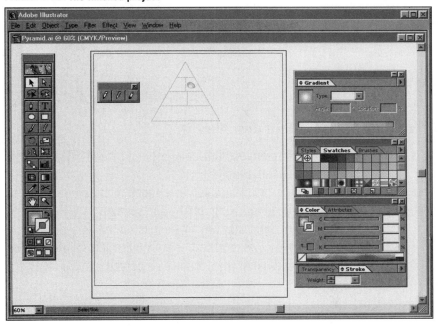

Practice

► Concepts Review

Label the Illustrator window elements shown in Figure D-21.

FIGURE D-21

Match each term with the statement that describes it.

7. **Smooth Tool**
8. **Place**
9. **Smooth point**
10. **Gradient**
11. **Path**
12. **Endpoints**

a. Straight or curved line composed of a series of anchor points between which line segments fall
b. A multicolor fill that can be applied to closed paths
c. A tool used for fixing bumpy line segments
d. Anchor points that are not connected to line segments on both sides
e. The ability to import text or a graphic picture into an Illustrator document
f. An anchor point that produces a curved line segment

13. Which tool selects a path so that you can move the anchor points?
   a. Smooth
   b. Selection
   c. Direct Selection
   d. Gradient

14. Which tool selects a path without allowing you to change it?
   a. Smooth
   b. Selection
   c. Direct Selection
   d. Gradient

15. Under which tool is the Smooth Tool hidden on the toolbox?
   a. Pen
   b. Pencil
   c. Eraser
   d. Gradient

16. Which of the following gradient types are available in Illustrator?
   a. Radial and linear
   b. Linear and circular
   c. Smooth and radial
   d. Curved and straight

Make sure that you have extra blank floppy disks on hand so that if you run out of room on your Project Disks while completing the Skills Review or Independent Challenges, you will have a place to save the files you create.

▶ Skills Review

1. Place and lock artwork in Illustrator.
   a. Start Illustrator.
   b. Open AI D-3 from the drive and folder where you store your project files.
   c. Save AI D-3 as *House*.
   d. Click File on the menu bar, then click Place.
   e. Click the drive containing your Project Disk, click AI D-4, then click Place.
   f. Drag the picture of the house below the cloud if necessary.
   g. Click Object on the menu bar, then click Lock.
   h. Drag a marquee around the entire house using the Zoom Tool to increase your view of the house.

2. Trace a bitmap with the Pen Tool.
   a. Make sure that the Fill icon is set to None on the toolbox.
   b. Make sure that the Stroke icon is set to Green on the toolbox.
   c. Increase the stroke weight to 3 pt.
   d. Click the Pen Tool.
   e. Starting with the left side, trace the outside border of the house using straight line segments, including the roof and chimney.
   f. Close the path by placing the Pen Tool over the first anchor point, then clicking.

g. Press [Ctrl] (Win) or [Command] (Mac) to switch temporarily to the Selection or Direct Selection Tool (whichever one you used last), then click the artboard to deselect the new path.

h. Release [Ctrl] (Win) or [Command] (Mac) to return to the Pen Tool pointer.

i. Trace the outside of the leftmost window. Press and hold [Shift] to create perfectly straight horizontal and vertical line segments.

j. Trace the remaining three windows, the front door, the small window inside the front door, and the picture window next to the front door using straight line segments. Don't forget to deselect each closed path before you begin the next one.

3. Create open paths with the Pen Tool.
   a. Trace the inside panes of each window using straight lines (open paths).
   b. Draw a straight line to separate the bottom of the roof from the house.
   c. Click Object on the menu bar, then click Unlock All.
   d. Delete the bitmap image of the black-and-white house.
   e. Save your work on the drive where you store your project files.

4. Work with smooth points and direction lines.
   a. Make sure the Fill icon is set to None on the toolbox.
   b. Make sure the Stroke icon is set to Black on the toolbox, and the stroke weight is set to 1 pt.
   c. Click the Pen Tool on the toolbox.
   d. Create another cloud next to the cloud on the left side of the artboard using smooth points.
   e. Remember to drag the Pen Tool as you create each line segment.
   f. When you are about to finish the cloud, place the Pen Tool directly on top of the first anchor point that you created.
   g. Click and drag to close the path.
   If you do not like the cloud that you created, undo your last few steps and try again.
   h. Click the Selection Tool when you are finished using the Pen Tool.
   i. Save your work.

5. Manipulate a closed path with the Direct Selection Tool.
   a. Double-click the Hand Tool to return to the Fit In Window view.
   b. Drag a marquee with the Zoom Tool around the two clouds.
   c. Click the Direct Selection Tool, then click the edge of the leftmost cloud.
   d. Drag a few of the anchor points to reshape the cloud so that it looks more like a cloud to you. (*Hint:* Place the Direct Selection Tool directly over the white anchor point that you want to move.) Drag the anchor point to a new location.
   e. Drag a few of the direction lines to force the line segments to move in a new direction.
   f. Press [Spacebar] to display the Hand Tool, then push the artboard to the left so that you can view the other cloud.
   g. Click the second cloud with the Direct Selection Tool.
   h. Drag a few of the anchor points, line segments, or direction lines to reshape the cloud slightly.

6. Use the Smooth Tool.
   a. Click the Selection Tool.
   b. Press [Spacebar] to display the Hand Tool, then push the artboard to the right to see the cloud on the left.
   c. Click the first cloud with the Selection Tool.
   d. Click the Pencil Tool, then drag the mouse over to the tearoff tab.
   e. Select the tearoff tab, then release the mouse to make a new toolbar.
   f. Click the Smooth Tool.
   g. Drag the Smooth Tool over areas of the cloud path that you would like to smooth out.

h. Repeat the same steps for the other cloud.

i. Click the Selection Tool, then click the artboard to deselect the cloud.

j. Save your work.

7. **Create a gradient and add it to the Swatches palette.**

a. Double-click the Hand Tool to return to the Fit In Window view.

b. Show the Gradient palette, the Swatches palette, and the Color palette, if necessary.

c. Separate the Gradient palette, if necessary.

d. Click the Show Options arrow ▶ on the Gradient palette, then click Show Options, if necessary.

e. Click the White, Black gradient on the Swatches palette.

f. Click the first color stop on the Gradient slider.

g. Create a light blue color for the first color of the gradient.

h. Click the last color stop on the Gradient slider.

i. Create a dark blue color for the second color of the gradient.

j. Click the Type list arrow on the Gradient palette, then click Radial.

k. Click the Gradient Fill icon on the Gradient palette and drag it to the Swatches palette, then release the mouse button.

l. Double-click the new gradient swatch. Then name it *Clouds*.

8. **Apply a gradient and use the Gradient Tool.**

a. Click one of the clouds with the Selection Tool.

b. Click the Clouds gradient on the Swatches palette.

c. Click the Gradient Tool on the toolbox.

d. Click the cloud to change the highlight point of the gradient.

e. Repeat these steps for the second cloud.

f. Save your work.

g. Place your name in the lower-left corner of the artboard.

h. Print one copy of *House*.

i. Exit (Win) or Quit (Mac) Illustrator.

▶ Independent Challenges

1. You work for the Human Resources Department of a multimedia company. Your job is to create a help wanted advertisement to attract new multimedia designers. You decide to use some visuals in addition to text to develop an eye-catching ad.

To complete this independent challenge:

a. Start Illustrator.

b. Open AI D-5 from the drive and folder where you store your project files.

c. Save AI D-5 as *Help*, and place it on the drive where you store your project files.

d. Create a radial gradient and apply it to the gold section of the CD. The radial gradient should have a metallic appearance; use shades of silver or gold.

e. Add the new gradient to the Swatches palette and name it **CD Fill**.

f. Use the Direct Selection Tool to select the gold section of the CD (the CD is one group).

g. Drag the Multimedia Designer Wanted text on top of the CD. Create another text object with a name and telephone number to call if interested in the job.

h. Place your name in the lower-left corner of the artboard.

i. Print one copy of Help.

j. Save your work and Exit (Win) or Quit (Mac) Illustrator.

2. You are an attorney representing a client who has been involved in an automobile accident. According to your client, he was hit while driving through a four-way intersection. The driver that hit him ran a red light. The collision occurred in the middle of the four-way intersection. You need to create an illustration of the intersection where the accident occurred for use in court.

To complete this independent challenge:

a. Start Illustrator.

b. Click File on the menu bar, then click New.

c. Name the new document *Accident*, then click **OK**.

d. Create a four-way intersection using the Pen Tool.

e. Create a Stop sign using the Polygon Tool and the Text Tool.

f. Use the letter C to represent your client's car and the letter D to represent the car of the other driver that hit your client.

g. Place your name in the lower-left corner of the artboard.

h. Print one copy of *Accident*.

i. Save your work on the drive where you store your project files.

j. Exit (Win) or Quit (Mac) Illustrator.

3. You are starting your own business as a carpenter. You want to create a business card that includes some images of tools. You began by tracing the head of a hammer in Illustrator and now need to finish drawing it.

To complete this independent challenge:

a. Start Illustrator.

b. Open AI D-6 from the drive and folder where you store your project files.

c. Save AI D-6 as *Hammer* and place it on the drive where you store your project files.

d. Zoom in on the picture of the hammer so that you have a good view of it.

e. Click the Red path that has already been drawn on the head of the hammer and lock it.

f. Trace the handle of the hammer with the Pen Tool.

g. Unlock all images using the Object menu.

h. Deselect all images by clicking the artboard with the Selection Tool.

i. Delete the bitmap image of the hammer.

j. Create two gradient fills: one for the handle, and one for the head of the hammer.

k. Group the two paths together.

l. Place your name on the lower-left corner of the artboard.

m. Print one copy of *Hammer*.

n. Exit (Win) or Quit (Mac) Illustrator, saving changes to your work.

4. You work for an office supplies company and have been asked to create a brochure showing products such as tape, pencils, paper clips, thumbtacks, and pens. You need a picture of some pencils to trace as an illustration.

To complete this independent challenge:

a. Connect to the Internet and go to *http://www.course.com*.

b. Navigate to the page for this book, then click the link for the Student Online Companion.

c. Click the links for this unit.

d. Type **pencils** in the Search text field.

e. Right-click a picture showing pencils and save it to the place where you store your project files, naming it *Pencils*.

f. Exit (Win) or Quit (Mac) your browser.

g. Start Illustrator.

h. Click File on the menu bar, then click New.

i. Name the new document *Office*, then click OK.

j. Click File on the menu bar, then click Place.

k. Navigate to the place where you just saved the Pencils picture.

l. Click the Pencils picture, then click Place.

m. Lock the Pencils image.

n. Zoom in on the Pencils image if necessary.

o. Trace a pencil on top of the locked Pencils image using the Pen Tool.

p. Unlock the Pencils image, then delete it.

q. Place your name in the lower-left corner of the artboard.

r. Save your work on the drive where you store your project files.

s. Print one copy of *Office*.

t. Exit (Win) or Quit (Mac) Illustrator.

► **Visual Workshop**

Re-create Figure D-22 by creating two new radial gradients and applying them to six circles. Use the Gradient Tool to give each circle the same highlight points as those in the circles below. Save your work as *Circles*. Place your name in the lower-left corner of the artboard. Print one copy of Circles, then Exit (Win) or Quit (Mac) Illustrator.

FIGURE D-22

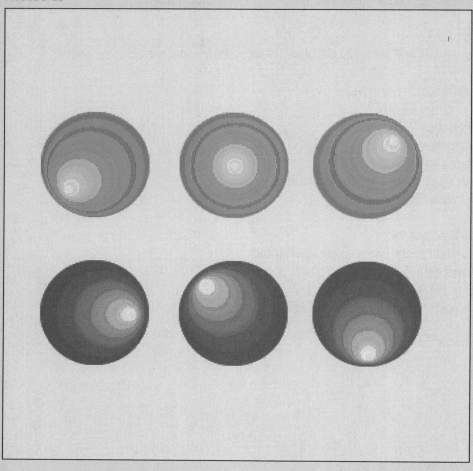

Illustrator 9.0

Working

with Paths and Layers

When you begin tracing objects that are more complex than circles and squares, you will discover how being able to manipulate direction lines on your path makes your work easier. You can delete direction lines or create new ones to help you follow precisely the outline of the object you are tracing. If you are creating an illustration that contains many paths, you can use the Layers palette to organize all of the elements in your illustration. ✐⬛ WHJY is introducing a new weekly feature called Health News on its six o'clock evening newscast. Bill has sketched a logo for Health News on paper and will recreate the sketch in Illustrator. Bill will save the illustration he creates as an EPS file so that it can be used in area newspapers for an advertisement about the health segment.

Deleting a Direction Line

Illustrator 9.0

Tracing with the Pen Tool requires a lot of practice and concentration. As your eye and your hand work in coordination to complete one segment of your path, you need to be thinking ahead about how you will handle the next segment. Will you need to create a smooth point or a corner point? Is the next area a straight line or a curved line? Direction lines on an anchor point control the direction and the height of the line segments coming into the anchor point and going out of the anchor point, as shown in Figure E-1. Sometimes you will be tracing in one direction and then find that you suddenly need to change direction. To trace in a new direction, you may have to delete a direction line. ⬛ Bill begins tracing a shape, then deletes a direction line to begin tracing in a new direction.

Steps

1. Start Illustrator

2. Open **AI E-1** from the drive and folder where you store your project files, then save it as **Health**

3. Increase the zoom level so that you have a good view, but so that you can still see all of the logo

4. Click the **Pen Tool** ⬛, then make sure that the Fill icon is set to **None**, the Stroke icon is set to **Black**, and the stroke weight is set to **3 pt**

5. Click the **top of the red object**, then release to add a corner anchor point as shown in Part A of Figure E-2

6. Click the **lower-right corner of the red object**, then without releasing the mouse button, drag to add a smooth point; continue to press the mouse button and drag downward to add the first line segment as shown in Part A of Figure E-2
   Watch the preview of the new line segment as you drag the mouse. Release the mouse when the preview of the new line segment falls into the desired position.

7. Click the **lower-left corner of the red object**, then without releasing the mouse button, drag downward until you notice that the preview of the new line segment is being forced in the wrong direction; release the mouse button
   Your new line segment will look similar to the one in Part B of Figure E-2 and will be fixed shortly. It's important to see an example like this that demonstrates how the last direction line, which was necessary to create the first line segment, is now forcing the new line segment in the wrong direction. Unless you eliminate the last direction line, it will be impossible to force the new line segment to curve inward.

8. Undo your last step by clicking **[Ctrl] [Z]** (Win) or **[Command] [Z]** (Mac)
   Your screen reverts back to Part A of Figure E-2.

9. Move the mouse pointer over the second anchor point until the cursor becomes ⬛. Click the second anchor point with ⬛, as shown in Part C of Figure E-2
   The direction line is deleted.

Trouble?

Printing, saving, and exporting are disabled in the Illustrator Tryout! software. To learn more about the Tryout! software that accompanies this book, see the Read This Before You Begin page.

Trouble?

If you released the mouse button too early and did not get a chance to see the preview of the second line segment, undo your last step and repeat Step 7.

Trouble?

Unless you click directly on top of the anchor point, you will receive a warning message stating that Illustrator can't convert the direction point. This message refers to another Illustrator feature with which you will not be working at this time. Click OK, then repeat Step 9. You may need to zoom in more to see your anchor points more clearly.

FIGURE E-1: The relationship between direction lines and line segments

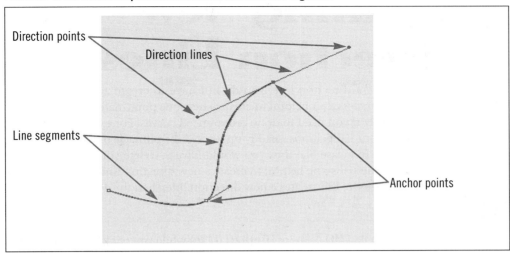

Direction points

Direction lines

Line segments

Anchor points

FIGURE E-2: Deleting direction lines

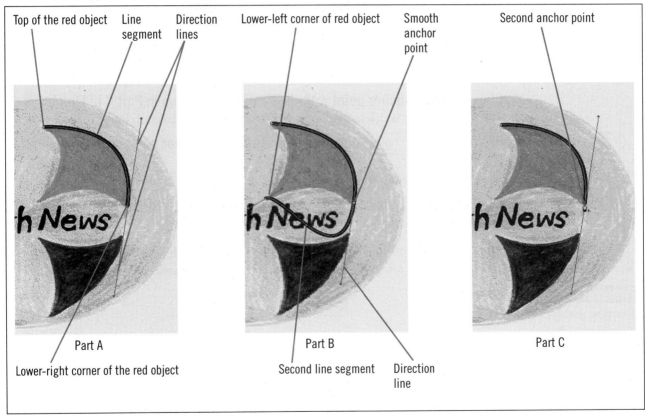

Top of the red object

Line segment

Direction lines

Lower-left corner of red object

Smooth anchor point

Second anchor point

Part A

Lower-right corner of the red object

Part B

Second line segment

Direction line

Part C

Reconnecting to a path

If you are working with the Pen Tool and get interrupted, your path may become deselected. When you return to your work, the next anchor point you add might start a new path instead of continuing the last unfinished one. If your path becomes disconnected, you can reconnect it simply by selecting the Pen Tool, and then pressing and holding [Alt] (Win) or [Option] (Mac) while you click the last anchor point of the path on which you were working. You can then finish tracing the rest of your path.

Illustrator 9.0

Creating New Direction Lines

After you delete a direction line, you do not have to create a new direction line before you proceed. Nevertheless, it is helpful to create a new one pointing in the direction your path needs to go—especially if you need to draw pronounced curves. For example, imagine tracing a roller coaster track. Your path climbs steadily up toward the pinnacle of the track, then dips in a downward direction. In a case like this, you would have to delete your last direction line before you proceeded. It would also be helpful to create a new direction line pointing in the same direction as the track. Bill creates a new direction line, then finishes tracing the red object.

Steps

1. Press and hold **[Alt]** (Win) or **[Option]** (Mac) while you click the **second anchor point** and drag until you see a new direction line appear, as shown in Part A of Figure E-3

2. Click ♟ on the **lower-left corner of the red object** and drag, until you see the new line segment fall into place as shown in Part B of Figure E-3
   The direction line that was just created when you made this new line segment will make it impossible for you to achieve the angle needed in your next line segment, which must curve upward and inward.

3. Click the **third anchor point** with the Pen Tool, as shown in Part C of Figure E-3
   The direction line is deleted. Bill opts not to create a new direction line.

4. Position the Pen Tool ♟ directly on top of the **first anchor point**, as shown in Part D of Figure E-3
   Your pointer becomes ♟₀.

5. Click and drag ♟₀ until you see the last line segment fall into the correct position, then release the mouse button

6. Click the Selection Tool ▶ then click the artboard to deselect the path
   Your path should resemble the one shown in Part E of Figure E-3.

7. Save your work

Trouble?

Because creating new direction lines is one of the most challenging aspects of Illustrator, you may need to do this lesson a few times to get it right.

Deciding on the length of line segments

As you trace an object with the Pen Tool, you always need to be thinking about where you will place the next anchor point. The location of the next anchor point determines the length of the next line segment. As you become more familiar with the relationship between direction line and line segment length, you will be able to position your anchor points more precisely. Keep in mind that if you must drag a direction line a long way (even going off the artboard), you have probably dropped your anchor point too far away from the last anchor point. The best thing to do in this situation is to undo your last step, then drop your next anchor point in a more reasonable location.

FIGURE E-3: Creating new direction lines

Part A

New direction line

Second anchor point

Part B

Lower-left corner of the red object

Second line segment

Part C

Third anchor point

Part D

First anchor point

Part E

Closed path

Unit E

Illustrator 9.0

Using the Reflect Tool

Illustrator includes five transformation tools: Move, Scale, Rotate, Reflect, and Shear. The **Reflect Tool** is used for flipping an object horizontally or vertically. You can duplicate and reflect an object at the same time to create a mirror image of an object. As with all transformation commands, you can reflect an object multiple times by using the Transform Again command. ✎ Bill realizes that it would be easier to reflect and duplicate his new path horizontally, and then vertically to create the green, blue, and purple pieces of the logo, rather than to trace each piece individually. This approach will not only be faster and easier, but will also ensure that all four shapes are identical.

Steps

Trouble?

If you have trouble selecting the new path on top of the red object, make sure that you click the edge of the path. Paths without fills cannot be selected by clicking the inside of the path.

1. **Click the Selection Tool ▶, then click the edge of the new closed path on top of the red object so that the three anchor points are solid blue as shown in Part A of Figure E-4**
   Direction lines will remain visible until you click the path with ▶. When you click a path with the ▶, the anchor points become blue again and are not editable.

2. **Click the Reflect Tool ⬚, then move your cursor over the artboard**
   Your pointer becomes ⊹. An icon called the **point of origin** ✣ appears in the center of the path. It determines the point around which the path will be reflected; it can be dragged to a new location, if desired.

3. **Click ⊹ between the red and green objects as shown in Part B of Figure E-4**
   The point of origin ✣ moves to the new location between the red and green objects. The path will now be reflected around this point instead of its center.

Trouble?

If you press [Alt] (Win) or [Option] (Mac) before you drag ⊹, the Reflect dialog box will appear. Undo your last step and repeat Step 4, making sure that you start dragging ⊹ *before* you press [Alt] (Win) or [Option] (Mac).

4. **Click the artboard anywhere near the point of origin ✣, drag until you see a preview of a new path emerge, then press [Alt] (Win) or [Option] (Mac) to duplicate the path and keep [Alt] (Win) or [Option] (Mac) pressed until after you release the mouse button**
   See Part A and Part B of Figure E-5. You may need to undo your last step and try this a few times. If you release [Alt] (Win) or [Option] (Mac) too early, you will lose your copy of the path. When you drag the mouse button using the Reflect Tool, your pointer becomes ▶. When you press and hold [Alt] (Win) or [Option] (Mac), your pointer becomes ▶▸ indicating that you are duplicating the selected object.

5. **Click the Selection Tool ▶, press and hold [Shift], then click the path on top of the red object so that both paths are selected as shown in Figure E-6**

6. **Click ⬚, then click directly above the small h in the word "Health" as shown in Figure E-6 to move the point of origin**
   You are now ready to reflect a copy of the two selected paths below the new point of origin ✣.

Trouble?

If you press [Alt] (Win) or [Option] (Mac) *before* you reflect the path, the Reflect dialog box appears. Undo your last step and repeat Step 4, making sure that you press [Alt] (Win) or [Option] (Mac) after you start reflecting the path.

7. **Click the artboard anywhere near the point of origin ✣, drag until you see a preview of the two new paths that appear on top of the blue and purple objects as shown in Figure E-7, then press and hold [Alt] (Win) or [Option] (Mac) to duplicate the paths**
   The new paths do not need to match up with the blue and purple objects as shown in Figure E-7.

8. **Release the mouse button, then save your work**
   You should now have four paths.

FIGURE E-4: Changing the point of origin

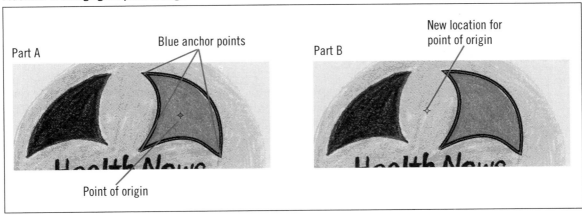

Part A — Blue anchor points — Point of origin

Part B — New location for point of origin

FIGURE E-5: Reflecting and duplicating an object

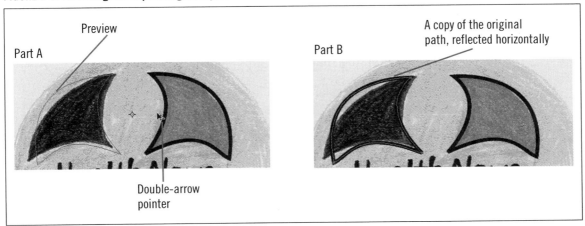

Part A — Preview — Double-arrow pointer

Part B — A copy of the original path, reflected horizontally

FIGURE E-6: Changing the point of origin

Point of origin

Make sure both paths are selected

FIGURE E-7: Reflecting and duplicating two objects

Preview of new path

Double arrow

Using the Layers Palette

You have already learned how objects on the artboard are "stacked" and how they can be sent backward or forward in that stack for lesser or greater visibility in an illustration. The Layers palette allows you to place objects on layers or sublayers and hide them or lock them without affecting other objects on the artboard. Sublayers within layers on the Layers palette form their own stack within that layer and can be sent forward or backward within it. Using the Layers palette, you can move, delete, and duplicate layers and sublayers. ✒ Bill will be adding the yellow circle and the text to his logo. He decides that it would be best to use the Layers palette for the remainder of his project. Because he no longer needs to look at the sketch of the Health News logo, he unlocks and deletes it, and then opens the Layers palette.

Steps 1 2 3 4

1. Click **Object** on the menu bar, then click **Unlock All**
   The sketch is unlocked and selected.

2. Press **[Delete]** (Win) or **[delete]** (Mac) to delete the sketch

3. Fill each path with the colors shown in Figure E-8
   You may need to switch to the Selection Tool ▶ to select each object.

4. Click the **Zoom menu** in the lower-left corner of the artboard, then click **100%**

Trouble?

If your menu option reads Hide Layers, the Layers palette is already showing.

5. Click **Window** on the menu bar, then click **Show Layers**
   The Layers palette appears as shown in Figure E-9. There is currently only one layer listed, called Layer 1. The small thumbnail picture to the left of Layer 1 displays the objects that are placed on Layer 1.

6. Click the **eye icon** 👁 on the Layers palette to the left of Layer 1 as shown in Figure E-9
   Everything on the artboard is temporarily hidden. Notice that the eye disappears from the icon.

7. Click the eye icon (which is now black) again 👁
   Everything reappears. Clicking the eye icon on a layer, toggles the visibility of objects on that particular layer.

8. Click the **gray square** ▢ to the right of the eye icon as shown in Figure E-9
   A padlock appears indicating that all objects on Layer 1 are locked. Your pointer becomes ✗. You cannot create an object or place a graphic on a locked layer.

9. Click 🔒 to unlock Layer 1, then save your work

FIGURE E-8: Filling each path with a color

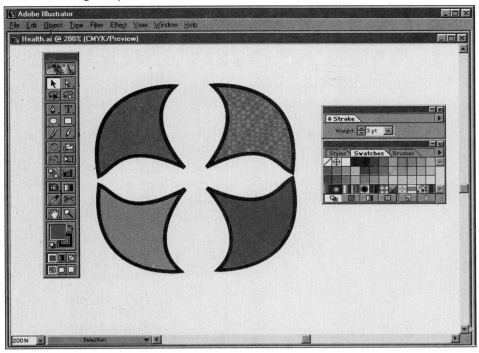

FIGURE E-9: The Layers palette

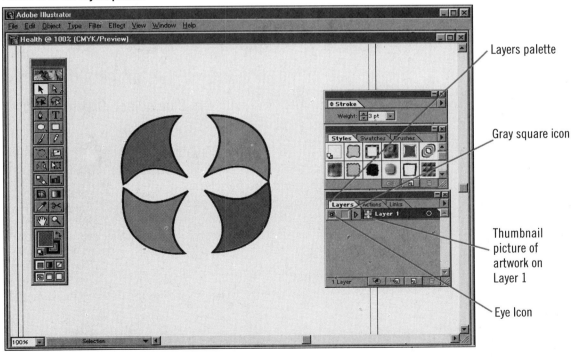

Layers palette

Gray square icon

Thumbnail
picture of
artwork on
Layer 1

Eye Icon

Viewing and Naming Layers and Sublayers

You can add new layers to the Layers palette and assign them names that describe that their contents. For example, if you were to design a calendar, you may want to place the days of the month on one layer called *Numbers* and all of the days of the week on another layer called *Days*. If you work on a project with other people, descriptive layer names make it easier for everyone to understand which objects belong on each layer. If you create multiple objects on one artboard, each new object created falls on a sublayer within that layer, as you can see from looking at the Layers palette. Sublayers fall in the order that the objects are created with the most recent object at the top of the list. Sublayers are given the name <path>; but like layers, they can be given new descriptive names. ✎ Bill renames Layer 1, views the four sublayers created within Layer 1, then gives them new names.

Steps

QuickTip

Clicking a layer in the Layers palette makes that layer the active layer. The active layer has a dark blue background color and a small white triangle in the upper-right corner of the layer name. Anything drawn or placed in Illustrator will be placed on a sublayer of the active layer.

QuickTip

Sublayers can contain grouped objects.

1. **Double-click Layer 1 on the Layers palette**
   The Layer Options dialog box opens. Notice the color assigned to Layer 1 is light blue. Light blue is the selection color for all objects placed on Layer 1 and sublayers assigned to Layer 1. Each time you click an object that is on Layer 1, you will see light blue selection lines.

2. **Rename Layer 1 Logo, then click OK**

3. **Click the gray triangle to the left of the Logo layer**
   The Sublayers on the Logo layer appear displaying a thumbnail picture of the object on each sublayer, as shown in Figure E-10. The gray triangle is used to expand and collapse the list of sublayers within a layer on the Layers palette.

4. **Double-click the first sublayer below the Logo layer on the Layers palette**
   The Options dialog box appears.

5. **Rename the sublayer Purple object, then click OK**

6. **Rename the remaining three sublayers Blue object, Green object, and Red object, as shown in Figure E-11**

7. **Click the circle to the right of the Red object sublayer, as shown in Figure E-12**
   The red object on the artboard is selected. If there were other objects assigned to the Red object sublayer, they would also be selected on the artboard. This is helpful in identifying which objects are on which sublayers or layers, if you are unsure. The circle on the Red object layer becomes a double circle, and a small light blue square appears next to the circle on the Red object sublayer. This square represents the selection color for objects placed on this sublayer.

8. **Click the green object on the artboard**
   Notice that the Green object sublayer now displays the double circle and the light blue selection square.

9. **Save your work**

FIGURE E-10: Viewing sublayers

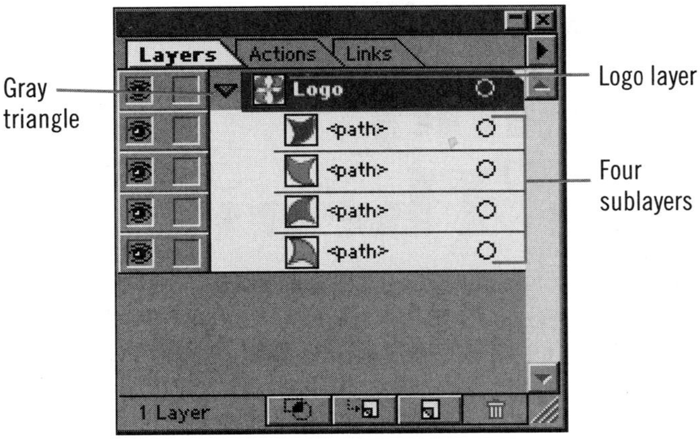
Layers
Actions
Links
Logo
<path>
<path>
<path>
<path>
1 Layer
Gray triangle
Logo layer
Four sublayers

FIGURE E-11: Renaming sublayers

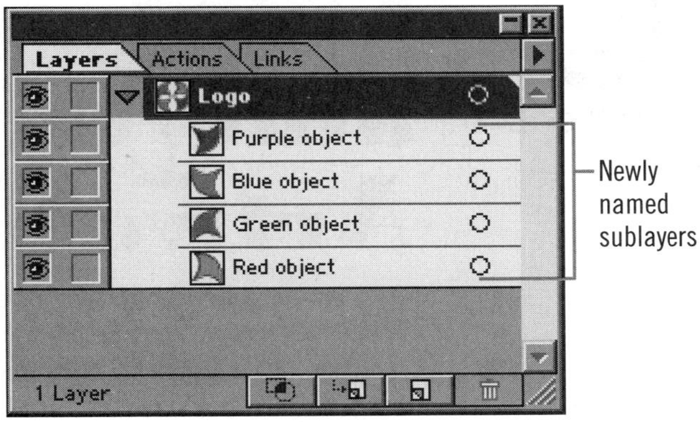
Layers
Actions
Links
Logo
Purple object
Blue object
Green object
Red object
1 Layer
Newly named sublayers

FIGURE E-12: Selecting a sublayer

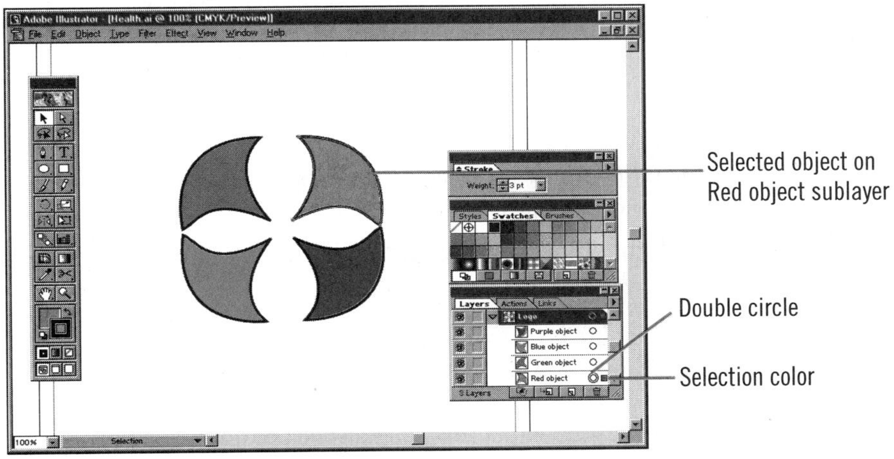
Selected object on Red object sublayer
Double circle
Selection color

CLUES TO USE

Paste Remembers Layers

You can use the Paste Remembers Layers feature when you would like to copy artwork and the layers on which the artwork is placed from one Illustrator document and then paste it into another Illustrator document. To use this feature, you must select Paste Remembers Layers from the Layers menu before you copy and paste objects on the artboard. Click the Show Option arrows ▶ on the Layers palette, then view the Layers menu items. If a check mark appears to the left of the Paste Remembers Layers menu item, this feature is already turned on; if no check mark is present, simply click to select it. Keep in mind that locked and hidden layers will not appear in the Layers palette of the new document.

Creating New Layers and Arranging Artwork on Them

When you create a new object or place a new object into an Illustrator document, that object will be placed on whichever layer is selected in the Layers palette. The selected layer, called the active layer, has a dark blue background color and a small white triangle in the upper-right corner of the layer name as shown in Part A of Figure E-13. It is possible to move objects from the active layer to new layers using the Layers palette. You can also change the stacking order of objects on the artboard by rearranging the order of layers, using the Layers palette. Bill creates a yellow circle and places it on a new layer called Yellow circle. He then drags the Yellow circle layer below the Logo layer on the Layers palette.

Steps

1. Click the **Logo layer** to make it the active layer

2. Click the **Ellipse Tool** on the toolbar, then click **Yellow** on the Swatches palette to change the fill color to yellow
   Make sure that the Fill icon is in front of the Stroke icon on the toolbar.

3. Place the pointer ⊹ in the center of the four filled paths as shown in Part A of Figure E-13

4. While pressing and holding **[Shift] [Alt]** (Win) or **[Option]** (Mac), drag ⊹ to create a perfect circle drawn from its center point, roughly the same size as the circle in Part B of Figure E-13
   The yellow circle is placed on a new sublayer underneath the Logo layer and is blocking the four colored objects as shown in Part B of Figure E-13.

5. Click the **Show Options arrow** on the Layers palette, then click **New Layer**
   The Layer Options dialog box opens.

QuickTip
You can also create a new layer by clicking the Create New Layer button on the Layers palette. Double-clicking a layer opens the Layer Options dialog box.

6. Rename Layer 2 **Yellow Circle**, then click **OK**
   The Yellow Circle layer appears above the Logo layer on the Layers palette as shown in Part A of Figure E-14. It is the active layer. Notice that the Yellow Circle layer is empty, indicated by the blank square that normally displays a thumbnail of the artwork on the layer.

QuickTip
Each new layer falls above the layer that is currently selected.

7. Locate the sublayer called **<path>** on which the yellow circle is currently placed, as shown in Part B of Figure E-14. Drag the **light blue square** (to the right of the double circle on the <path> sublayer—see Part B of Figure E-14) to the new Yellow Circle layer, then release the mouse button
   Your pointer becomes a pointing finger 🖑 as you move the artwork to a new layer. The yellow circle is placed on the Yellow Circle layer as shown in Part C of Figure E-14. The yellow circle on the artboard has a new selection color of red, indicated by the red square on the Yellow Circle layer.

8. While pressing and holding the mouse button on the **Yellow Circle layer** in the Layers palette, drag the layer **below the Red object sublayer**, then release the mouse button
   Your pointer becomes a closed fist 🤛 as you drag the layer to its new location. See Part A of Figure E-15. A heavy black line appears below the Red object layer, as shown in Part A of Figure E-15, indicating the new location of the layer when you release the mouse button. The yellow circle on the artboard is now behind the four colored objects as shown in Part B of Figure E-15.

9. Save your work

FIGURE E-13: Creating the yellow circle

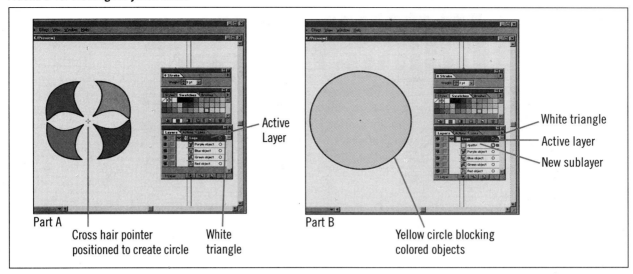

Active Layer

White triangle
Active layer
New sublayer

Part A

Cross hair pointer
positioned to create circle

White
triangle

Part B

Yellow circle blocking
colored objects

FIGURE E-14: Creating a new layer

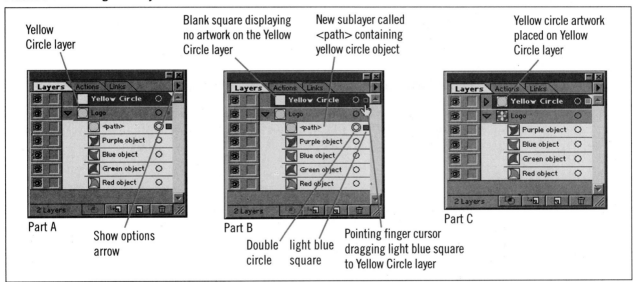

Yellow
Circle layer

Blank square displaying
no artwork on the Yellow
Circle layer

New sublayer called
<path> containing
yellow circle object

Yellow circle artwork
placed on Yellow
Circle layer

Part A

Show options
arrow

Part B

Double
circle

light blue
square

Pointing finger cursor
dragging light blue square
to Yellow Circle layer

Part C

FIGURE E-15: Moving layers in the Layers palette

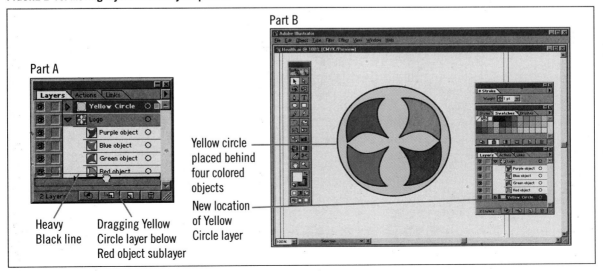

Part B

Part A

Yellow circle
placed behind
four colored
objects

New location
of Yellow
Circle layer

Heavy
Black line

Dragging Yellow
Circle layer below
Red object sublayer

Illustrator 9.0

Illustrator 9.0

Locking and Hiding Layers

The ability to lock and hide layers and sublayers may help you organize a complex illustration and allow you to focus on an object or objects without being distracted by others. For example, if you have created an illustration of a roadmap and all of the highways appear on one layer, all of the secondary streets appear on another layer, and all of the railroad tracks appear on a third layer, and you now need to add tiny signs to the highways, you may find it easier to work on them by temporarily hiding the secondary street and railroad track layers. You may also find it helpful to lock the highway layer so that you do not select or move part of the highway accidentally when you place the highway signs on it. In addition, you can hide layers and sublayers for viewing, printing, and saving variations of one illustration. Bill creates a new layer called Health Text and places a text object on it. He hides the Yellow Circle layer so that he can view the logo without it, and then hides everything except the Health Text layer to determine whether he likes the typeface he chose.

Steps

1. Click the **gray triangle** to the left of the Logo layer on the Layers palette to collapse the sublayers

2. Click the **Logo Layer** on the Layers palette to make it the active layer, if necessary

3. Click the **Show Options arrow** ▶ on the Layers palette, then click **New Layer**

4. Name the new layer **Health Text**, then click **OK**

5. Create a **text object** on top of the logo, as shown in Figure E-16, which reads "Health News" and position it using the Selection Tool

   You can choose a font that you like from the Type menu. Choose a font size that is similar to the one shown in Figure E-16 (24 pt). The text object is placed on the Health Text layer since it was the active layer when the text object was created.

6. Click the **eye icon** 👁 on the Yellow Circle layer to hide the yellow circle, then click the blank eye icon on the Yellow Circle layer again to show the yellow circle

7. Click the **Health Text layer** to make it the active layer, if necessary

QuickTip

You can also hide all layers except the active layer by clicking the eye icon 👁 on the active layer of the Layers palette while pressing [Alt] (Win) or [Option] (Mac).

8. Click the **Show Options arrow** ▶ on the Layers palette, then click **Hide Others**

   The contents on all layers, except the Health Text layer, are temporarily hidden.

QuickTip

Objects on hidden layers will not print.

9. Click ▶ on the Layers palette, click **Show All Layers**, then save your work

   Your screen should resemble Figure E-16.

FIGURE E-16: Adding the Text layer

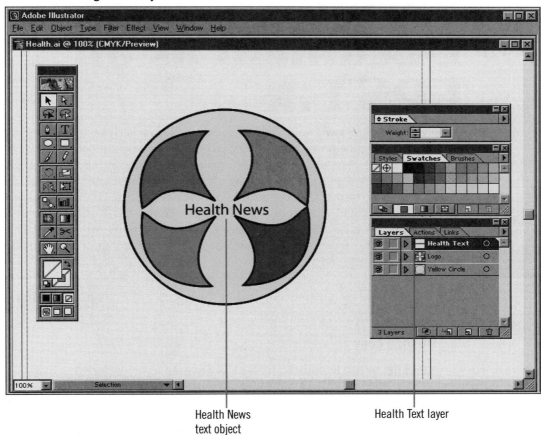

Health News
text object

Health Text layer

Suppressing the printing of Illustrator layers

You can suppress the printing of an Illustrator layer without hiding or deleting it by using the Layers menu. For example, if you were an interior decorator who designed floor plans in Illustrator, and you wanted to print a particular living room scene without the rug but without removing the image from the artboard, you could select the Rug layer, click the Show

Options arrow ▶ on the Layers palette, then click Options for Rug. When the Layer Options dialog box opened, you would click the check mark in the Print check box to remove it, click OK, then print your document. Even though the rug would be visible, it would not print.

Saving an Illustrator Document as an EPS File

When you are finished with your illustrations, you will most likely want to use them in a Web page, a multimedia presentation, or some other type of software program, such as a page layout software. To import one of your illustrations into a page layout program like Adobe PageMaker, Adobe InDesign, or QuarkXPress, you need to save it first as an **Encapsulated PostScript (EPS)** file. EPS is the preferred file format for illustrated line art because it is based on PostScript printer definition language and results in crisp, vector-based images. Bill is ready to deliver his file to the Advertising Department. First, he prints a copy of the logo for his own files. Next, he saves the logo as an EPS file so that the Advertising Department can import it into its page layout software to create the newspaper ad.

Steps

1. Compare your completed illustration to Figure E-17, then place **your name** in the lower-left corner of the artboard

2. Print **one copy** of Health

3. Click **File** on the menu bar, then click **Save As**
   The Save dialog box opens as shown in Figure E-18.

4. Click the **Save in list arrow** (Win) or the **Desktop button** (Mac), then navigate to the drive where you store your project files

5. Click the **Save as Type list arrow** (Win) or the **Format list arrow** (Mac), then click **Illustrator EPS**
   If you are working on a PC, the extension .eps will be added to the end of the filename. If you are working on a Macintosh, click the Append File Extension check box, if necessary, to add the .eps extension to the filename.

6. Click **Save**
   The EPS Format Options dialog box opens, offering you Compatibility and Preview options. Do not make any changes in this dialog box.

7. Click **OK**, then **Exit** (Win) or **Quit** (Mac) Illustrator

FIGURE E-17: **The finished illustration**

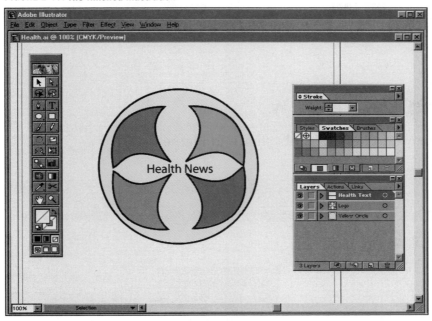

FIGURE E-18: **Saving an illustration as an EPS file on a PC and a Macintosh**

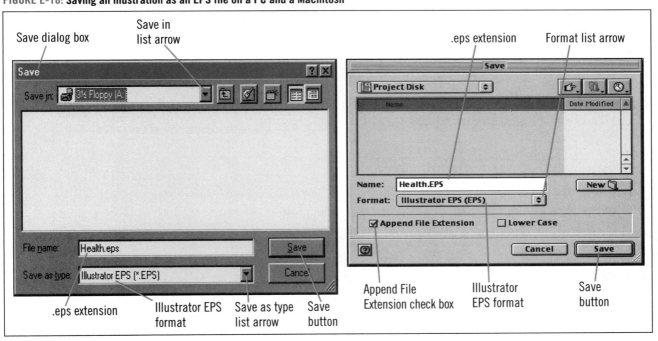

Illustrator 9.0

Practice

▶ Concepts Review

Label the Illustrator window elements shown in Figure E-19.

FIGURE E-19

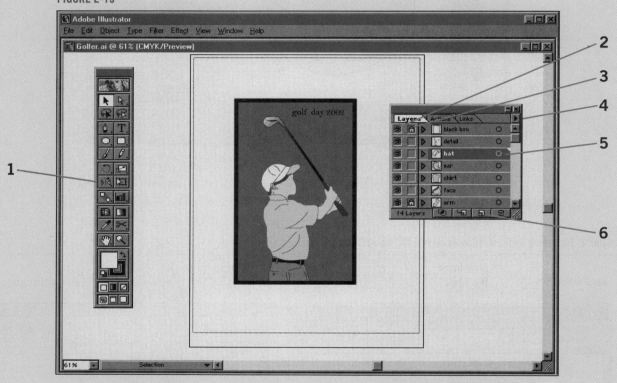

Match each term with the statement that describes it.

7. EPS
8. Reflect Tool
9. Layers palette
10. Eye icon
11. Locked layer
12. Active layer

a. Tool that flips objects horizontally or vertically
b. An icon on the Layers palette that hides the layer when clicked
c. The layer that is currently selected in the Layers palette
d. Layer whose objects cannot be selected or moved
e. Palette used for placing objects on individual layers
f. File format required for printing illustrations in a page layout software program

13. Which pointer does your cursor become when you press and hold [Alt] (Win) or [Option] (Mac) while dragging an object?
    a. ▨
    b. 🖑
    c. ▶
    d. ⬚₊

14. The layer that is selected in the Layers palette is considered:
    a. locked.
    b. nonprinting.
    c. active.
    d. hidden.

15. What does the colored square to the right of a layer's name in the Layers palette indicate?
    a. The color of the object(s) on that layer
    b. The selection color of the object(s) on that layer
    c. The visibility of object(s) on that layer
    d. The number of object(s) on that layer

16. Which pointer does your cursor become when you drag a layer to a new location in the Layers palette?
    a. ▨
    b. 🖑
    c. ✋
    d. ▶

Make sure that you have extra blank floppy disks on hand so that if you run out of room on your Project Disks while completing the Skills Review or Independent Challenges, you will have a place to save the files you create.

▶ Skills Review

1. Delete direction lines.
    a. Start Illustrator.
    b. Open AI E-2 from the drive and folder where you store your project files. A picture of a snowman has been placed and locked in this document. Nine black dots with corresponding numbers have been added to the artboard to help you trace the snowman.
    c. Save AI E-2 as *Snowmen*.
    d. Click the Pen Tool.
    e. Set the fill color to None.
    f. Set the stroke color to Black.
    g. Set the stroke weight to 2 pt.
    h. Increase the zoom level so that you have a good view of the snowman.
    i. Click the Pen Tool on top of the first black dot, then release it to add a corner anchor point.
    j. Click-and-drag the Pen Tool on the second black dot until you see a preview of the first line segment fall into place.
    k. Click the second anchor point (on the second black dot) to delete the direction line.

Illustrator 9.0

2. Create new direction lines.

a. Click-and-drag the Pen Tool on the third black dot until you see a preview of the second line segment fall into place.

b. Click the third anchor point (on the third black dot) to delete the direction line.

c. Keep the Pen Tool pointer on the third anchor point, then while pressing [Alt] (Win) or [Option] (Mac) click-and-drag to the left to create a new direction line that points to the number 3 on the artboard. This new direction line will help you draw the next line segment.

d. Click-and-drag the Pen Tool on the fourth black dot until you see a preview of the third line segment fall into place.

e. Continue to trace the snowman by placing new anchor points on each of the black dots. Delete direction lines and create new direction lines, when necessary.

f. When you get to the tenth point, close the path by clicking the first anchor point with the Pen Tool.

g. Save your work.

3. Use the Reflect Tool.

a. Click the edge of the new path to select it.

b. Click the Reflect Tool.

c. Click a point on the artboard to the right of the snowman to change the point of origin from the center point of the snowman.

d. Drag the Reflect Tool pointer on the artboard to reflect the snowman. When the preview of the snowman is completely vertical, press [Alt] (Win) or [Option] (Mac) to duplicate the original snowman.

e. Release the mouse button first, then release [Alt] (Win) or [Option] (Mac).

f. Scale one of the snowmen 75% using the Scale Tool.

g. Fill each snowman with white.

h. Save your work.

4. Use the Layers palette.

a. Click the Selection Tool.

b. Click Object on the menu bar, then click Unlock All.

c. Press [Delete] (Win) or [delete] (Mac) to delete the picture, the numbers, and the black dots.

d. Make sure that the Layers palette is showing. If you do not see the Layers palette, click Window on the menu bar, then click Show Layers.

e. Notice the thumbnail picture of the two snowmen on Layer 1 of the Layers palette.

f. Click the Eye icon on Layer 1 of the Layers palette to hide the snowmen.

g. Click the empty square where the eye icon was to show the snowmen.

5. View and name layers and sublayers.

a. Double-click Layer 1, then rename it **Snowmen**.

b. Click the gray triangle to the left of the Snowmen layer to view the sublayers.

c. Rename the first sublayer **Snowman One**

d. Rename the second sublayer **Snowman Two**

e. Click the gray triangle to the left of the Snowmen layer to hide the sublayers.

6. Create new layers and arrange artwork on them.

a. Click the Show Options arrow on the Layers palette, then click New Layer.

b. Double-click Layer 2, then rename it **Eyes**.

c. Make sure that the Eyes layer is the active layer by selecting it.

d. Use the Ellipse Tool, the Paintbrush Tool, or the Pencil Tool to create eyes for the two snowmen. The eyes are now assigned to the Eyes layer.

    e. Continue to create new layers for items that you would like to add to the snowmen, for example, nose, mouth, buttons, hat, arms, and legs. Create the new layer, rename it, then create the artwork to be placed on that layer.

    f. Create a new layer called **Background**.

    g. Make sure that the Background layer is the active layer, then draw a large rectangle on the artboard that covers the snowmen.

    h. Fill the rectangle with a color of your choice.

    i. Drag the Background layer beneath the Snowmen layer on the Layers palette so that the rectangle falls behind the snowmen on the artboard.

    j. Save your work.

7. Lock and hide layers.

    a. Click the eye icon to the left of each layer to hide the objects that are assigned to that layer, then show them again by clicking the empty gray square.

    b. Lock each layer except for the Snowmen layer and the Background layer

    c. Save your work.

8. Save an Illustrator document as an EPS file.

    a. Place your name in the lower-left corner of the artboard.

    b. Print one copy of Snowmen.

    c. Click File on the menu bar, then click Save As.

    d. Click the Save in list arrow (Win) or the Desktop button (Mac), then navigate to the drive where you store your project files.

    e. Click the Save as Type list arrow (Win) or the Format list arrow (Mac), then click Illustrator EPS. If you are working on a PC, the extension .eps will be added to the end of the filename. If you are working on a Macintosh, click the Append File Extension check box, if necessary, to add the .eps extension to the filename.

    f. Click Save. The EPS Format Options dialog box opens, offering you Compatibility and Preview options. Do not make any changes in this dialog box.

    g. Click OK, then Exit (Win) or Quit (Mac) Illustrator.

▶ Independent Challenges

1. You are a designer working for a frame company. You use Illustrator to create your designs. Recently, your manager asked you to design a frame that has identical graphics in each of its four corners. You can refer to the example in Figure E-20 as you work.

    To complete this independent challenge:

    a. Start a new document in Illustrator.

    b. Save the new Illustrator document as *Frame*.

    c. Use the Pen Tool, the Paintbrush Tool, or a Basic Shape Tool to create a design. This design can be a squiggle, a star, an hourglass, or anything you want.

    d. Make sure that the object is selected, then click the Reflect Tool.

    e. Click the artboard to the right of the object to change the point of origin from the object's center.

    f. After you start reflecting the object, press [Alt] (Win) or [Option] (Mac) to duplicate the object, releasing the mouse button first and [Alt] (Win) or [Option] (Mac) last.

    g. Select both objects.

    h. Click the artboard about 2 inches below the selected objects to change the point of origin.

    i. After you start reflecting the objects, press [Alt] (Win) or [Option] (Mac) to duplicate them, releasing the mouse button first and [Alt] (Win) or [Option] (Mac) last.

j. Place the four objects on a new layer called **Corners**.

k. Create a frame using the Rectangle Tool.

l. Place the frame on a new layer called **Frame**.

m. Drag the Frame layer below the Corners layer on the Layers palette.

n. If necessary, adjust the locations of the objects placed on the four corners.

o. Choose fill and stroke colors for the design objects and the frame.

p. Lock the Corners layer.

q. Place your name in the lower-left corner of the artboard.

r. Print one copy of Frame.

s. Save your work and Exit (Win) or Quit (Mac) Illustrator.

FIGURE E-20

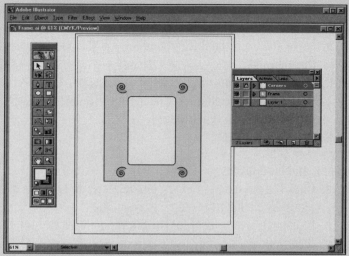

2. You are employed by your town's Parks and Recreation Department. You have been asked to create a flyer to post at the local duck pond describing the different types of ducks that can be seen there. You decide to draw illustrations of ducks, rather than use photographs. You will trace a bitmap of a duck to help you get started.

To complete this independent challenge:

a. Start Illustrator.

b. Open AI E-3 from the drive and folder where you store your project files.

c. Save AI E-3 as *Duck*.

d. Using the Pen Tool, trace a path of the duck. You do not need to trace a path of the water.

e. When you are finished tracing the duck, unlock the bitmap of the duck using the Object menu, then delete it.

f. Use the Shape tools, the Paintbrush Tool, and the Brushes palette to add detail to the duck, such as feathers and eyes.

g. Group all of the pieces of the duck together.

h. Double click Layer 1 on the Layers palette, then rename it **Duck**.

i. Click the gray triangle to the left of the Duck layer to view the sublayers. Notice the sublayer is called <group>.

j. Create a new layer and rename it **Water**.

k. Keep the Water layer selected.

l. Create a rectangle on the artboard that covers the duck.

m. Fill the rectangle with a color or a gradient representing water.

n. Drag the Water layer beneath the Duck layer on the Layers palette.

o. Place your name in the lower-left corner of the artboard.

p. Print one copy of Duck.

q. Save your work, then Exit (Win) or Quit (Mac) Illustrator.

3. You are a graphic designer who specializes in corporate identity projects. Corporate identity involves creating a look and feel for a company that is indicative of its product, style, philosophy, and personality—all of which need to be reflected in the company logo. You are designing a logo for a sporting goods manufacturer. You need to meet with your client to show her variations of a possible logo that you have created in Illustrator. To display all of the possibilities easily, you will place each element of the logo on its own layer.

To complete this independent challenge:

a. Start Illustrator.

b. Open AI E-4 from the drive and folder where you store your project files.

c. Save AI E-4 as *Logo*.

d. Create a new layer for each object that is part of the completed logo, using titles that are indicative of the objects on those layers, such as Red Circle and Black Circle.

e. Place each object on its respective layer.

f. If necessary, rearrange the layers in the Layers palette to make all of the logo elements visible.

g. Leave Layer 1 empty.

h. Practice hiding and showing each layer as you would for your client.

i. Place your name in the lower-left corner of the artboard.

j. Print one copy of Logo.

k. Save your work.

l. Save Logo as an EPS file with the same name.

m. Exit (Win) or Quit (Mac) Illustrator.

4. You are an art director for a furniture store. Your newest project is to create a living room scene for an upcoming magazine advertisement. You have completed most of the living room scene; however, you still need an illustration of a sofa to be placed in the picture.
To complete this independent challenge:

a. Connect to the Internet and go to *http://www.course.com*.

b. Navigate to the page for this book, then click the link for the Student Online Companion.

c. Click the links for this unit.

d. Look for a picture of a sofa.

e. [Right-click (Win) or [Ctrl] click (Mac)] the sofa picture, then click Save Picture As. The Save Picture dialog box opens.

f. Rename the picture **Sofa**.

g. Click the Save as Type list arrow in the Save Picture dialog box, then click Bitmap.

h. Click Save.

i. Exit (Win) or Quit (Mac) your Web browser.

j. Start Illustrator.

k. Open AI E-5 from the file and folder where you store your project files.

l. Save AI E-5 as *Living room*.

m. Click the Bookcase layer on the Layers palette to make it the active layer.

n. Create a new layer called Sofa. The Sofa layer should be placed above the Bookcase layer.

o. Place the Sofa picture in the Living room document. The Sofa picture should be assigned to the Sofa layer.

p. Zoom in on the picture of the sofa in order to trace it with the Pen Tool.

q. After tracing the sofa with the Pen Tool, fill the sofa with a new color.

r. Delete the bitmap image of the sofa so that you are left with the vector illustration of the sofa.

s. Click the circle to the right of the Sofa layer on the Layers palette to select the sofa. If you have created many individual paths for the sofa, they will all be selected. Group the sofa or scale the sofa, if necessary.

t. Move any layers on the Layers palette, if necessary. For example, if you would like the plant in front of the sofa, move the Plant layer above the Sofa layer.

u. Place your name in the lower-left corner of the artboard.

v. Print one copy of Living room.

w. Exit (Win) or Quit (Mac) Illustrator, saving changes to the document.

Illustrator 9.0

► Visual Workshop

Re-create Figure E-21 by creating the shapes and then creating layers for each of the shapes. Place each object on the appropriate layer, then move the layers around in the Layers palette, if necessary, so that your screen looks like Figure E-21. Save your document as *Layers*. Place your name in the lower-left corner of the artboard, print one copy of Layers, then Exit (Win) or Quit (Mac) Illustrator.

FIGURE E-21

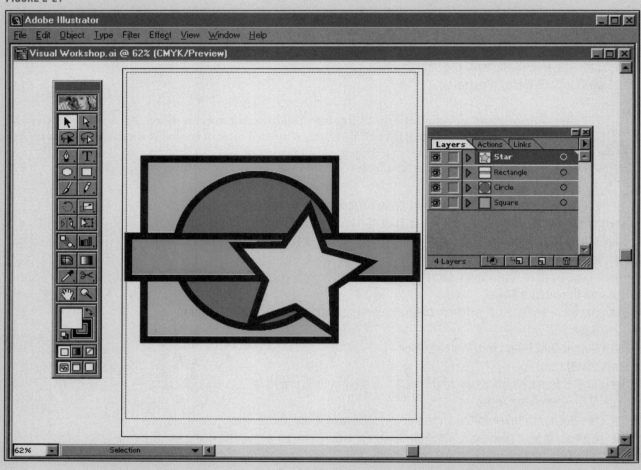

Designing

Logos with Text and Gradient Tools

► **Create new views**
► **Create outlines and apply gradient fills**
► **Change the colors in a gradient**
► **Add and delete anchor points**
► **Unite objects**
► **Type on a path**
► **Move text along a path**
► **Use Outline and Preview mode**

Illustrator includes many ways to enhance text graphically. In addition to typing along a straight or curved line using the Path Type Tool, you can convert text into objects called **outlines** that you can then fill with gradients and unite as one object for strong visual effect. While working on a project you can toggle between Preview mode and Outline mode. Outline mode is useful for finding objects that you should remove from the artboard, such as stray anchor points and empty text boxes. The designers at WHJY have been asked to come up with ideas for the 2004 presidential election news logo. They are supposed to present their logos to the CEO of WHJY in three weeks. Bill has already started working on his logos, but needs to finish the job.

Illustrator 9.0

Creating New Views

You have already experienced some of the benefits of zooming in on different areas of the artboard to create better working views. The **New View** feature allows you to save the views that you will be using frequently. To create a new view, you first zoom in on a specific area of the artboard, then save the view with a unique name. The view becomes an item on the View menu, which you can then select to display the exact area you defined when you created it. ✎ Bill creates a new view for each of the logos on which he's been working.

Steps

1. Start Illustrator

2. Open **AI F-1** from the drive and folder where you store your project files, then save it as **Election**
   One of the logo designs is placed at the top of the artboard, and one is placed at the bottom.

Trouble?

If you zoom in too much or not enough, double-click the Hand Tool to return to the Fit In Window view of the artboard, and try again.

3. Click the **Zoom Tool** 🔍, then drag ⊕ to create a marquee around the top logo so that it fills the screen as shown in Figure F-1
   You should be able to see the entire logo.

4. Click **View** on the menu bar, then click **New View**
   The New View dialog box opens.

QuickTip

You can also zoom out in smaller increments by pressing [Alt] (Win) or [Option] (Mac) while clicking ⊕. When you press the key combination, ⊕ becomes ⊖.

5. Name the view **Election One** as shown in Figure F-2, then click **OK**
   It is helpful to be as descriptive as possible when defining views on your artboard.

6. Double-click the **Hand Tool** 🖐 to return to the Fit In Window view of the artboard

7. Zoom in on the second logo, then create a new view called **Election Two**
   Remember to make sure that you can see the entire logo on the artboard.

8. Click **View** on the menu bar, then click **Election One**

Trouble?

Printing, saving, and exporting are disabled in the Illustrator Tryout! software. To learn more about the Tryout! software that accompanies this book, see the Read This Before You Begin page.

9. Click **View** on the menu bar, click **Election Two**, then save your work
   Notice how easy it is to navigate to specific areas on the artboard.

FIGURE F-1: Zooming in on the top logo

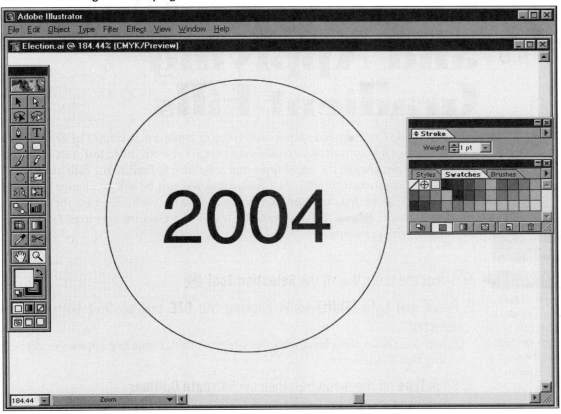

FIGURE F-2: Creating a New View

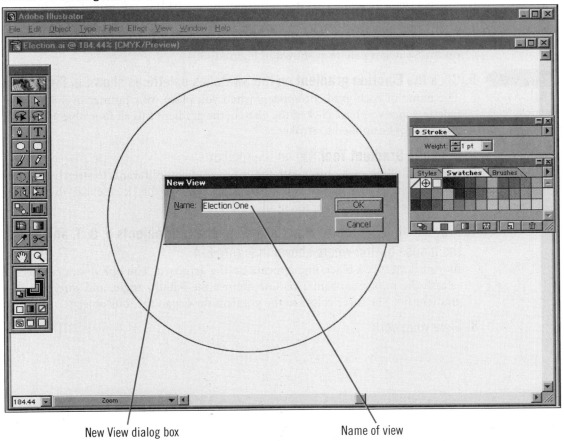

New View dialog box

Name of view

Illustrator 9.0

Creating Outlines and Applying Gradient Fills

Text can be filled and stroked with a solid color or a pattern. It cannot be filled with a gradient, however, unless it is converted into individual vector objects, called **outlines**. Converting text to outlines does not change the text's appearance. Be sure to finalize the font and font size of your text before converting it to outlines, because you will not be able to change the font once your text has been converted. You can convert your text to outlines using the Illustrator **Create Outlines** feature. Bill converts the text in the Election Two logo to outlines, then fills the outlines with gradients.

Trouble?

You may also see the bounding box appear around your selected objects. It's OK to leave it on, but you can hide the use Bounding Box feature using the View menu.

1. Select the large **V** with the **Selection Tool**

2. Press and hold **[Shift]** while clicking the **OTE** text so that both text objects are selected

When you click a text object with the Selection Tool, a blue line appears underneath it, indicating that it is selected.

3. Click **Type** on the menu bar, then click **Create Outlines**

The four characters that make up the word "VOTE" are now vector objects with anchor points and line segments, as shown in Figure F-3.

4. Resize the Swatches palette by dragging (Win) or (Mac) so that you see a new gradient called **Election**.

If you do not see any gradients on the Swatches palette click the Show All Swatches button on the Swatches palette as shown in Figure F-3.

Trouble?

If you do not see the Swatches palette, click Window on the menu bar, then click Show All Swatches.

5. Click the **Election gradient** on the Swatches palette as shown in Figure F-3

The name of each gradient appears when you place your pointer over it on the Swatches palette. Once you have clicked the swatch, the gradient fills all four objects. Note that gradients cannot be applied to strokes.

6. Click the **Gradient Tool** on the toolbox

Instead of filling each object with the entire gradient, Bill wants to stretch the three colors in the gradient so that they start on the "V" and end on the "E". He uses the Gradient Tool to change the length of the gradient fill.

7. Drag ╬ in a horizontal direction across **the four objects V, O, T, and E**, then release the mouse button where shown in Figure F-4

As you drag ╬, a black line appears on the artboard. The line disappears as soon as you release the mouse button. This line defines the length, angle, and direction of the entire gradient fill. The three colors in the gradient now span the four objects.

8. Save your work

FIGURE F-3: Converting text to outlines and applying a gradient fill

Anchor points

Four objects filled with Election gradient

Election gradient

Show All swatches button

Line segments

FIGURE F-4: Changing the length of a gradient fill

Gradient Tool

Black line that appears when you drag -¦- to change the length and direction of the gradient

Election gradient

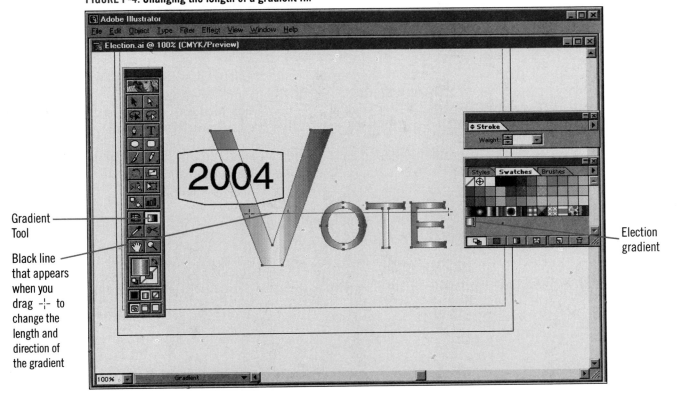

Changing the Colors in a Gradient

Illustrator 9.0

You may want to change something about a gradient fill after you see it applied to one or more objects on the artboard. To see how a change in the gradient will appear in your objects, keep those objects selected while you make changes to the gradient in the Gradient palette. As you add, remove, or move colors on the gradient slider, the gradient fill will keep updating its appearance inside the selected objects. Bill keeps the V, O, T, and E objects selected while he modifies the Election gradient.

Steps

1. Show the **Gradient palette** and the **Color palette** if you do not already see them
   Take a moment to separate the Gradient palette from other palettes as shown in Figure F-5.

2. Make sure that the **V, O, T**, and **E objects** are still selected and that you can see a full view of the Gradient palette
   If you do not see a full view of the Gradient palette, click the Show Options arrow ▶ on the Gradient palette, then click Show Options.

3. Click the **second color stop** on the Gradient slider to select it as shown in Part A of Figure F-5

QuickTip

You can also enter values in the Color palette manually.

4. Drag the **K slider** on the Color palette to **10%**, then drag the **C slider** on the Color palette to **10%** to change the second color in the gradient

QuickTip

If you do not click close enough to the bottom edge of the Gradient slider, a new color stop will not appear.

5. Click the **bottom edge of the Gradient slider** to add a third color stop at approximately the **65% location**, as shown in Part B of Figure F-5
   A new color stop appears wherever you click the bottom edge of the Gradient slider. The location of the color stop appears in the Location field on the Gradient palette. You can drag the color stop to adjust the location of it on the Gradient slider. Anything close to 65% is fine.

6. Keeping the new color stop selected, press **[Alt]** (Win) or **[Option]** (Mac), while you click the **25% Azure swatch** on the Swatches palette
   If you do not press [Alt] (Win) or [Option] (Mac) when you apply a swatch to a gradient, the selected objects on the artboard are filled with the swatch color and not the gradient.

7. Drag the **gradient fill icon** on the Gradient palette to the Swatches palette
   The gradient fill icon, as shown in Figure F-6, is the square in the upper-left corner of the Gradient palette. It displays a preview of the gradient as it is created.

8. Double-click the **new gradient swatch** on the Swatches palette, then name it **New Election**

9. Click the **Selection Tool** �, click the artboard to deselect the logo, then save your work
   Notice the new gradient fill applied to the V, O, T, and E objects in Figure F-6.

FIGURE F-5: Changing colors in a gradient

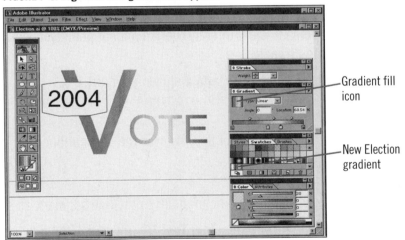

Gradient slider

Second color stop

Bottom edge of gradient slider

Second color stop

Location field

Gradient slider

Third color stop

25% Azure swatch

Part A

Part B

FIGURE F-6: Logo with new gradient fill applied

Gradient fill icon

New Election gradient

CLUES TO USE

Document Info

The Document Info dialog box includes information about Illustrator documents including the number of objects it contains, fonts, colors, gradients, and patterns used in the document, and the names of linked and embedded images. This information can be saved as a report, which is a text file that you can print, e-mail to a coworker, or store in a folder on your computer. To access information about your document, click File on the menu bar, then click Document Info. Click the Show Options arrow ▶, then click the item that you are interested in. To create a report, click ▶, then click Save. You will then be prompted to rename and save the report somewhere on your computer system. The Document Info menu item will not be available if you have anything selected on the artboard; instead, you'll find the Selection Info menu. To make the Document Info menu available, deselect all objects by clicking [Ctrl] [Shift] [A] (Win) or [Command] [Shift] [A] (Mac) before you click the File menu.

Illustrator 9.0

Adding and Deleting Anchor Points

In earlier units, you learned about using the Pen Tool to trace bitmaps in Illustrator. Sometimes, you may need to edit a path that has already been created. Using the Pen Tool, you can add anchor points to a line segment or delete them as necessary. Adding an anchor point to a line segment breaks the line segment into two parts, thereby giving you more sides and curves to manipulate in your path. On the other hand, using too many anchor points yields unnecessary curves and line segments, frequently resulting in jagged-looking paths. Removing extra anchor points allows you to smooth out these paths. ✐━━ Bill edits the rectangle by adding and deleting anchor points.

Steps 1234

1. Click the **Selection Tool** � on the toolbox, then click the **edge of the shape that resembles a rectangle** around the 2004 text

2. Click the **Pen Tool** 🖋 on the toolbox

3. Place 🖋 directly on top of **Point 1** as shown in Figure F-7
   Your pointer becomes 🖋_.

Trouble?
If you make a mistake, undo your last few steps and try again. Zoom in using the Zoom Tool to see the anchor points more easily.

4. Click 🖋_ to remove the anchor point. If the Pen Tool is not directly on top of the anchor point, you will not see 🖋_ and will not be able to delete the point. If you click the Pen Tool when it is not directly over an anchor point, you will add a new stray anchor point on the artboard.

5. Remove **Points 2, 3, and 4** shown in Figure F-7
   The shape should now be a rectangle with four corner anchor points as shown in Part A of Figure F-8.

6. Position the Pen Tool directly over the vertical line segment in the location shown in Part A of Figure F-8
   Your pointer becomes 🖋+.

7. Click 🖋+ to add an anchor point to the line segment as shown in Part B of Figure F-8

8. Click the **Direct Selection Tool** ▸, then click the **new anchor point** and pull it to the left to change the angle of the two new line segments as shown in Part C of Figure F-8
   If you begin dragging an anchor point that is not connected to the line segment, you probably added an anchor point next to the line segment on the artboard, instead of directly on the line segment. Undo a few steps until the new anchor point is gone, then repeat Steps 6, 7, and 8.

9. Save your work

FIGURE F-7: **Removing anchor points**

Point 2

Point 1

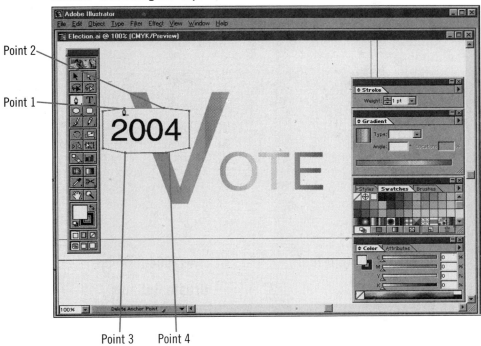

Point 3   Point 4

FIGURE F-8: **Adding an anchor point to a line segment**

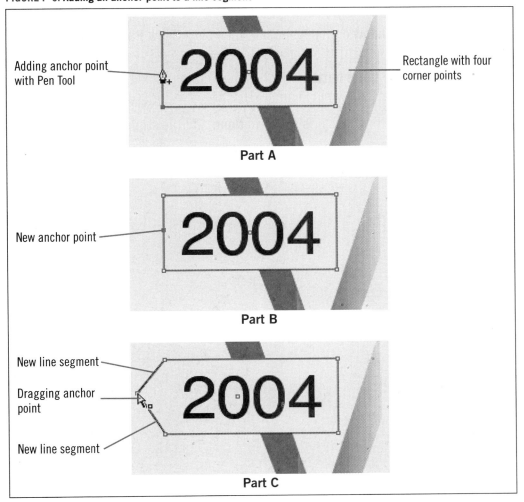

Adding anchor point
with Pen Tool

Rectangle with four
corner points

Part A

New anchor point

Part B

New line segment

Dragging anchor
point

New line segment

Part C

Uniting Objects

The **Unite** command is one of the Pathfinder commands found on the Pathfinder palette. **Pathfinders** are Illustrator commands that combine and divide overlapping objects, thereby creating new objects in the process. The Unite command may be helpful if you have created pieces of an illustration separately and now want to combine them into a single closed path. Unlike grouping objects, which also combines two or more objects into one unit, uniting removes the overlapping line segments from the objects and places one stroke around the perimeter of the new object. It changes the appearance of objects, whereas grouping does not. For example, if you created the base and handle of a coffee mug as two separate objects, but wanted the handle to look as though it stemmed directly from the mug, you would overlap the handle and the mug, select both the handle and the mug, and then unite them. Bill converts the 2004 text to outlines, overlaps the four objects, and then unites them to make it look as though 2004 is one continuous object.

Steps

1. Click the **Selection Tool** , then click the **2004** text object

2. Click **Type** on the menu bar, then click **Create Outlines**

3. Click **Object** on the menu bar, then click **Ungroup**

4. Click the **artboard** to deselect the four objects

5. Drag each object so that it overlaps with the one before it, as shown in Figure F-9

6. Press and hold **[Shift]** while you click the V, O, T, and E objects to select all of them

7. Click **Window** on the menu bar, then click **Show Pathfinder**
   The Pathfinder palette appears.

8. Click the **Unite button**, which is the first button in the Combine row of the Pathfinder palette, as shown in Figure F-10

9. Change the fill color of 2004 to **None** and the stroke color to **Red**

10. Click the **artboard** to deselect 2004, then save your work
    Compare your screen with Figure F-10.

FIGURE F-9: Overlapping objects

Overlapping objects

FIGURE F-10: Uniting objects

Pathfinder palette

Unite button

United object

Typing on a Path

Illustrator provides six Type tools that you can use to create text. They include the Type, Area Type, Path Type, Vertical Type, Vertical Area Type, and the Vertical Path Type tools. **Area Type** tools are used to fill the inside of a closed path with text. **Path Type** tools are used to place text along an open or closed path. When you type on a path, the fill and stroke colors of the path are removed. If you want to retain the fill or stroke colors of the path, you must duplicate the path before you start typing. ➤ Bill types the word "Election" along the circle path in the Election One logo.

Steps

1. Click **View** on the menu bar, then click **Election One**

2. Close the Gradient, Pathfinder, and Color palettes
   The artboard becomes cluttered when too many palettes are showing.

3. Click the **Selection Tool** �, then click the **edge of the circle** to select it

4. Click **Edit** on the menu bar, then click **Copy**

5. Click **Edit** on the menu bar, then click **Paste in Front**
   A copy of the circle is pasted directly on top of the original. You will not see anything change on your artboard. Since the fill and stroke colors of the duplicate path will be removed when you type on it, the original paths stroke color will appear underneath the duplicate path.

6. Click **Type** on the menu bar, point to **Size**, then click **24**

7. Press and hold the mouse button on the **Type Tool** T; when the hidden toolbar appears, drag the pointer until it is over the **Path Type Tool** to select it, then release the mouse button
   Your cursor becomes ⌐. A table of Illustrator Type Tools and their uses can be seen in Table F-1.

> **Trouble?**
> If you do not click directly on the path, you will see a warning message indicating that you must click on the path. Undo your last step and try again.

8. Click the **edge of the circle** with ⌐ where shown in Figure F-11, then type **Election**

9. Compare your screen to Figure F-12, then save your work

FIGURE F-11: Positioning the Path Type Tool on a path

Path Type Tool

Path Type cursor

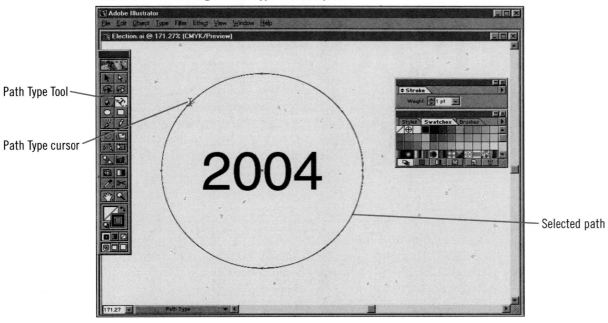

Selected path

FIGURE F-12: Typing on path

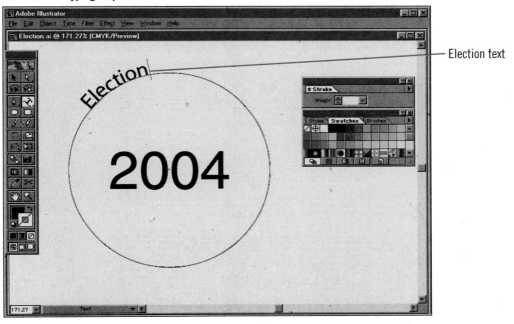

Election text

TABLE F-1: Type tools

tool name	tool	use
Type Tool	T,	For typing horizontally on the artboard or inside a text box
Area Type Tool	T	For filling a closed path with horizontal text
Path Type Tool	↖	For typing horizontally along an open or closed path
Vertical Type Tool	T	For typing vertically on the artboard or inside a text box
Vertical Area Path Tool	T	For filling a closed path with vertical text
Vertical Path Type Tool	↖	For typing vertically along an open or closed path

Moving Text Along a Path

Text on a path can be moved horizontally along the path as well as to the reverse side of the path. In addition, you can move text vertically by changing the baseline shift amount of the text. The **baseline** is the invisible line on which text sits. You can move text above or below its baseline by using the Character palette. Bill moves the text to the right so that it is centered on the top of the circle, then moves the text slightly above the circle by increasing the baseline shift amount.

Steps

1. Click the **Selection Tool**

   The flashing text cursor disappears, and an I Beam appears to the left of the word "Election" as shown in Figure F-13. If the bounding box is turned on and you find it distracting, click View on the menu bar, then click Hide Bounding Box.

2. Drag the **I Beam** to move the word "Election" to the top of the circle as shown in Figure F-13

   The I Beam is very sensitive. As a result, you may accidentally drag the text too far or to the other side of the baseline. If so, you can undo your last step and start again, or try dragging the I Beam up or down in the vertical direction that you want the text to move.

3. Click **Type** on the menu bar, then click **Character**

   The Character palette appears.

4. Click the **Show Options arrow** on the Character palette, then click **Show Options**

   The Character palette includes settings for formatting text. The baseline shift list arrow is in the lower-left corner of the Character palette.

5. Click the **Baseline shift list arrow**, then click **9 pt** as shown in Figure F-14

   The text moves 9 points above its original baseline, putting a little space between the circle and the text. After you change the baseline shift, you may need to move the word "Election" a little more to the right.

6. Double-click the **Hand Tool** to return to the Fit In Window view

7. Save your work

CLUES TO USE

Importing text files into Illustrator

You can import text from another document into Illustrator by using the Place command. Text should be saved in either the RTF (Rich Text Format) or Text Only file format—common Save As options in word-processing programs such as Microsoft Word. Saving in one of these file formats removes formatting applied to the text in the word-processing program that will be unintelligible to Illustrator. To place text into an Illustrator document, you must first create a text box. To create a text box, drag the Type Tool to make a box. A flashing cursor will appear in the upper-left corner of the box. Click File on the menu bar, click Place, then locate the text document with which you want to fill the text box.

FIGURE F-13: Moving type along a path

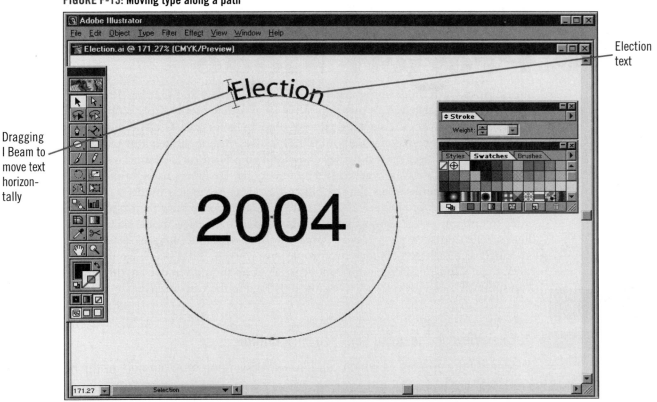

Dragging I Beam to move text horizontally

Election text

FIGURE F-14: Changing the baseline shift amount

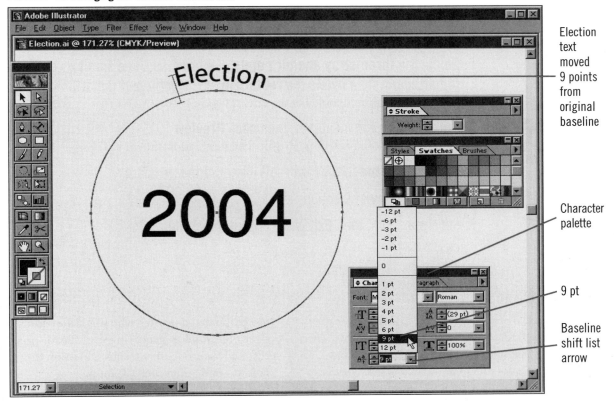

Election text moved 9 points from original baseline

Character palette

9 pt

Baseline shift list arrow

Using Outline and Preview Mode

Illustrator has two modes in which you can work: Preview and Outline. **Preview** mode is the mode in which you have been working thus far. Preview mode displays objects with fills and strokes and recognizes the stacking order of objects. In contrast, **Outline** mode displays objects on the artboard as paths only, without fills or strokes. Although the paths may appear to you as having a stroke of black, in reality they do not. All objects are on the same layer in Outline mode, regardless of how they are stacked in Preview mode. Designers use Outline mode when they need to select something that may be difficult to select in Preview mode, such as an object that accidentally gets placed behind another object. Designers also view their documents in Outline mode to find unwanted objects that would not appear in Preview mode, such as objects without fill or stroke colors, empty text boxes, and stray anchor points. Because this document is a rough composition on which two people have worked, Bill thinks it would be a good idea to check the document in the Outline mode to see if he should remove anything from it. He will then submit his two ideas for the Election 2004 logo to the CEO of WHJY.

QuickTip

The word Preview or Outline appears in the title bar, depending on which mode you are in.

1. Click **View** on the menu bar, then click **Outline**

2. Identify the objects on which you have been working, making note of the objects that should not be on the artboard
   Notice that the center anchor point of objects is displayed as a small x.

3. Click the **edge of the rectangle** on the right side of the artboard with the **Selection Tool** as shown in Figure F-15
   Notice that the Fill and Stroke icons on the toolbox change to None. This is why you could not see the rectangle in Preview mode. You must click the edge of objects to select them in Outline mode.

4. Press **[Delete]** (Win) or **[delete]** (Mac) to delete the rectangle

5. Delete the **three stray anchor points** displayed as three small x's on the left side of the artboard, then delete the **rectangle** at the bottom of the artboard
   Your window should look like the one in Figure F-16.

QuickTip

Press [Ctrl] [Y] (Win) or [Command] [Y] (Mac) to toggle between Preview and Outline mode.

6. Click **View** on the menu bar, then click **Preview**
   Your screen should resemble the finished illustration shown in Figure F-17.

7. Place your **name** in the lower-left corner of the artboard

8. Print **one copy** of Election

9. Save your work, then **Exit** (Win) or **Quit** (Mac) Illustrator

Cleanup

The Cleanup dialog box will find and delete stray points, empty text paths and unpainted objects, which are objects that have fills and strokes set to None. Cleaning up a document at the end of a project is a good idea, especially if you are sending your document to a commercial printer, who might be confused by stray objects when preparing your file for printing. To clean up your document, click Object on the menu bar, point to Path, then click Cleanup.

FIGURE F-15: **Viewing the artboard in the Outline mode**

Outline mode

Stray anchor points

Fill and Stroke set to None

Selected rectangle to be removed

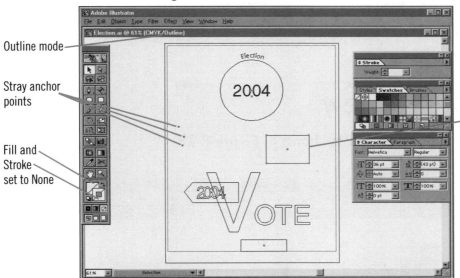

FIGURE F-16: **Removing unwanted objects from the artboard**

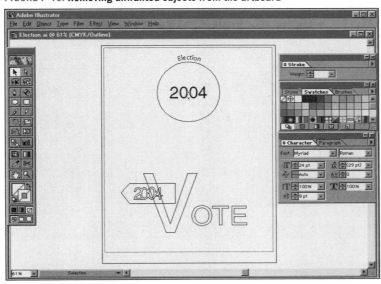

FIGURE F-17: **The finished illustration**

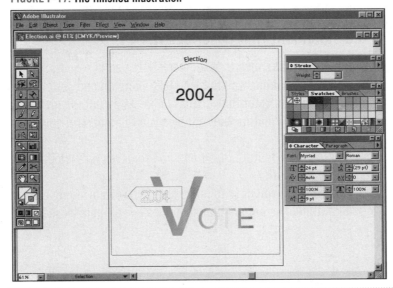

Illustrator 9.0

Practice

► Concepts Review

Label the Illustrator window elements shown in Figure F-18.

FIGURE F-18

Match each term with the statement that describes it.

7. New View
8. Create outlines
9. Unite
10. Path Type Tool
11. I Beam
12. Outline mode
13. Cleanup

a. A feature that converts text objects into vector objects
b. A tool that enables you to place text along an open or closed path
c. A view in Illustrator that displays objects as paths only
d. An Illustrator feature that enables you to name and save specific views of the artboard
e. An Illustrator feature that finds and removes stray points, unpainted objects, and empty text paths
f. The icon that you drag to move type horizontally along a path
g. A Pathfinder command that combines two or more closed paths into one closed path

14. **What is the name of the tool used to fill the inside of a closed path with text?**
    a. Type Tool
    b. Vertical Type Tool
    c. Area Type Tool
    d. Path Type Tool

15. **What do you call the invisible line on which text sits?**
    a. Hairline
    b. Baseline
    c. Pathline
    d. I Beam

16. **What does the Pen Tool pointer look like when it is directly on top of an anchor point?**
    a. [icon]
    b. [icon]
    c. [icon]
    d. [icon]

▶ Skills Review

1. **Create new views.**
    a. Start Illustrator.
    b. Open AI F-2 from the drive and folder where you store your project files.
    c. Save AI F-2 as *Pizza*.
    d. Zoom in on the purple circle at the top of the artboard so that you can see the entire circle.
    e. Click View on the menu bar, then click New View.
    f. Change the view name to **Logo One**.
    g. Double-click the Hand Tool to return to the Fit In Window view.
    h. Zoom in on the words "Pete's Pizza" at the bottom of the artboard.
    i. Click View on the menu bar, then click New View.
    j. Change the view name to **Logo Two**.
    k. Click View on the menu bar, then click Logo One.
    l. Click View on the menu bar, then click Logo Two.

2. **Create outlines and apply gradient fills.**
    a. Click the words "Pete's Pizza" with the Selection Tool.
    b. Click Type on the menu bar, then click Create Outlines.
    c. Show the Gradient palette and the Swatches palette, if necessary.
    d. Click the Rainbow gradient on the Swatches palette.
    e. Click the Gradient Tool on the toolbox.
    f. Drag the Gradient Tool straight across the words "Pete's Pizza."
    g. Save your work.

Illustrator 9.0

3. Change the colors in a gradient.
a. Make sure that you have a full view of the Gradient palette, including the Gradient slider, if necessary.
b. Click the third color stop (green) on the Gradient slider and pull it straight down to remove it from the Gradient slider.
c. Click the third color stop (blue) on the Gradient slider and drag it to the 48% location (approximately).
d. Click Window on the menu bar, then click Show Color, if necessary.
e. Keeping the third color stop (blue) selected, change the color in the Color palette to 50% C, 0% M, 0% Y, and 0% K.
f. Drag the new gradient from the gradient fill on the Gradient palette to the Swatches palette.
g. Double-click the new gradient and name it **Pizza Gradient**.
h. Save your work.

4. Add and delete anchor points.
a. Click the Selection Tool, then click the black rectangle underneath the words "Pete's Pizza."
b. Click the Pen Tool, then click the two anchor points in the middle of the bottom line segment to remove them.
c. Click the Pen Tool in the middle of the top line segment of the rectangle, directly above the center anchor point of the rectangle. Be careful to click on the line segment.
d. Click the Direct Selection Tool, then drag the new anchor point straight up slightly so that the two line segments that meet at the new anchor point are angled slightly. The black object should not overlap with the Pete's Pizza objects. (Hint: Remember, if you make a mistake, undo your last few steps and try again.)
e. Save your work.

5. Unite objects.
a. Click the Selection Tool, then click the Pete's Pizza objects.
b. Click Object on the menu bar, then click Ungroup.
c. Click the artboard to deselect the objects.
d. Click Window on the menu bar, then click Show Pathfinder, if necessary.
e. Click-and-drag each object in the word Pete's so that each one overlaps with the one before it. The objects can be overlapped any way that you like; you can drag them slightly up or down in addition to overlapping them.
f. Select the objects in the word "Pete's," then click Unite on the Pathfinder palette. The gradient fill has not changed, however, its appearance has changed because the objects that are filled with the gradient have been placed in new locations on the artboard.
g. Click the Selection Tool, then drag the objects in the word "Pizza" so that they overlap with each other any way that you like.
h. Select the objects in the word "Pizza," then click Unite on the Pathfinder palette. The gradient fill has not changed, however, its appearance has changed because the objects that are filled with the gradient have been placed in new locations on the artboard.
i. Save your work.

6. Type on a path.
a. Click View on the menu bar, then click Logo One.
b. Click the purple circle to select it.
c. Click Edit on the menu bar, then click Copy.
d. Click Edit on the menu bar, then click Paste in Front.
e. Click Type on the menu bar, then click Character, if necessary.
f. Change the font size to 24 pt, if necessary. Choose any font that you like.

g. Change the baseline shift amount to 12 pt, if necessary. (*Hint:* The baseline shift amount appears in the lower-left section of the Character palette when it is in full view.)

h. Click the Path Type Tool on the toolbox. (*Hint:* It may be underneath the Type Tool.)

i. Click the Path Type Tool on the purple circle at about where 11:00 would be on a clock (a little to the left of the top of the circle).

j. Type **Pete's Pizza**.

k. Save your work.

7. **Move text along a path.**

a. Click the Selection Tool.

b. Drag the I Beam to the left of the word "Pete's" and move the text horizontally so that it is centered.

c. Double-click the Hand Tool to return to the Fit In Window view.

d. Save your work.

8. **Use Outline and Preview mode.**

a. Click View on the menu bar, then click Outline.

b. Remove anything on the artboard that should not be there.

c. Click View on the menu bar, then click Preview.

d. Place your name in the lower-left corner of the artboard.

e. Print one copy of Pizza.

f. Save your work.

g. Exit (Win) or Quit (Mac) Illustrator.

▶ Independent Challenges

1. You are building an addition on your house that will include a new fireplace. You have created an illustration of your new house dimensions to present to your architect, but you forgot to include the chimney on the drawing. To complete this independent challenge:

a. Start Illustrator.

b. Open AI F-3 from the drive and folder where you store your project files.

c. Save AI F-3 as *House*.

d. Select the house.

e. Zoom in on the roof area where the word "chimney" points to the roof so that you have a good view of the right side of the roof.

f. Add four anchor points along the roof of the house to create a chimney that stems from the roof so that the roof and chimney are one object. After you add four anchor points, switch to the Direct Selection Tool, then drag the new points to create the sides of the chimney. Compare your screen to Figure F-19.

g. Place your name in the lower-left corner of the artboard.

h. Print one copy of House.

i. Save your work and Exit (Win) or Quit (Mac) Illustrator.

Illustrator 9.0

FIGURE F-19

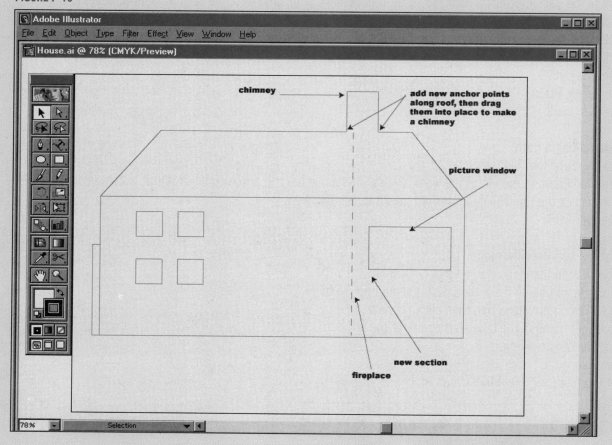

2. You are an Illustrator professor preparing a lesson about gradients for your class. The lecture will cover how to add and remove colors on the Gradient slider, apply gradient fills to text, and change the length and direction of a gradient fill.
   To complete this independent challenge:

a. Start Illustrator.

b. Open AI F-4 from the drive and folder where you store your project files.

c. Save AI F-4 as *Gradient*.

d. Convert the word "Creative" to outlines.

e. Click the Rainbow gradient on the Swatches palette, then change it to a four-color gradient using colors of your choice. You may need to show the Gradient palette.

f. Add the new gradient to the Swatches palette and name it *My Gradient*.

g. Use the Gradient Tool to change the length and direction of the gradient. If you don't like the angle, you can either undo your last step or change the Angle field on the Gradient palette to 0, and try again.

h. Place your name in the lower-left corner of the artboard.

j. Print one copy of Gradient.

k. Save your work and Exit (Win) or Quit (Mac) Illustrator.

3. You are a designer for an advertising agency. Your client, the golf pro at Rolling Greens Golf Course, has asked you to design a new logo for his course. You decide to create a golf ball sitting on a golf tee, with the course's name, *Rolling Greens*, along the top of the golf ball.

To complete this independent challenge:

a. Start Illustrator.

b. Open AI F-5 from the drive and folder where you store your project files.

c. Save AI F-5 as *Golf*.

d. Zoom in on the golf ball so that you have a good view of it.

e. Copy the golf ball and paste it in front. Otherwise, you will lose the stroke of the golf ball when you type on the path.

f. Change the settings on the Character palette, if necessary, so that your font size is 18 points and the baseline shift amount is 9 points. Remember that the Character palette is found under the Type menu, not the Window menu.

g. Using the Path Type Tool, type **Rolling Greens** at the top of the golf ball.

h. Switch to the Selection Tool to drag the text horizontally, if necessary.

j. Change the fill color of the text to Orange to match the golf tee.

k. Place your name in the lower-left corner of the artboard.

l. Save your work, then print one copy of *Golf*.

m. Exit (Win) or Quit (Mac) Illustrator.

4. You are pursuing a career as a creative director for a design firm. You have a strong interest in type and how combinations of type and image convey personality. To keep abreast of current design trends, you search the Internet for examples of unusual type designs before you create one of your own in Illustrator.

To complete this independent challenge:

a. Connect to the Internet and go to *http://www.course.com*

b. Navigate to the page for this book, then click the link for the Student Online Companion.

c. Click the links for this unit and look for examples of interesting type.

d. Exit (Win) or Quit (Mac) your browser.

e. Start Illustrator.

f. Create a new document and save it as *Type*.

g. Create a text object consisting of your first and last names.

h. Design the type by either filling it with a gradient or typing your name along a path that you create using the drawing tools. You can also unite the letters in your name. Try combining some of these features—for example, type your name on a path and then fill it with a gradient, or fill your name with a gradient and then overlap and unite it.

j. Place your name in the lower-left corner of the artboard.

k. Save your work.

l. Print one copy of Type, then Exit (Win) or Quit (Mac) Illustrator.

Illustrator 9.0

► **Visual Workshop**

Re-create the picture shown in Figure F-20. Start by creating a spiral. (*Hint:* To access the Spiral Tool, press and hold the mouse button on the Ellipse Tool until the hidden toolbar appears, then click the Spiral Tool). Change the fill of the spiral to None and the stroke of the spiral to Black. Copy the spiral and paste the copy in front. Use any font that you like. Change the baseline shift amount of the text to 12 points. Save the document as *Spiral*. Place your name in the lower-left corner of the artboard, print one copy of Spiral, then Exit (Win) or Quit (Mac) Illustrator.

FIGURE F-20

Using

Advanced Illustrator Features

Objectives

- ► **Use the Knife Tool**
- ► **Rasterize an object**
- ► **Apply a filter to a rasterized object**
- ► **Create a clipping mask**
- ► **Create a compound path**
- ► **Apply a drop shadow**
- ► **Create a pattern swatch**
- ► **Edit a pattern**

In addition to transforming and layering objects in Illustrator, you can manipulate objects by using the advanced tools and commands. You can cut a single path into two or more paths, cut holes through closed paths, and convert vector objects into bitmaps. Illustrator offers many special effects, called filters, that can be applied to both vector and bitmap objects. ✒ The 50th Cincinnati Marathon will take place on April 15, 2002. Each year WHJY provides live coverage of the marathon, hosted by the station's popular sports anchor, Ben Prince. Bill has been asked to create a banner with marathon graphics, including a picture of Ben, that will run at the bottom of the television screen below the marathon coverage.

Using the Knife Tool

Illustrator 9.0

At times you may want to modify shapes or create a certain effect in your illustration by "cutting" your open or closed paths into two or more paths with the **Knife Tool**. You can achieve interesting results depending on the type of cut marks you make through an object. For example, you can drag the Knife Tool in a zigzag line, a curvy line, or even a line that looks like a puzzle piece. Bill creates a circle, then cuts it into two closed paths using the Knife Tool.

Steps

Trouble?

Saving and exporting are disabled in the Illustrator Tryout! software. To learn more about the Tryout! software that accompanies this book, see the Read This Before You Begin Page.

1. Start Illustrator, open AIG-1 from the drive and folder where you store your project files, then save it as **Marathon**

2. Show the **Swatches** and the **Layers palettes** and close any other palettes that may be open

3. Click the **Show Color Swatches button** on the Swatches palette as shown in Figure G-1 to hide the gradient and pattern swatches
   Notice the five new colors in the fourth row of the Swatches palette.

4. Click **View** on the menu bar, then click **Banner**

5. Click the **Fill icon** on the toolbar, click **Lavender** on the Swatches palette, click the **Stroke icon**, then click **None**

6. Click the **Ellipse Tool** , click the **Marathon logo layer** on the Layers palette, then while pressing **[Shift] [Alt]** (Win) or **[Shift] [Option]** (Mac), create a circle on top of the green background as shown in Figure G-1
   The circle is automatically placed on the Marathon logo layer.

7. Press and hold the mouse button over the **Scissors Tool** ; when the hidden toolbar appears, drag the pointer until it is over the **Knife Tool** , then release the mouse button

8. Hide the Banner background layer by clicking on its layer on the Layers palette
   Hiding the rectangle on this layer will make it easier for you to concentrate on cutting the circle.

Trouble?

If you have trouble dragging the Knife Tool in a curved line, undo your last step and try again. It may take you a few tries to achieve the desired curve. Refer to Figure G-2 for help.

9. Place the outside the artboard, then drag in a curved line that goes well beyond the circle as shown in Figure G-2
   If you start and stop cutting an object too close to the object's edge, you will not successfully cut it into two objects. To drag the Knife Tool in a perfectly straight line, press [Shift] [Alt] (Win) or [Shift] [Option] (Mac).

10. Click the **Selection Tool** , click the **artboard** to deselect both objects, then select the **top part of the circle** and fill it with **Raspberry** as shown in Figure G-3, then save your work
    Make sure the Fill icon is active before you change the fill color to Raspberry. When you cut an object, the two new objects are selected. You need to deselect them so that you can select one and manipulate it.

FIGURE G-1: Creating a circle on the green background

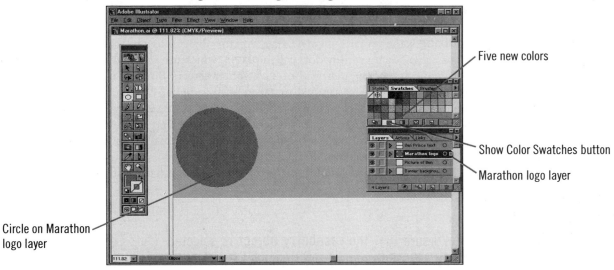

Five new colors

Show Color Swatches button

Marathon logo layer

Circle on Marathon logo layer

FIGURE G-2: Cutting the circle with the Knife Tool

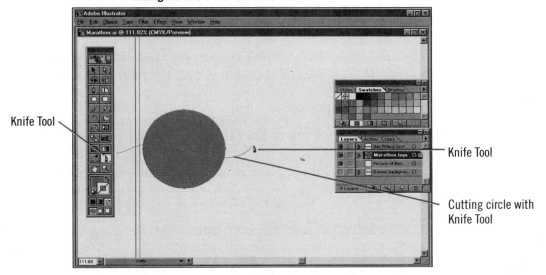

Knife Tool

Knife Tool

Cutting circle with Knife Tool

FIGURE G-3: Filling the top part of the circle with Raspberry

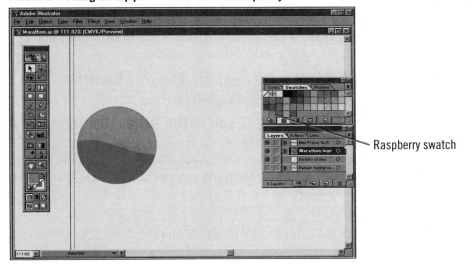

Raspberry swatch

Illustrator 9.0

Rasterizing an Object

Rasterizing is the process of converting a vector object into a bitmap object. As you may recall, bitmaps are made up of tiny dots called **pixels**, which are small squares used to display a digital image on the rectangular grid of a computer screen. Bitmaps may be illustrations or photographs that have been scanned or taken with a digital camera, or pictures that have been created out of pixels (rather than mathematical equations) in paint software programs, such as Adobe Photoshop. Illustrator has several **filters** that you can use to add special effects to objects in your illustration—some of which can be applied only to bitmap graphics. If you want to use one of these bitmap filters on a vector graphic, you can simply rasterize the object first. ➤ Bill types "Marathon 2002" along the top half of the circle path, converts it to outlines, then rasterizes it.

Steps

QuickTip

Whenever you use the Path Type Tool, the fill and stroke of the path are removed. If you want to retain the fill or stroke of the path you are typing on, copy the object and then paste it in front. When you type on the top-layered object, its fill and stroke will be removed, but the fill and stroke of the original object will still be visible.

1. Make sure that the **raspberry object** is selected, click **Edit** on the menu bar, click **Copy**, click **Edit** again, and then click **Paste in Front** to duplicate it

   Although you will not see anything change on your artboard, there are now two identical raspberry objects one on top of the other. To make sure that you did this step correctly, drag the top raspberry object until you see the other raspberry object underneath it, then undo your last step so that the top raspberry object moves back into position.

2. Press and hold the mouse button over the **Type Tool** 🔲; when the hidden toolbar appears, move your pointer until it is over the **Path Type Tool** 🔲, then release the mouse button

   Your pointer changes to ↓.

3. Place ↓ along the **top of the raspberry object** as shown in Figure G-4, then type **Marathon 2002**

   If you get a message that says you must click on a non-compound, non-masking path to create text along a path, you did not click directly on the path with the Path Type Tool. Click OK, and repeat Step 3 again.

4. Click the **Selection Tool** 🔲, click **Type** on the menu bar, then click **Character**

   The Character palette appears on the artboard.

Trouble?

If you do not see the baseline shift amount on the Character palette, click the Show Options arrow 🔲 on the Character palette, then click Show Options. If Arial Black or Arial is not an option on the palette, choose another font.

5. Change the **font** to **Arial Black** or **Arial**, the **type size** to **24 pt**, the **baseline shift** to **6 pt**, and the **fill color** to **Royal Blue**

   Compare your screen to Figure G-5.

6. Click **Type** on the menu bar, then click **Create Outlines**

   Keep the outlines selected for the next step.

7. Click **Object** on the menu bar, then click **Rasterize**

   The Rasterize dialog box opens.

8. Click the **Screen (72 ppi) option button**, the **Transparent option button**, and the **Anti-Alias check box**, as shown in Figure G-6, then click **OK**

   The Screen (72 ppi) option is meant for objects that will be output on a television screen or computer monitor. The Anti-Alias option ensures that the rasterized object will have a smooth edge, and the Transparent option makes the inside area of the bounding box around a rasterized object transparent.

9. Click the artboard to deselect the rasterized object, then save your work

FIGURE G-4: Positioning the Path Type Tool

Path Type Tool

Path Type cursor

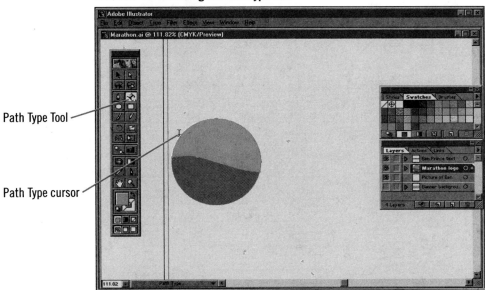

FIGURE G-5: Typing along the path

I Beam

Royal Blue swatch

Show options arrow

Type size

Baseline shift amount

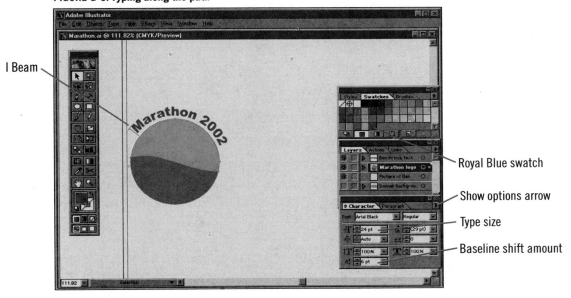

FIGURE G-6: Rasterize Options dialog box

Screen (72 ppi) option

Transparent option

Anti-Alias check box

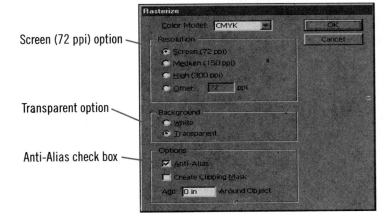

Applying a Filter to a Rasterized Object

The Filter menu is divided into two sections. The top section includes filters that are designed for vector objects only, like the Punk and Bloat filter that you used in a previous lesson. The bottom section includes filters that are designed for bitmap objects only. Some of these filters apply lighting and blur effects and distort images. Others imitate traditional art media such as watercolors, charcoal, and Conté crayon. Bill applies the Gaussian Blur filter to the Marathon 2002 bitmap.

Steps

1. Close the **Character palette**, then click the **artboard** to deselect the bitmap if you have not already deselected it

2. Zoom in on the **M** in **Marathon** to see the pixels, as shown in Figure G-7

3. Click the **Zoom menu list arrow** in the lower-left corner of the artboard, then click **400%**

4. Adjust your view of the Marathon 2002 image by moving the artboard with the Hand Tool and dragging palettes out of the way, if necessary
   You should have a good view of the Marathon 2002 image before you apply a filter to it.

5. Click the **Selection Tool**, then click the **Marathon 2002 image**

6. Click **Filter** on the menu bar, point to **Blur**, then click **Gaussian Blur**
   The Gaussian Blur dialog box opens. Some filters require a lot of memory. You may see a message indicating that your computer cannot apply the filter or provide a preview of the filter in the Filter dialog box. Contact your instructor or technical support person for help if you receive this kind of warning.

7. Drag the **Radius slider** to **1.5** as shown in Figure G-8, then click **OK**

8. Click the **artboard** to deselect Marathon 2002

Trouble?

If your Marathon 2002 text is not completely contained within the boundaries of the green rectangle, click the rectangle and move it up slightly.

9. Click **View** on the menu bar, then click **Banner**
   The Banner background layer, which includes the green banner, reappears as shown in Figure G-9.

10. Save your work

FIGURE G-7: Zooming in to see pixels

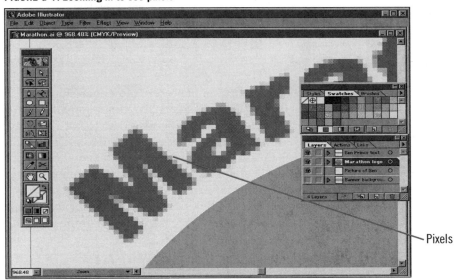

Pixels

FIGURE G-8: The Gaussian Blur dialog box

Filter preview window

Radius slider

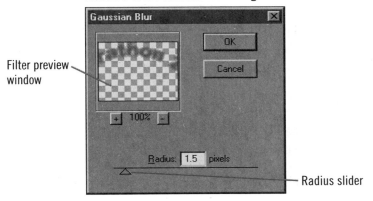

FIGURE G-9: The Gaussian Blur filter applied to the Marathon 2002 text

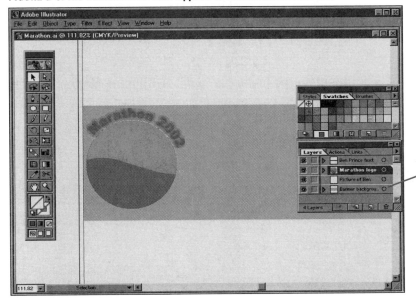

Banner background layer

Illustrator 9.0

Illustrator 9.0

Creating a Clipping Mask

Steps 1 2 3 4

If you were to cut a hole in a piece of paper and move it around while looking through it, your view would be focused but always changing. The clipping mask feature in Illustrator uses this same concept. A **mask** is a closed path that is placed on top of a bitmap or vector illustration. It exposes only the area of the picture that is under the mask. The rest of the picture is "covered up." As a result, moving the mask around the artboard exposes different views of the underlying picture. The mask feature is useful for cropping a picture with a specific shape like an oval or a star. Bill needs a picture of Ben for the banner. The most recent picture of Ben on file at WHJY was taken with his wife at a fundraiser. Bill places the picture in Illustrator and then uses the clipping mask feature to crop Bill's face from the rest of the picture.

1. Click **View** on the menu bar, then click **Work Area**

2. Make sure the Marathon logo layer is selected on the Layers palette

3. Click **File** on the menu bar, then click **Place**
   The Place dialog box opens.

4. Click the **Look in list arrow** (Win) or click the **Desktop button** (Mac), click the drive containing your Project Disk, click **AI G-2**, make sure to remove the checkmark next to Link, if necessary, then click **Place**
   The picture of Ben and his wife appears. Notice that the picture is placed on the Marathon logo layer because it was the active layer at the time the image was placed.

5. Drag the **small red square** on the **Marathon logo layer** to the **Picture of Ben layer** to place the **picture of Ben and his wife** on the **Picture of Ben layer**
   The selection color changes to bright green. See Figure G-10.

Trouble?
If your circle is not big enough, enlarge it by using the Scale Tool or change the circle's width and height using the Transform palette.

6. Click the **Ellipse Tool**, click **Gold** on the Swatches palette, then create a circle around Ben's face as shown in Part A of Figure G-11
   The circle, which represents the mask, does not have to be perfect. When you are creating a mask, it's easier to select it if you apply a fill or stroke color to it, even though these colors will disappear when the mask is created.

7. Click the **Selection Tool**, press and hold [Shift], then click the **picture of Ben** so that both the circle and the picture are selected.

QuickTip
You can also make a clipping mask by pressing [Ctrl] [7] (Win) or [Command] [7] (Mac)

8. Click **Object** on the menu bar, point to **Clipping Mask**, then click **Make**
   The circle crops the picture and loses its fill color. The mask (circle) and the masked object (picture) remain selected as shown in Part B of Figure G-11.

9. Click the **artboard** to deselect both objects

Trouble?
If you start moving the picture but not the mask, undo your last step. Be very careful to click the edge of the circle to select the mask properly.

10. Click **Edit** on the menu bar, point to **Select**, then click **Masks**
    Only the mask is selected this time. If you carefully select the edge of the mask, you can move it to expose different views of the picture as shown in Part C of Figure G-11. If you do move the mask, make sure you move it back so that you can see all of Ben's face.

11. Save your work

FIGURE G-10: Placing the picture on the correct layer

Bright green
selection color

Picture of Ben
layer

FIGURE G-11: **Creating a mask**

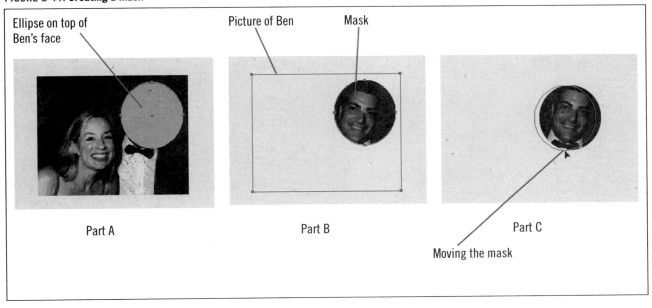

Ellipse on top of
Ben's face

Picture of Ben   Mask

Moving the mask

Part A   Part B   Part C

Creating a Compound Path

A **compound path** is a group of two or more overlapping closed paths in which the objects on the top become transparent where they overlap with the objects on the bottom. Compound paths are useful in illustrations when you need to show part of something underneath an object. For example, if you draw eyeglasses, the lens areas of the eyeglass frame would need to be transparent for the eyes underneath the eyeglasses to be visible. ✎ Bill creates a hole through the purple section of the Marathon logo. This hole is a window through which Ben's face can show.

Steps

1. Click **View** on the menu bar, then click **Banner**

2. Click the **Ellipse Tool** ⬭, then click **Gold** on the Swatches palette

Trouble?

If you do not see the circle, it may be on the wrong layer. Undo your last step, then click the Marathon logo layer before you create the circle.

3. Click the **Marathon logo layer**, then create a circle about the size of a quarter on top of the purple object as shown in Part A of Figure G-12
   The circle is automatically placed on the Marathon logo layer.

4. Click the **Selection Tool** ▶, press [**Shift**], then click the **purple object** so that both objects are selected

5. Click **Object** on the menu bar, point to **Compound Path**, then click **Make**
   The gold circle is knocked out, and the circle is transparent. You can see the green banner beneath the circle as shown in Part B of Figure G-12.

6. Double-click the **Hand Tool** ✋ to see the entire artboard

Trouble?

If the mask and the picture of Ben did not become selected after Step 7, they may be located on the wrong layer. Place the mask and the picture of Ben on the Picture of Ben layer, then repeat Step 7.

7. Click the **circle** on the **Picture of Ben layer** on the Layers palette
   The circle becomes a double circle and the objects on the Picture of Ben layer are selected on the artboard.

8. Click ▶, then drag the picture of Ben underneath the transparent circle as shown in Figure G-13
   Use the arrow keys on your keyboard to move the picture of Ben in small increments if necessary.

9. Scale the picture of Ben using the Scale Tool 🔲 if it is smaller than the window created by the compound path

FIGURE G-12: **Making a compound path**

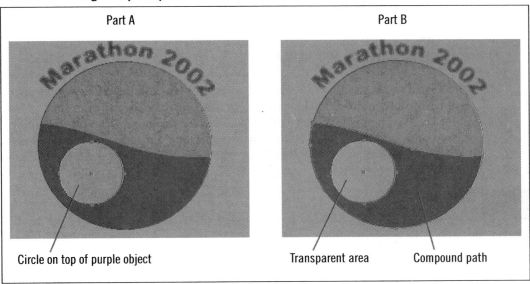

Part A   Part B

Circle on top of purple object   Transparent area   Compound path

FIGURE G-13: **Placing the picture underneath the compound path**

Circle on Picture of Ben layer

Picture of Ben underneath compound path

Applying a Drop Shadow

Drop shadows placed behind text and vector objects add depth to your elements and place emphasis on them in your illustrations. You can customize your drop shadow by choosing its color and darkness, the X and Y offset (how far the drop shadow is offset from the object vertically and horizontally), the amount of blur and opacity, and the drop shadow mode. Bill places the "host: Ben Prince" text on top of the green banner and then places a drop shadow behind it.

Steps

1. Drag the **host: Ben Prince text** inside of the green rectangle as shown in Figure G-14
   Notice that the host: Ben Prince text object has already been assigned to the Ben Prince text layer on the Layers palette.

2. Make sure that the text is still selected

3. Click the **Fill icon** on the toolbox if necessary, then click **Raspberry** on the Swatches palette

4. Click **Filter** on the menu bar, point to **Stylize** in the top section of the Filter menu, then click **Drop Shadow**
   The Drop Shadow dialog box opens as shown in Figure G-15.

5. Click the **Mode list arrow**, then click **Normal**

6. Click the **Color option button**
   The color icon fills with Black

7. Click **OK**

8. Click the **artboard** to deselect the text

9. Click **View** on the menu bar, then click **Banner** to see a better view of the drop shadow as shown in Figure G-16

10. Save your work

> **QuickTip**
>
> If you click the Color icon on the Drop Shadow dialog box, the Color Picker dialog box opens allowing you to pick a new color for your drop shadow.

FIGURE G-14: **Dragging the text on top of the green rectangle**

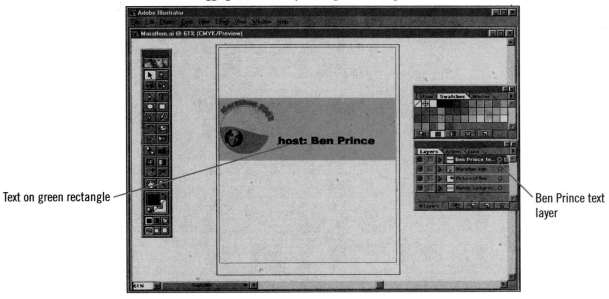

Text on green rectangle

Ben Prince text
layer

FIGURE G-15: **Drop Shadow dialog box**

X Offset

Y Offset

Color option button

Color icon

Mode list arrow

Opacity amount

Blur amount

Darkness amount

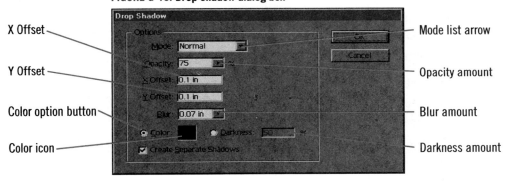

FIGURE G-16: **Drop Shadow filter applied to text**

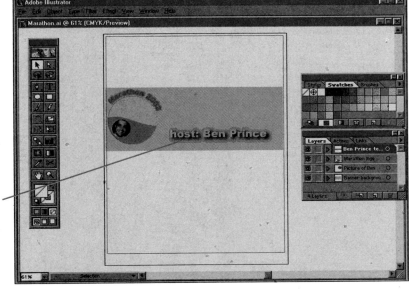

Drop shadow applied
to text

Creating a Pattern Swatch

Illustrator comes with six patterns on the Swatches palette: **Red Tablecloth, Pyramids, Azure Rings, Red Stripe, Clown Attack,** and **Camouflage**. Patterns can be used for object fills and strokes. Like colors and gradients, they can be edited using new colors. In addition, you can create new patterns using Illustrator objects. New patterns are made from open or closed paths with solid color fills. You cannot use bitmaps, paint objects (objects created with the Paintbrush Tool), or objects filled with gradients for creating new patterns. Patterns created for the Swatches palette can also be used to create new Pattern brushes. ⬦ Bill creates a pattern using stars, adds it to the Swatches palette, then applies it to the Marathon logo.

Steps

1. Click **View** on the menu bar, then click **Work Area**

2. Click **Window** on the menu bar, then click **Show Transform**, if necessary
   Your Transform palette may already be visible.

3. Click the **Show All Swatches button** on the Swatches palette to show the gradient and pattern swatches

4. Resize the Swatches palette using the **Resize button** 🔲 (Win) or 🔳 (Mac) on the Swatches palette so that you have a full view of all of the Swatches as shown in Figure G-17

Trouble?

The Star Tool is hidden underneath the Ellipse Tool.

5. Create **three small stars** using any colors except for Light Green to fill them, making sure that the height and width of each star is about **0.25"**
   Use the Transform palette to view the width and height of each star, as shown in Figure G-17.

6. Select the **three stars**, then drag them on top of the Swatches palette
   Your pointer becomes 🔖, and the new pattern is added to the Swatches palette as shown in Figure G-18.

7. Press **[Delete]** (Win) or **[delete]** (Mac) to remove the three stars from the artboard

8. Double-click the **stars pattern** on the Swatches palette, name it **Stars**, then click **OK**

9. Click **View** on the menu bar, then click **Banner**

10. Click the **Selection Tool** ▶, then click the **raspberry-colored object** beneath the words "Marathon 2002"

11. Click the **Stars pattern**, click the **Stroke icon** on the toolbox, click **Black**, then deselect the object
    Your screen should resemble Figure G-18.

12. Save your work

FIGURE G-17: Creating a pattern swatch

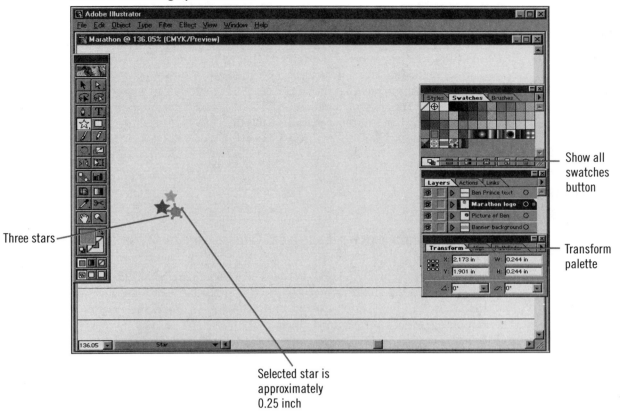

Show all
swatches
button

Three stars

Transform
palette

Selected star is
approximately
0.25 inch

FIGURE G-18: Applying a pattern to an object

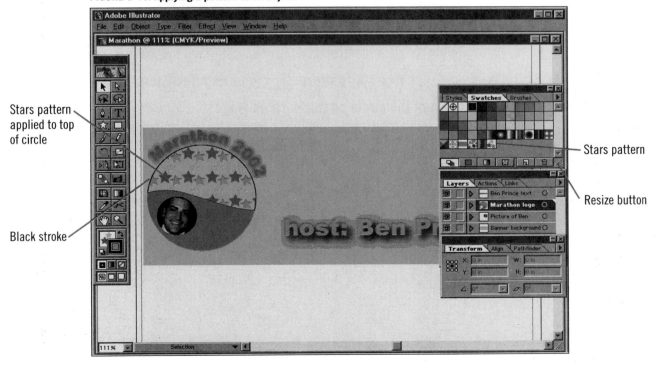

Stars pattern
applied to top
of circle

Stars pattern

Resize button

Black stroke

Illustrator 9.0

Editing a Pattern

You can edit patterns that already exist on the Swatches palette. For example, you may like the existing Camouflage pattern, but prefer to change the colors in it. You can change the colors in a pattern, which creates a new pattern on the Swatches palette, leaving the original pattern intact. ━━━ Bill decides that the stars in the Stars pattern look too uniform. He edits the pattern by changing the size and rotation angle of the stars, adds the new pattern to the Swatches palette, and then applies it to the Marathon logo.

Steps

1. Drag the **Stars pattern** from the Swatches palette to the artboard as shown in Figure G-19
   Your pointer becomes ⬚ as you drag. The pattern remains on the Swatches palette and a copy of it appears on the artboard with a box around it. This bounding box is automatically placed around new patterns as they are added to the Swatches palette. The stars and the bounding box are one grouped object.

2. Click the **artboard** to deselect the copy of the pattern

3. Click the **Direct Selection Tool** �k, then click **one of the stars**
   Because the three stars are grouped together, you'll need the Direct Selection Tool to modify them individually.

4. Change the size, color, or the rotation angle of each star using the Scale Tool ▦ and the Rotate Tool ▣ on the toolbox

5. Click the **Selection Tool** ▶, then click the **copy of the pattern on the artboard** and drag it to the Swatches palette

6. Press **[Delete]** (Win) or **[delete]** (Mac) to remove the copy of the pattern from the artboard

7. Double-click the **new star pattern**, then rename it **New Stars**

8. Click the **top of the circle on the Marathon logo** that is filled with the Stars pattern, then click the **Fill icon** on the toolbox to make sure it is in front of the Stroke icon

Trouble?

If your object does not fill with the new pattern, you probably changed the stroke of the object and not the fill. Undo your last step. Make sure that the Fill icon is in front of the Stroke icon, then click the New Stars pattern on the Swatches palette.

9. Click the **New Stars pattern** on the Swatches palette, then click the **artboard** to deselect the object
   Compare your illustration with Figure G-20.

10. Double-click the **Hand Tool** 🖐 to fit the entire artboard in your window
    Your screen should resemble Figure G-21.

11. Place **your name** in the lower-left corner of the artboard, print one copy of Marathon, then **Exit** (Win) or **Quit** (Mac) Illustrator, saving changes to your work

FIGURE G-19: **Drag pattern swatch to artboard**

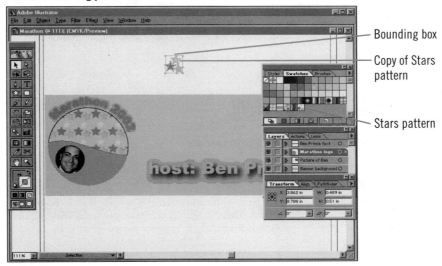

Bounding box

Copy of Stars pattern

Stars pattern

FIGURE G-20: **Applying new pattern to an object**

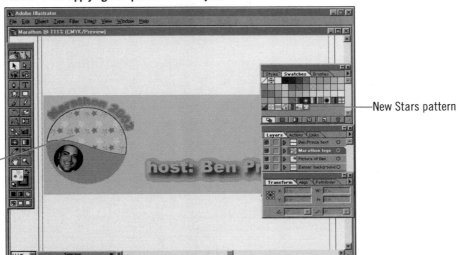

New Stars pattern

New Stars pattern applied to top of circle

FIGURE G-21: **The finished illustration**

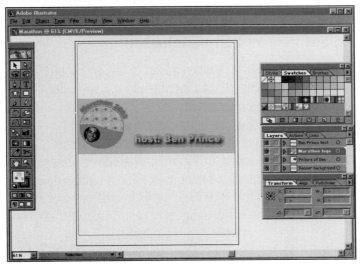

Practice

► Concepts Review

Identify the following objects in Figure G-22.

FIGURE G-22

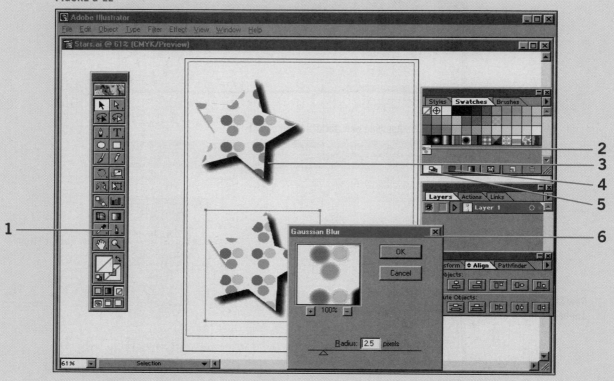

Match each term with the statement that describes it.

7. **Mask**	**a.** A filter that, when added to text or an object, adds depth to it
8. **Bitmap**	**b.** A vector shape that acts like a view finder, cropping the view of a bitmap or a vector illustration
9. **Pattern**	
10. **Knife Tool**	**c.** An object made up of pixels
11. **Compound path**	**d.** A group of two or more overlapping closed paths in which the objects on the top become transparent where they overlap with the objects on the bottom
12. **Drop shadow**	
13. **Rasterize**	**e.** To convert a vector object into a bitmap object
	f. Used to cut through paths to create two or more new paths
	g. A type of fill made up of vector objects that cannot be made from bitmaps and cannot contain gradients

14. **Out of which of the following can patterns be made?**
    a. Objects created with the Paintbrush Tool
    b. Objects with gradient fills
    c. Bitmaps
    d. None of the above

15. **Patterns created for fills can also be used to create new**
    a. Masks
    b. Pattern brushes
    c. gradients
    d. compound paths

16. **Which of the following Illustrator features help you organize objects on the artboard?**
    a. Organize Tool
    b. Layers
    c. Masks
    d. Filters

 # Skills Review

Make sure that you have extra blank floppy disks on hand so that if you run out of room on your Project Disks while completing the Skills Review or Independent Challenges, you will have a place to save the files you create.

1. **Use the Knife Tool.**
   a. Start Illustrator.
   b. Open AI G-3 from the drive and folder where you store your project files.
   c. Save AI G-3 as *Winter*.
   d. Click View on the menu bar, then click Window.
   e. Click the purple rectangle with the Selection Tool.
   f. Cut the rectangle into four quadrants to create a window with four panes using the Knife Tool. If you want to cut the rectangle using perfectly straight lines, press [Shift] [Alt] (Win) or [Shift] [Option] (Mac) while dragging the Knife Tool. (You do not have to use perfectly straight lines.)
   g. Click the Selection Tool, then click the artboard to deselect the four window quadrants.
   h. Move each quadrant slightly away from the others so that white space appears between all four objects.
   i. Change the stroke color to Black on all four objects.
   j. Change the stroke weight to 5 points on all four objects.
   k. Change the fill color to None on all four objects.

2. **Create a compound path.**
   a. Click View on the menu bar, then click Grandmother.
   b. Select the eyeglass frame and the two purple circles on top of the eyeglass frame.
   c. Click Object on the menu bar, point to Compound Path, then click Make.
   d. Drag the glasses on top of the grandmother's eyes.
   e. Save your work.

3. Apply a drop shadow.

a. Click View on the menu bar, then click Text.

b. Change the fill color of the text to the color of your choice.

c. Click Filter on the menu bar, point to Stylize, then click Drop Shadow.

d. Click the Mode list arrow, then click Normal.

e. Click the Color option button, if necessary.

f. Keep the rest of the settings as they are.

g. Click OK.

h. Deselect the text object.

i. Save your work.

4. Create a pattern swatch.

a. Click View on the menu bar, then click Grandmother.

b. Click Window on the menu bar, then click Show Transform, if necessary.

c. Create a new pattern out of circles, stars, rectangles, or a combination of all three.

d. Make sure that each object is approximately 0.25 inch high and wide.

e. Drag the new pattern to the Swatches palette.

f. Double-click the new pattern and name it **Collar**.

g. Apply the Collar pattern to the collar of the grandmother's dress.

h. Delete the objects that you used to create the pattern from the artboard.

i. Save your work.

5. Edit a pattern swatch.

a. Drag the Collar pattern from the Swatches palette onto the artboard.

b. Click the artboard to deselect it.

c. Click the Direct Selection Tool and change the colors in each of the objects used to create the original pattern.

d. Click the Selection Tool, then click the copy of the pattern swatch on the artboard.

e. Drag the new pattern to the Swatches palette.

f. Double-click the new pattern swatch and name it **New Collar**.

g. Apply the New Collar pattern to the collar of the grandmother's dress.

h. Remove the copy of the pattern from the artboard by deleting it.

6. Rasterize an object.

a. Double-click the Hand Tool on the toolbox to see the Fit In Window view.

b. Click the circle on the Grandmother layer on the Layers palette to select every object on the Grandmother layer.

c. Click Object on the menu bar, then click Group.

d. Click Object on the menu bar, then click Rasterize.

e. Click the Screen (72 ppi) resolution option button, if necessary.

f. Click the Transparent option button, if necessary.

g. Click the Anti-Alias check box, if necessary.

h. Click OK.

i. Save your work.

7. Apply a filter to a rasterized object.

   a. Make sure the grandmother is still selected.

   b. Click Filter on the menu bar, point to Blur, then click Gaussian Blur.

   c. Drag the Radius slider to 1.5 pixels, then click OK.

   d. Drag the grandmother behind the window panes. The Grandmother layer is underneath the Window layer on the Layers palette so the grandmother is placed underneath the window panes.

   e. Drag the Winter text closer to the window panes, underneath the window or next to the window.

   f. Click the Text layer to make it the active layer.

   g. Place your name in the lower-left corner of the artboard.

   h. Save your work.

   i. Print one copy of Winter.

   j. Exit (Win) or Quit (Mac) Illustrator.

▶ Independent Challenges

1. You are a professional photographer designing a business card for yourself. You would like to include a small photograph on the card to make it more interesting than a standard business card with only text.

   To complete this independent challenge:

   a. Start Illustrator.

   b. Open AI G-4 from the drive and folder where you store your project files.

   c. Save AI G-4 as *Card*.

   d. Zoom in on the picture of the duck and the business card so that you have a better view of them.

   e. Create a clipping mask to crop the picture of the duck so that it will fit on the business card. Use an oval or a rectangle for the mask and place it on top of the duck.

   f. Select the shape and the picture of the duck.

   g. Click Object on the menu bar, point to Clipping Mask, then click Make.

   h. Drag the mask on top of the business card. Both the mask and the masked object (picture) will be selected.

   i. Place a 2-point Black stroke on the mask.

   j. Change the font of the text on the business card.

   k. Add any other design elements that you want to the business card.

   l. Place your name in the lower left corner of the artboard.

   m. Print one copy of Card.

   n. Save your work and Exit (Win) or Quit (Mac) Illustrator.

Illustrator 9.0 | Practice

2. You are a professional illustrator for children's books. You have been asked to create a picture of a mouse eating a piece of Swiss cheese. You are almost done with the illustration, however, you need to punch holes through the cheese to make it look like Swiss cheese. You decide to use the Compound Path feature to accomplish this task.

To complete this independent challenge:

a. Start Illustrator.

b. Open AI G-5 from the drive and folder where you store your project files.

c. Save AI G-5 as *Mouse*.

d. Create five or six circles on top of the yellow piece of cheese. The fill and stroke color of the circles does not matter as the circles will eventually become transparent. The circles represent holes in the cheese that will be knocked out using the Compound Path feature.

e. Switch to the Selection Tool, then press [Shift] as you click each circle and the yellow piece of cheese.

f. Click Object on the menu bar, point to Compound Path, then click Make. You should see holes in the cheese and the blue tablecloth underneath the holes. See Figure G-23.

FIGURE G-23

g. Place a drop shadow behind the piece of cheese. Experiment with the drop shadow settings in the Drop Shadow dialog box. After applying a drop shadow, you can undo your last step and try another type of drop shadow.

h. Place your name in the lower-left corner of the artboard.

i. Print one copy of *Mouse*.

j. Save your work and Exit (Win) or Quit (Mac) Illustrator.

3. You are a wallpaper designer and create your initial designs in Illustrator using the pattern feature. You have presented two ideas to a client for approval and have been asked to change the colors in the pattern designs.

To complete this independent challenge:

a. Start Illustrator.

b. Open AI G-6 from the drive and folder where you store your project files.

c. Save AI G-6 as *Wallpaper*.

d. Locate the two patterns in the fifth row of the Swatches palette. You may need to resize the Swatches palette.

e. Drag each pattern to the artboard.

f. Zoom in on the pattern swatches so that you have a good view of them.

g. Using the colors on the Swatches palette and the Direct Selection Tool, change the colors of the objects in each pattern.

h. Drag each pattern back to the Swatches palette, using The Selection Tool.

i. Fill the two samples with the new pattern swatches.

j. Delete the new pattern swatches from the artboard.

k. Place your name in the lower-left corner of the artboard.

l. Print one copy of *Wallpaper*.

m. Save your work and Exit (Win) or Quit (Mac) Illustrator.

4. You are a fabric designer for a company that manufactures curtains for commercial buildings like hotels and hospitals. You have been asked to design a pattern for a new curtain that will be used in a doctor's office. The pattern should be cheerful and use bright colors. You decide to look at some patterns on the Internet to get ideas.

To complete this independent challenge:

a. Connect to the Internet and go to *http://www.course.com*.

b. Navigate to the page for this book, then click the link for the Student Online Companion.

c. Click the links for this unit and look for examples of fabrics.

d. Print a page from one of the Web sites containing a fabric you like.

e. Exit (Win) or Quit (Mac) your browser.

f. Start Illustrator.

g. Create a new file and save it as *Pattern*.

h. Using the tools that you are familiar with in Illustrator, create a pattern similar to the one that you printed.

i. Add the new pattern to the Swatches palette and give it a unique name.

j. Apply the new pattern to a large rectangle on the artboard.

k. Place your name in the lower-left corner of the artboard.

l. Save your work.

m. Print one copy of Pattern, and Exit (Win) or Quit (Mac) Illustrator.

► Visual Workshop

Re-create the picture shown in Figure G-24. Start Illustrator and save your document as *Blur*. Create a square with a fill color of your choice. Cut the square into four pieces using the Knife Tool. Separate each piece as shown in Figure G-24, and apply four different fill colors to the pieces. Select the four pieces and apply a drop shadow with a 0.2" X Offset and a 0.2" Y Offset. Rasterize the four pieces, then apply the Radial Blur filter. Choose 10 for the Blur Amount, Spin for the Blur Method, and Good for the Quality. Place your name in the lower-left corner of the artboard, print one copy of Blur, and Exit (Win) or Quit (Mac) Illustrator, saving the changes to your work.

FIGURE G-24

Creating
Graphs in Illustrator

Objectives

► **Create a graph**
► **Edit data in the Graph Data palette**
► **Use the Group Selection Tool**
► **Use the Graph Type dialog box**
► **Create a combination graph**
► **Create a custom graph design**
► **Apply a custom design to a graph**
► **Create a sliding scale design and apply it to a graph**

A **graph** is a diagram of data that shows a quantitative relationship among a set of numbers. A **series**, or a set of data, can be represented by a graphic element, such as a bar, line, or point. Different types of graphs are used to emphasize different aspects of a display. Illustrator offers nine types of graphs: column, stacked column, pie, bar, stacked bar, line, area, scatter, and radar. These visual displays can simplify complex data and help to communicate a message. You can convert one type of graph into another type and create custom designs to apply to graphs. Bill will create two graphs: one showing the lowest, highest, and average temperatures for the months of January, February, and March; and another showing the amount of snow that fell in the area over the last three years. He will use a custom design for the graph columns.

Unit H

Illustrator 9.0

Creating a Graph

Before you create a graph, it is important to understand how data is plotted in Illustrator's Graph Data palette. The first column of the Graph Data palette is reserved for **category labels**, while the first row is reserved for **legend labels**. Category labels describe nonnumeric data, such as the months of the year, the days of the week, or a group of salespersons' names. They appear on the x-axis (horizontal axis) of the graph. Legend labels describe numeric data that may change, such as weekly sales totals, payroll amounts, or daily temperatures and appear in a box next to the graph, called the Legend. The **Legend**, similar to a map legend, contains the legend labels and small boxes filled with colors that represent the columns on the graph. Bill is given an Illustrator file with the data that he needs to enter into the Graph Data palette to create his first graph. Bill creates a Column Graph that is 6 " wide and 4" tall.

Steps 1 2 3 4

1. Start Illustrator

Trouble?

Printing, saving, and exporting are disabled in the Illustrator Tryout! software. To learn more about the Tryout! software that accompanies this book, see the Read This Before You Begin page.

2. Open **AI H-1** from the drive and folder where you store your project files, then save it as **Graph**

3. Click the **Column Graph Tool** on the toolbox, then click the artboard
   The Graph dialog box opens. It displays 0 in (inches) in the Width field and 0 in (inches) in the Height field, assuming that inches has been chosen in the General Units and Undo Preferences or in the Document Setup dialog box. If you see "pt" in the Width and Height fields, change your unit of measure to inches before you proceed.

QuickTip

You can change the size of a graph after it is created by using the Scale Tool.

4. Enter **6** in the Width field and **4** in the Height field as shown in Figure H-1, then click **OK**
   The Graph Data palette appears in front of the graph. The Graph Data palette consists of horizontal rows and vertical columns. The intersection of a row and a column is called a **cell**. The first cell, which is selected, contains the number 1.00 as sample data to create a temporary structure for the graph. The appearance of the graph will change after you enter your own data.

Trouble?

If the open palettes disappear when you press [Tab], press [Tab] again and they will reappear. If the Graph Data palette does not reappear, undo your last few steps until the graph is gone and start over. When you repeat Step 5, make sure you click the cell containing 1.00 before you press [Tab].

5. Press **[Delete]** (Win) or **[delete]** (Mac), then press **[Tab]** to eliminate the 1.00 from the first cell and select the next cell in the first row
   You must always remove the number 1.00 from the first cell before entering your new data.

6. Type **Low**, press **[Tab]**, type **High**, press **[Tab]**, then type **Average**
   You have entered three legend labels.

7. Click the **second cell in the first column**, type **Jan**, press **[Enter]** (Win) or **[return]** (Mac), type **Feb**, press **[Enter]** (Win) or **[return]** (Mac), type **March**, then press **[Enter]** (Win) or **[return]** (Mac)
   You have entered three category labels. Compare the positions of your labels with those shown in Figure H-2.

QuickTip

Some labels consist of numbers such as a ZIP code or the year 2002. These labels are meant to describe categories and must be set in quotes ("2002") so that Illustrator will not mistake them for data that should be plotted.

8. Enter the rest of the data that is supplied in the upper-left corner of the artboard, using **[Tab]**, **[Enter]** (Win) or **[return]** (Mac), and the four arrow keys on your keyboard to move between cells; refer to Figure H-2 if you need help

9. Click the **Close button** (Win) in the upper-right corner of the Graph Data palette or (Mac) in the upper-left corner of the Graph Data palette, click **Yes** (Win) or **Save** (Mac) when prompted to save changes to the graph data, then save your work
   The column graph, the category axis data, and the legend now appear on the artboard. For now, don't worry if the labels in the legend are outside the boundaries of the artboard.

FIGURE H-1: **Graph dialog box**

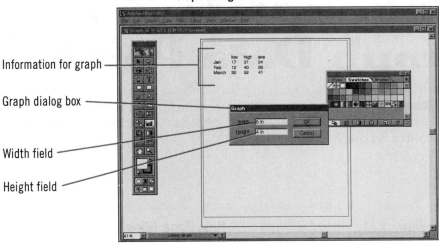

Information for graph

Graph dialog box

Width field

Height field

FIGURE H-2: **Entering data in the Graph Data palette**

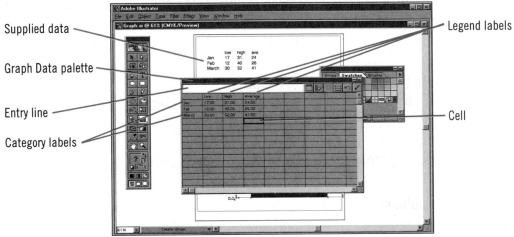

Supplied data

Graph Data palette

Entry line

Category labels

Legend labels

Cell

Choosing a chart type

Keep in mind the following guidelines when choosing a chart type:
- Pie or column charts are typically used to show quantitative data as a percentage of the whole.
- Line or bar charts are used to compare trends or changes over time.

- Area charts emphasize volume and are used to show a total quantity rather than to emphasize a portion of the data.
- Scatter or radial charts show a correlation between variables.

Importing data from other software programs

You can import graph data from a text file or a Microsoft Excel worksheet into the Graph Data palette in Illustrator. To import data, you must be in the Graph Data palette. Click the Import Data button ▦ (Win) or ▦ (Mac). If you are working on a Windows computer, the Import Graph Data dialog box will open; if you are working on a Macintosh, the

Please open a text file window will open. In either case, you are prompted to open a file from your hard disk or floppy disk. If you are importing a text file, it must be saved as a text-only file with commas separating each number. If you are importing an Excel worksheet, it must be saved as a text (tab-delimited) file for Illustrator to support it.

Illustrator 9.0

Editing Data in the Graph Data Palette

Once you have created a graph, it's easy to go back and change data if necessary in the Graph Data palette. While Bill is changing the artboard orientation from tall to wide and hiding the imageable area dotted line, he receives two new numbers from the Weather Department that need to be inserted in the Graph Data palette.

Steps

1. Click **View** on the menu bar, then click **Hide Page Tiling**
   The dotted line that represents the imageable area is hidden.

2. Click **File** on the menu bar, point to **Document Setup**, click the **Landscape button** as shown in Figure H-3, then click **OK**
   The artboard is now 11" wide by 8.5" high. It is easier to view the graph on the artboard.

3. Delete the text at the top of the artboard
   Since the numbers have already been plotted, it is no longer necessary to keep them in the document.

4. Click the **graph** to select it if it is not already selected

5. Click **Object** on the menu bar, point to **Graph**, then click **Data**
   The Graph Data palette may block your view of the graph.

QuickTip

To remove data from cells in the Graph Data palette, select the cells from which you want to delete the data, click Edit on the menu bar, then click Clear.

6. Click the **cell that contains the number 30**, type **34**, then press **[Enter]** (Win) or **[return]** (Mac)
   When you click a cell, the number in the cell becomes highlighted in the entry line of the Graph Data palette, allowing you to change it to a new number. See Figure H-4.

7. Click the **cell that contains the number 41**, type **43**, then press **[Enter]** (Win) or **[return]** (Mac)

QuickTip

Category labels are listed vertically and legend labels are listed horizontally, in the Graph Data palette. If you enter your labels incorrectly, you can click the Transpose Cell/Column button on the Graph Data palette to switch them.

8. Click the **Apply button** in the upper-right corner of the Graph Data palette, then drag the **Graph Data palette** down slightly to view the graph on the artboard as shown in Figure H-4
   The lets you see changes made to the graph, but keeps the Graph Data palette open in case you need to make additional changes. Once you have applied changes to the Graph Data palette, your pointer will become if you try to click the again.

9. Close the **Graph Data palette**, then save your work

FIGURE H-3: Document Setup dialog box

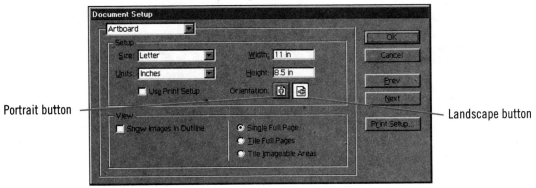

Portrait button

Landscape button

FIGURE H-4: Changing data in the Graph Data palette

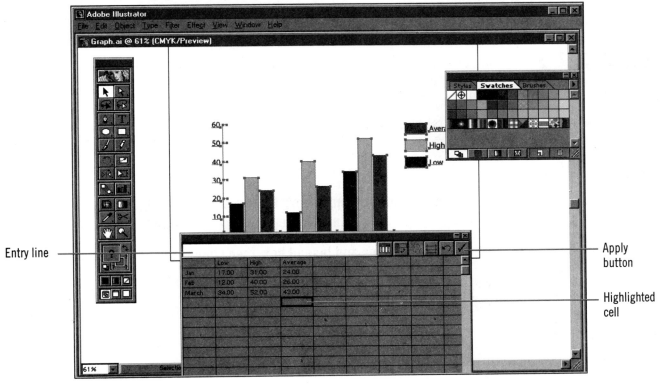

Entry line

Apply button

Highlighted cell

CLUES TO USE

Changing the cell style in the Graph Data palette

Numbers in the Graph Data palette are initially displayed with two decimals. For example, if you type the number 86, it appears as 86.00. To modify the number of decimals in any or all cells in the Graph Data palette, click the cells that you want to change, then click the Cell Style button ▣ in the upper-right corner of the Graph Data palette. The Cell Style dialog box will open. Increase or decrease the number in the Number of decimals box to change the decimal place—setting it to 0 if you do not want any decimal place—and then click OK. You can also increase or decrease the column width in the Cell Style dialog box by changing the default 7 in the Column Width field.

Illustrator 9.0

Using the Group Selection Tool

Graphs are grouped objects, consisting of many individual groups grouped together. Each set of colored columns represents an individual group within the larger group. For example, all of the black columns in Figure H-5 represent the low temperatures for each month. The gray columns are the average-temperature group, and the light gray columns are the high-temperature group. The Group Selection Tool allows you to select entire groups within the larger group for the purpose of editing them with the Illustrator tools and menu commands. ✒ Bill changes the color of each group of columns using the Group Selection Tool.

Steps

1. Make sure that your graph is not selected by clicking the artboard to deselect it if necessary

2. Press and hold the mouse button over the **Direct Selection Tool** ▣; when the hidden toolbar appears, drag the pointer until it is over the **Group Selection Tool** ▣, then release the mouse button

Trouble?

If you click too many times, you will eventually select the entire graph instead of an individual group. In that case, deselect the graph and try again.

3. Click the **first black column above the Jan label**, then click again
Notice that the first click selects the first column, and the second click selects the two remaining columns.

4. Click the **first black column** a third time to select the low-temperature legend box
The entire low-temperature group is selected.

QuickTip

The text labels, value axis labels, and legend labels are also individual groups within the larger graph group. Click twice to select them, then change their font, size, or color as desired.

5. Change the fill color of the selected columns to **Red** as shown in Figure H-6

6. Click the **first light gray column above the Jan label**, click it again, click it a third time, then change the fill color of the high-temperature columns and legend box to **Yellow**

7. Select the **gray columns and legend box**, then change the fill color to **Green**
Your graph should resemble the one shown in Figure H-7.

8. Save your work

FIGURE H-5: Elements of the graph

Low-temperature group

Legend

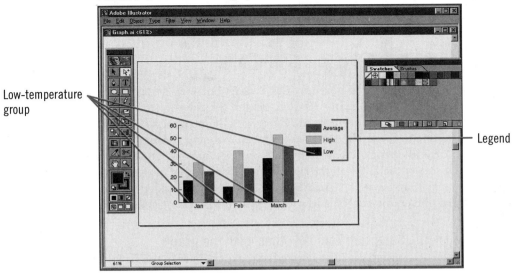

FIGURE H-6: Using the Group Selection Tool

Group Selection Tool

Low-temperature group with new fill color

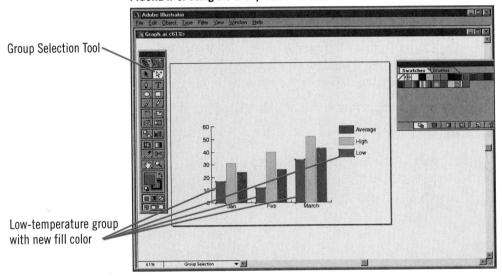

FIGURE H-7: Changing the fill color of the columns

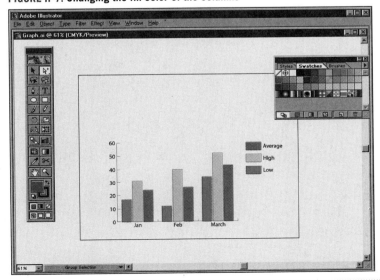

Illustrator 9.0

Using the Graph Type Dialog Box

The Graph Type dialog box provides a variety of ways to change the look of your graph. For example, you can add a drop shadow behind the columns in a graph or change the appearance of the tick marks. **Tick marks** are short lines that extend out from the **value axis**, which is the vertical line to the left of the graph. Tick marks help viewers interpret the meaning of column height by indicating incremental values on the value axis. You can also move the value axis from the left side of the graph to the right side or display it on both sides. Values on the value axis can be changed, and symbols such as $, %, and ° can be added to the numbers for clarification. ✏ Bill adds a drop shadow to the graph, then changes the appearance of the tick marks.

Steps 1 2 3 4

1. Click the **Selection Tool** �, then click the **graph**
   The entire graph must be selected to make changes in the Graph Type dialog box.

2. Click **Object** on the menu bar, point to **Graph**, then click **Type**
   The Graph Type dialog box opens.

3. Click the **Add Drop Shadow check box** as shown in Figure H-8

4. Click the **Graph Options list arrow**, then click **Value Axis** as shown in Figure H-9
   All of the options in this window now refer to the value axis, which is the vertical line containing values located to the left of the columns on the graph.

5. Click the **Length list arrow** in the Tick Marks section of the window, then click **Full Width**

6. Click **OK**

7. Deselect your graph to view the changes made to it
   Your screen should resemble Figure H-10.

8. Save your work

FIGURE H-8: **Graph Type dialog box**

Graph Options list arrow

Graph types

Add Drop Shadow check box

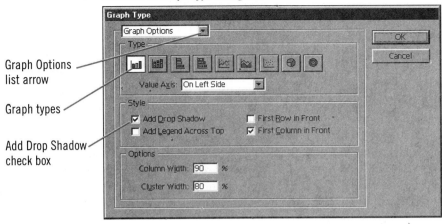

FIGURE H-9: **Changing the length of the tick marks**

Graph Options list arrow

Tick Marks section

Length list arrow

Prefix field

Suffix field

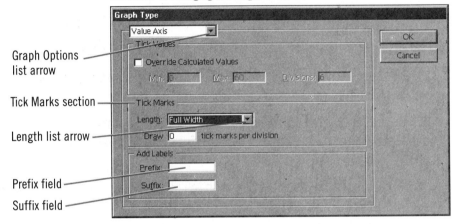

FIGURE H-10: **Graph with full width tick marks and a drop shadow**

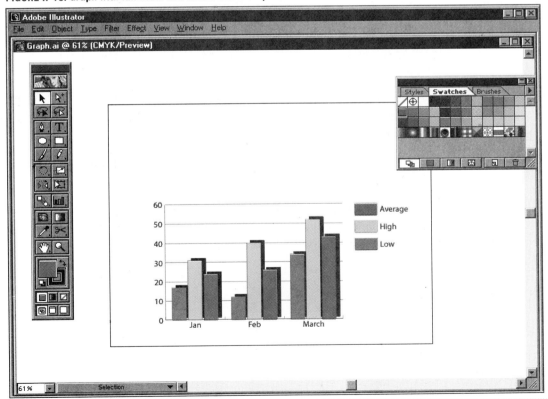

Illustrator 9.0

Creating a Combination Graph

A **combination graph** is a graph that uses two graph styles to plot numeric data. This type of graph is useful if you want to emphasize one set of numbers in comparison to others. For example, if you needed to create a column graph showing how much more paper than glass, plastic, or aluminum is recycled in a major city over a one-year period, you could plot the paper recycling data as a line graph, leaving the other recycling categories as columns. Your audience would be able to compare how much more paper is recycled than the other three products by looking at the line in relationship to the columns on the graph. ✎ Bill needs to emphasize the average temperature for the three months. He decides to plot the average temperature data as a line graph set against the other columns.

Steps

1. Click the **Group Selection Tool** ▶, then select the entire **green group** on the graph

2. Click **Object** on the menu bar, point to **Graph**, then click **Type**

3. Click the **Line graph type**, then click the **Add Drop Shadow check box** to deselect it as shown in Figure H-11

4. Click the **Edge-to-Edge Lines check box**, make sure that there are check marks in the **Mark Data Points** and **Connect Data Points check boxes** as shown in Figure H-11, then click **OK**

5. Click the **artboard** to deselect the graph, click ▶ then select the **line group** as shown in Figure H-12
   Although the line graph is behind the columns, it may appear to be in front of the columns when it is selected. Notice the three small squares on the line. These **markers** represent the numeric values entered in the Graph Data palette.

6. Click **Object** on the menu bar, point to **Arrange**, then click **Bring to Front**
   The line graph moves in front of the columns. This effect will be more readily apparent later when you deselect the graph.

7. While the line is still selected, change the stroke weight of the line to **10 pts** (you may need to show the Stroke palette to do so), the fill color of the line to **None**, and the stroke color of the line to **Green** as shown in Figure H-13

8. Click the **artboard** to deselect the graph, then place your **name** in the lower-left corner of the artboard

9. Print one copy of **Graph**, then close the **Graph document**, saving your changes to it
   ✎ Bill hands the graph over to the Weather Department for final approval, then moves on to finish the second graph.

FIGURE H-11: **Creating a combination graph**

Line graph type

Graph Options list arrow

Add Drop Shadow option deselected

Options for line graphs

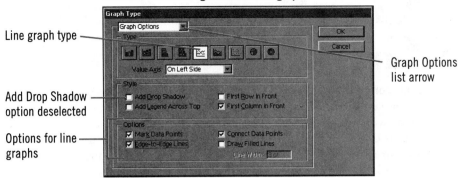

FIGURE H-12: **Selecting the line graph**

Group Selection Tool

Line selected

Markers

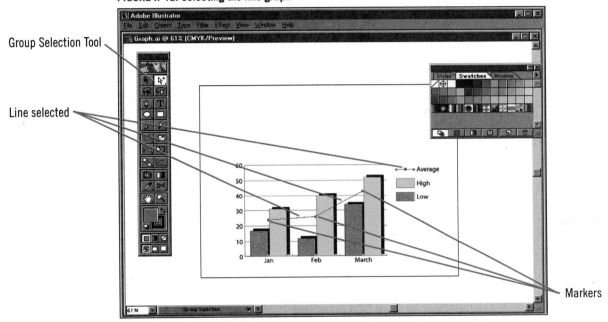

FIGURE H-13: **Changing the fill and stroke colors and the stroke thickness of the line**

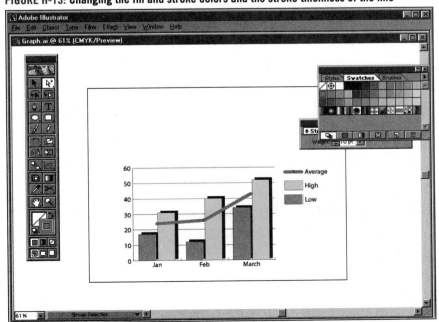

Creating a Custom Graph Design

A **custom graph design** is simply a picture of something used to replace traditional columns, bars, or markers in Illustrator graphs. For example, newspapers, such as *USA Today,* may print graphs made with custom designs of coins or dollars instead of columns and bars. Only vector-based objects can be used for custom graph designs. You cannot use bitmaps, objects created with the Paintbrush Tool, or objects filled with gradients for custom graph designs. ✎ Bill began his work on the snowfall graph by creating a picture of a shovel and plotting the data for the years 2001, 2002, and 2003. His next step is to make a custom design using the shovel.

Steps

1. Open **AI H-2** from your Project Disk, then save it as **Snow**

2. Click **View** on the menu bar, then click **Shovel**

QuickTip

It is important to group your illustration before you use it as a custom design.

3. Click **View** on the menu bar, click **Show Rulers**, then drag **two guides from the horizontal ruler** that line up with the top and the bottom of the shovel as shown in Part A of Figure H-14

4. Make sure that the fill and stroke colors are set to **None** on the toolbox as shown in Part B of Figure H-14, then click the **Rectangle Tool** ▣

Trouble?

If your rectangle is not the correct size, undo your last step and try again. If your rectangle becomes deselected by accident, you can temporarily switch to outline mode to select it. Just make sure that you switch back to Preview mode when you are finished.

5. Create a **rectangle** that snaps to the top and bottom guides as shown in Part B of Figure H-14
   The rectangle represents the height of the column. It is very important that the height of the rectangle exactly match the height of the custom design to ensure that data values are represented correctly on the graph.

6. While the rectangle is still selected, click **Object** on the menu bar, point to **Arrange**, then click **Send to Back**
   The rectangle must be behind the illustration. Otherwise, you will receive an error message when you create the custom design.

Trouble?

If you drag the shovel or rectangle instead of selecting them with the Selection Tool, undo your last step. When you start over, position the Selection Tool farther away from the objects before you start dragging the Selection Tool.

7. Select both the **rectangle** and the **shovel** as shown in Part C of Figure H-14
   An easy way to ensure that you select both objects is to drag a marquee across the shovel using the Selection Tool. Otherwise, it may be difficult to select the rectangle once it becomes deselected. You can also temporarily switch to Outline mode to select the shovel and the rectangle.

8. Click **Object** on the menu bar, point to **Graph**, then click **Design**
   The Graph Design dialog box opens.

9. Click **New Design**, click **Rename**, name the design **Shovel**, click **OK**, then click **OK** again to close the Graph Design dialog box
   See Figure H-15.

FIGURE H-14: **Creating a custom graph design**

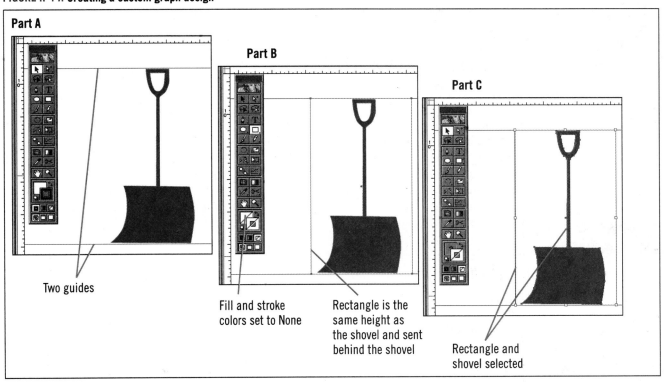

Part A

Two guides

Part B

Fill and stroke
colors set to None

Rectangle is the
same height as
the shovel and sent
behind the shovel

Part C

Rectangle and
shovel selected

FIGURE H-15: **Graph Design dialog box**

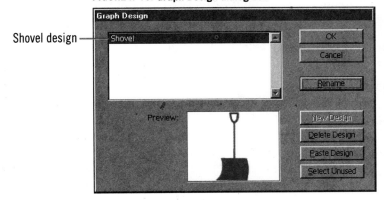

Shovel design

Custom graph designs

Illustrator comes with two documents full of custom designs that you can apply to graphs. These designs include flags, cats, hammers, diamonds, dollar signs, stars, and men and women. In addition, three-dimensional objects such as cylinders, hexagons, cubes, arrows, and pyramids are available. To use a column or marker design, start Illustrator, then open

Column & Marker Designs1.ai or Column & Marker Designs2.ai, located in the Illustrator 9.0\Sample Files\Graphs & Graph Designs folder. Start a new document and create a graph. Select the graph, click Object on the menu bar, then click Column. All of the column designs will appear in the Graph Column dialog box.

Applying a Custom Design to a Graph

Custom designs are typically applied to column graphs and line graphs. Illustrator provides four options for displaying custom designs on a graph: uniformally scaled, vertically scaled, repeating, and sliding. **Uniformly scaled designs** are resized vertically and horizontally, whereas **vertically scaled designs** are resized only vertically. **Repeating designs** assign a value to the custom design and repeat it as many times as necessary. For example, if the shovel is assigned a value of 1 foot of snow, 3 shovels would represent 3 feet of snow. **Sliding-scale designs** allow you to define a point on the custom design from which the design will stretch, thereby leaving everything below that point uniform. ✎ Bill applies the shovel design to the graph he has created using the vertically scaled design style.

Steps

1. Click **View** on the menu bar, then click **Graph Area**

2. Select the **graph** with the **Selection Tool** ▰

3. Click **Object** on the menu bar, point to **Graph**, then click **Column**
   The Graph Column dialog box opens.

4. Click **Shovel**, then make sure that **Vertically Scaled** is selected for the **Column Type** as shown in Figure H-16

5. Click the **Rotate Legend Design check box** to remove the check mark as shown in Figure H-16, then click **OK**
   The three columns on the graph are replaced with shovels, each a different height, indicating how many feet of snow fell in each year.

6. Click the **artboard** to deselect the graph
   Your screen should resemble Figure H-17.

7. Save your work

FIGURE H-16: Graph Column dialog box

Graph Column dialog box

Shovel design

Column Type list arrow

Rotate Legend Design check box

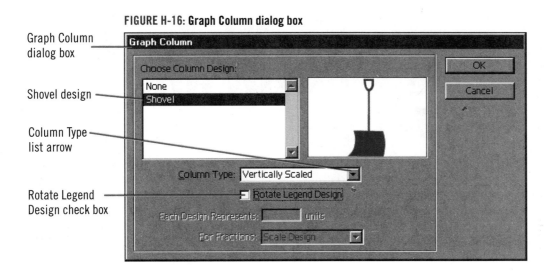

FIGURE H-17: The graph with the shovel design applied to it

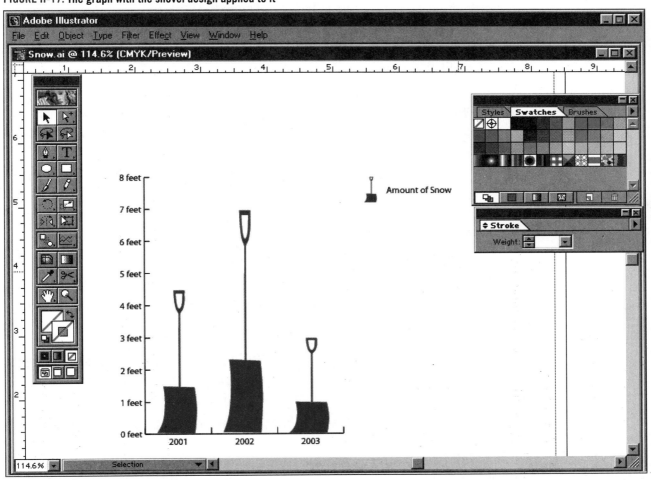

Illustrator 9.0

Creating a Sliding Scale Design and Applying It to a Graph

When you apply a vertically scaled design style to a column graph, the entire design stretches to accommodate the value assigned to it. This expansion may present a problem if the custom design needs to maintain an aspect ratio. For example, a logo custom design might become unreadable if it is stretched too far. As you learned in the previous lesson, a sliding scale design allows you to define a point on the custom design from which the graph should stretch. Thus a portion of the design remains at its original size. 🖌 Bill thinks that the graph columns would look better if the handle and the rod of the shovel stretched, but the scoop of the shovel stayed the same size. He creates a sliding scale design called Sliding Shovel and applies it to the graph.

1. Using the **View** menu, return to the **Shovel** view, click the **View** menu again, point to **Guides**, click **Clear Guides,** then set the stroke color to **Black** on the tool box

2. Using the **Pen Tool** 🖊, click the **artboard** to drop an anchor point where shown in Part A of Figure H-18; then while pressing and holding **[Shift]**, click again to create a straight line where shown in Part A of Figure H-18
Make sure that the fill color is still set to None.

3. Switch to the **Selection Tool** 🖈, click **View** on the menu bar, point to **Guides**, then click **Make Guides**
The black line turns into a guide as shown in Part B of Figure H-18.

4. Click **View** on the menu bar again and point to **Guides** to make sure your guides are unlocked; if there is a check mark to the left of Lock Guides, click **Lock Guides** to unlock them
If the check mark is not present, your guides are already unlocked, and you do not need to click Lock Guides to deselect the option.

5. Use 🖈 to drag a **marquee** around the **shovel**, the **rectangle**, and the **guide**, so that all three objects are selected as shown in Part C of Figure H-18

6. Click **Object** on the menu bar, point to **Graph**, then click **Design**

7. Click **New Design**, click **Rename**, name the design **Sliding Shovel** as shown in Figure H-19, click **OK**, then click **OK** again to close the Graph Design dialog box

8. Click **View** on the menu bar, click **Graph Area**, then select the **graph** with 🖈

9. Click **Object** on the menu bar, point to **Graph**, click **Column**, click **Sliding Shovel**, click **Sliding** from the **Column Type list** as shown in Figure H-20, then click **OK**
Notice that the scoop of the shovel remains equal in all three columns.

10. Deselect the **graph**, click **View** on the menu bar, point to **Guides**, click **Hide Guides**, place your **name** in the lower-left corner of the artboard, print one copy of **Snow**, then **Exit** (Win) or **Quit** (Mac) Illustrator, saving your changes to the document
Your screen should resemble Figure H-21 once you have deselected the graph.

FIGURE H-18: Creating a sliding-scale design

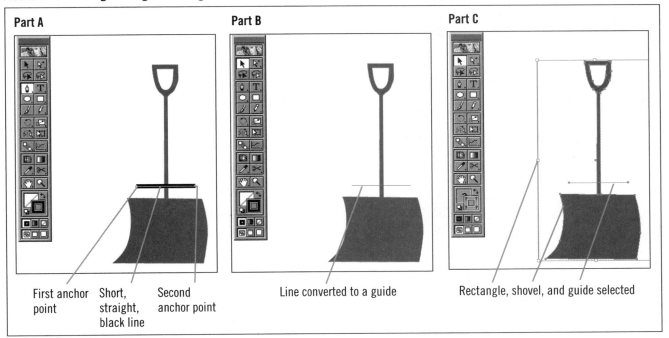

Part A

First anchor point   Short, straight, black line   Second anchor point

Part B

Line converted to a guide

Part C

Rectangle, shovel, and guide selected

FIGURE H-19: Graph Design dialog box

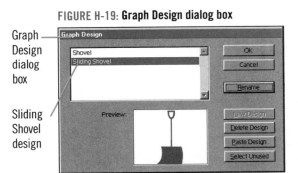

Graph Design dialog box

Sliding Shovel design

FIGURE H-20: Graph Column dialog box

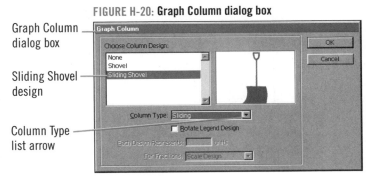

Graph Column dialog box

Sliding Shovel design

Column Type list arrow

FIGURE H-21: The finished illustration

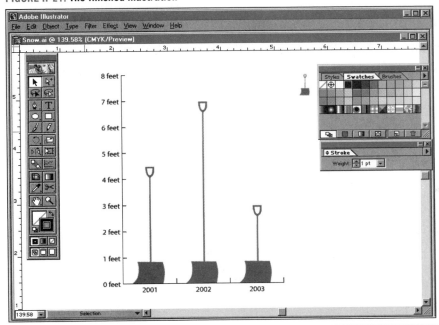

Illustrator 9.0

Practice

▶ Concepts Review

Label the Illustrator window elements shown in Figure H-22.

FIGURE H-22

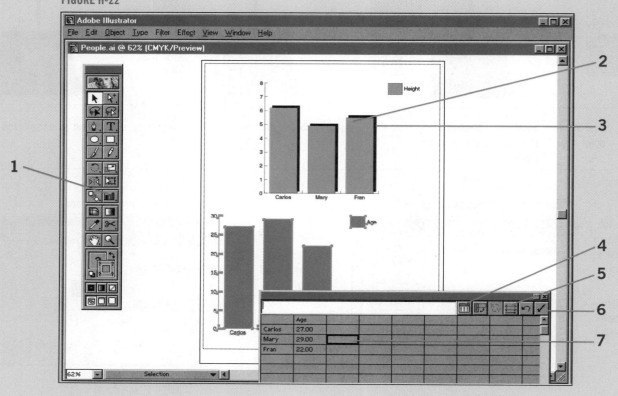

Match each term with the statement that describes it.

8. Graph Data palette
9. Sliding Scale design
10. Cells
11. Custom design
12. Group Selection Tool
13. Graph

a. A tool that allows you to select individual groups within larger groups.
b. A vector-based picture used in place of traditional columns or markers in a graph.
c. A diagram that shows a quantitative relationship among a set of numbers.
d. Where you enter graph data before the information is plotted.
e. A type of custom graph design that uses a guide to determine the point from which a design stretches.
f. Small boxes in the Graph Data palette that are displayed horizontally in rows and vertically in columns.

14. Which button do you click to apply graph data without closing the Graph Data palette?
   a. ▦   b. ✓   c. ▦   d. ▦

15. Illustrator comes with _____ types of graph tools.
   a. 8   b. 11   c. 9   d. 7

16. A graph that uses two different graph styles to plot data is called a _____.

a. column graph   **b.** combination graph   **c.** sliding-scale graph   **d.** double graph

Make sure that you have extra blank floppy disks on hand so that if you run out of room on your Project Disks while completing the Skills Review or Independent Challenges, you have a place to save the files you create.

▶ Skills Review

1. Create a graph.
   a. Start Illustrator.
   b. Open AI H-3 from the drive and folder where you store your project files.
   c. Save AI H-3 as *Weather*.
   d. Click the Column Graph Tool.
   e. Click the artboard.
   f. Enter "6" in the Width field.
   g. Enter "4" in the Height field.
   h. Click OK.
   i. Press [Delete] (Win) or [delete] (Mac) to remove the number 1.00 from the first cell in the Graph Data palette.
   j. Press [Tab] to select the next cell in the first row.
   k. Type "Rain", press [Tab], type "Sun", press [Tab], type "Clouds", then press [Tab].
   l. Click the second cell in the first column, type "August", press [Enter] (Win) or [return] (Mac), type "September", press [Enter] (Win) or [return] (Mac), type "October", then press [Enter] (Win) or [return] (Mac).
   m. Enter the rest of the data that is supplied in the upper-left corner of the artboard to fill in the cells underneath Rain, Sun, and Clouds.
   n. Close the Graph Data palette, then save your changes to it.

2. Edit data in the Graph Data palette.
   a. Click View on the menu bar, then click Hide Page Tiling.
   b. Click File on the menu bar, click Document Setup, click the Landscape button, then click OK.
   c. Delete the text at the top of the artboard.
   d. Click the graph to select it, if necessary.
   e. Click Object on the menu bar, point to Graph, then click Data.
   f. Click the cell that contains the number 7, and change it to **8**.
   g. Click the cell that contains the number 20, and change it to **19**.
   h. Click the Apply button in the upper-right corner of the Graph Data palette, then drag the Graph Data palette down slightly to view the artboard.
   i. Close the Graph Data palette.
   j. Save your work.

3. Use the Group Selection Tool.
   a. If the Group Selection Tool is not visible, press and hold the Direct Selection Tool; when the hidden toolbar appears, drag the pointer until it is over the Group Selection Tool, then release the mouse button.
   b. Click the first black column above the August label, click a second time, then click a third time to select the Rain group.
   c. Change the fill color of the selected columns to Green.
   d. Change the fill color of the Sun group to Yellow.
   e. Change the fill color of the Clouds group to Violet.
   f. Save your work.

4. Use the Graph Type dialog box.
   a. Click the Selection Tool, then click the graph.
   b. Click Object on the menu bar, point to Graph, then click Type.
   c. Click the Add Drop Shadow check box.
   d. Click the Graph Options list arrow, then click Value Axis.
   e. Click the Length list arrow in the Tick Marks section of the window, then click Full Width.
   f. Click OK.
   g. Save your work.

5. Create a combination graph.
   a. Using the Group Selection Tool, select the yellow columns and the yellow box in the legend.
   b. Click Object on the menu bar, point to Graph, then click Type.
   c. Click the Line Graph type.
   d. Click the Add Drop Shadow check box to deselect the option.
   e. Click the Edge-to-Edge Lines check box.
   f. Click the Mark Data Points and Connect Data Points check boxes to ensure that there are check marks in both boxes.
   g. Click OK.
   h. Click the artboard to deselect the graph.
   i. Using the Group Selection Tool, select the line segments and the small corresponding line in the legend.
   j. Change the stroke weight of the line to 10 pts.
   k. Change the fill color of the line to None, and the stroke color of the line to Yellow.
   l. Place your name in the lower-left corner of the artboard.
   m. Print one copy of Weather.
   n. Close the Weather document, saving your changes to it.

6. Create a custom graph design.
   a. Open AI H-4 from the drive and folder where you store your project files.
   b. Save AI H-4 as *Flowers*.
   c. Click View on the menu bar, then click Flower.
   d. Click View on the menu bar, then click Show Rulers, if necessary.
   e. Drag two guides from the horizontal ruler: one that touches the top of the flower, and one that touches the bottom of the stem.
   f. Lock the guides using the View menu.
   g. Set the fill and stroke colors to None on the toolbox.
   h. Create a rectangle that snaps to the top and bottom of the guides and that is slightly wider than the width of the flower.
   i. While the rectangle is still selected, click Object on the menu bar, point to Arrange, then click Send to Back.
   j. Select the flower and the rectangle.
   k. Click Object on the menu bar, point to Graph, then click Design.
   l. Click New Design, click Rename, name the design **Flower**, click OK, then click OK again.

7. Apply a custom design to a graph.
   a. Click View on the menu bar, then click Graph Area.
   b. Select the graph with the Selection Tool.
   c. Click Object on the menu bar, point to Graph, then click Column.
   d. Click Flower, then make sure that Vertically Scaled is chosen for the Column Type.

e. Click the Rotate Legend Design check box to remove the check mark.

f. Click the artboard to deselect the graph.

g. Save your work.

8. **Create a sliding-scale design graph.**

a. Click View on the menu bar, then click Flower.

b. Click View on the menu bar, point to Guides, then click *Clear Guides*.

c. Set the stroke color to Black and the fill color to None.

d. Click the Pen Tool and create a short, straight line directly above the two flower leaves. To do so, click the artboard directly above the leaf on the left side of the flower to create an anchor point. Press and hold [Shift], then click the artboard about 1" to the right of the first anchor point.

e. Click View on the menu bar, point to Guides, then click Make Guides.

f. Click View on the menu bar, and if there is a check mark to the left of Lock Guides, click Lock Guides to select it and unlock the guides.

g. Click the Selection Tool, then drag a marquee around the flower, rectangle, and guide.

h. Click Object on the menu bar, point to Graph, then click Design.

i. Click New Design, click Rename, name the design **Sliding Flower**, then click OK twice to close the Graph Design dialog box.

j. Click View on the menu bar, click Graph Area, then select the graph.

k. Click Object on the menu bar, point to Graph, then click Column.

l. Click Sliding Flower, then click Sliding from the Column Type list arrow.

m. Click View on the menu bar, point to Guides, then Click *Hide Guides*.

n. Deselect the graph.

o. Place your name in the lower-left corner of the artboard.

p. Print one copy of Flowers.

q. Exit (Win) or Quit (Mac) Illustrator, saving your changes to Flowers.

▶ Independent Challenges

1. You are applying for financial aid to pursue a master's degree in nutrition, and have been asked to submit your monthly living expenses. You decide to present the information in a simple column chart.

To complete this independent challenge:

a. Start Illustrator.

b. Open AI H-5 from the drive and folder where you store your project files.

c. Save AI H-5 as *Expenses*.

d. Create a 6" wide by 4" tall column graph.

e. Delete 1.00 from the first cell, then press [Tab].

f. Type **Monthly Expenses**.

g. Using the information at the top of the artboard, enter the rest of the data. Remember to skip over the first cell in the first column.

h. Close the Graph Data palette, saving your changes to the data.

i. Using the Type Tool, create numbers that correspond to the columns in the graph as shown in Figure H-23; for example, type **400** and place it above the Rent column.

j. Change the fill color of the graph columns and legend box to Red.

k. Place a drop shadow behind the columns.

l. Enter $ as a Prefix in the Graph Type dialog box. (*Hint:* Click Value Axis in the Graph Options list box to display the Prefix text box.)

m. Delete the information at the top of the artboard.

n. With the Direct Selection Tool, make sure that the graph is not selected, then click the red rectangle and the words Monthly Expenses and drag them to the left to move them closer to the rest of the graph.

o. Place your name in the lower-left corner of the artboard.

p. Print one copy of Expenses.

q. Exit (Win) or Quit (Mac) Illustrator, saving your changes to Expenses.

FIGURE H-23

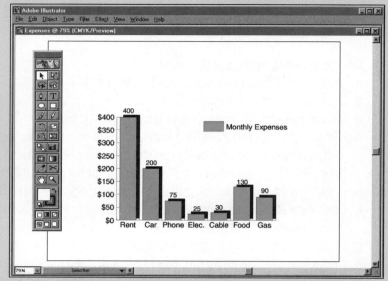

2. You work for your town's recycling office and have been asked to speak at an upcoming town meeting about recycling. You decide to discuss how aluminum can recycling has increased over the past five years and how that increase has made more money available for community projects.

To complete this independent challenge:

a. Start Illustrator.

b. Open AI H-6 from the drive and folder where you store your project files.

c. Save AI H-6 as *Recycle*.

d. Create a rectangle around the cola can that is the same height as the can. If you use guides when drawing the rectangle, clear the guides after you have finished with them.

e. Change the fill and stroke colors of the rectangle to None and send the rectangle behind the can.

f. Deselect the rectangle, click the Pen Tool, then change the stroke color to Black.

g. Create a short, straight line above the word cola on the can.

h. Make the line into a guide.

i. Make sure that the guides are unlocked using the View menu.

j. Select the can, rectangle, and guide.

k. Click Object on the menu bar, point to Graph, then click Design.

l. Click New Design, then click Rename.

m. Name the design **Sliding Can**, click OK, then click OK again.

n. Select the graph and apply the Sliding Can type to the graph. (*Hint:* Don't forget to choose Sliding from the Column Type list.)

o. Clear the check mark next to Rotate Legend Design, then click OK.

p. Deselect the graph; clear the guides; then delete the can, rectangle, and guide from the top of the artboard.

q. Place your name in the lower-left corner of the artboard.

r. Print one copy of Recycle.

s. Exit (Win) or Quit (Mac) Illustrator, saving your changes to Recycle.

3. You are a salesperson at a computer store. You sell computers, printers, and scanners. Your boss has asked you to prepare a graph that shows how these three products are selling in comparison to one another over the last four weeks. You decide to create a combination graph that emphasizes how many more scanners you sell each week than computers or printers.

To complete this independent challenge:

a. Start Illustrator.

b. Create a new document and save it as *Sales*.

c. Create a column graph that is 4 " wide by 4" tall using the following data:

	Computers	Printers	Scanners
Week One	11	13	55
Week Two	12	15	40
Week Three	14	6	61
Week Four	9	11	35

d. Enter your data in the Graph Data palette.

e. Close the Graph Data palette, saving changes to it.

FIGURE H-24

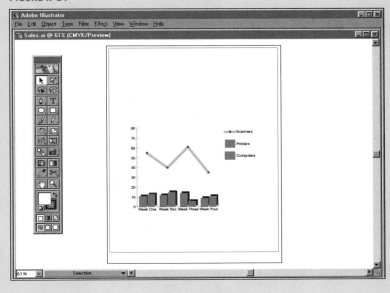

f. Select the Scanners group using the Group Selection Tool, then apply the line graph type to it, as shown in Figure H-24.

g. Change the color and thickness of the line graph so that it is easy to see, as shown in Figure H-24.

h. Use the Group Selection Tool to apply formatting to the rest of the graph (labels, printers group, and computers group) as shown in Figure H-24.

i. Place your name in the lower-left corner of the artboard.

j. Print one copy of Sales.

k. Exit (Win) or Quit (Mac) Illustrator, saving your changes to Sales.

4. You are a sports writer for a local newspaper and would like to create a graph showing the number of wins of one of your local sports teams and two of their rivals. The wins may be from the current season or from the previous year.

To complete this independent challenge:

a. Connect to the Internet and go to *http://www.course.com*

b. Navigate to the page for this book, then click the link for the Student Online Companion.

c. Click the links for this unit.

d. Find three teams you want to graph, and write down on paper how many games they each won.

e. Exit (Win) or Quit (Mac) your browser.

f. Start Illustrator.

g. Create a new document and save it as *Wins*.

h. Create a graph using the information you wrote down and the names of the teams.

i. Use the Graph Type dialog box and the Group Selection Tool to format the graph any way you like.

j. Place your name in the lower-left corner of the artboard.

k. Print one copy of Wins.

l. Exit (Win) or Quit (Mac) Illustrator, saving your changes to Wins.

► Visual Workshop

Re-create the graph shown in Figure H-25 using the following data:

	Oranges	Bananas	Apples
Monday	88	56	45
Tuesday	67	44	61

Create a new document and save it as *Fruit*. Place your name in the lower-left corner of the artboard, then print one copy of Fruit. Exit (Win) or Quit (Mac) Illustrator, saving your changes.

FIGURE H-25

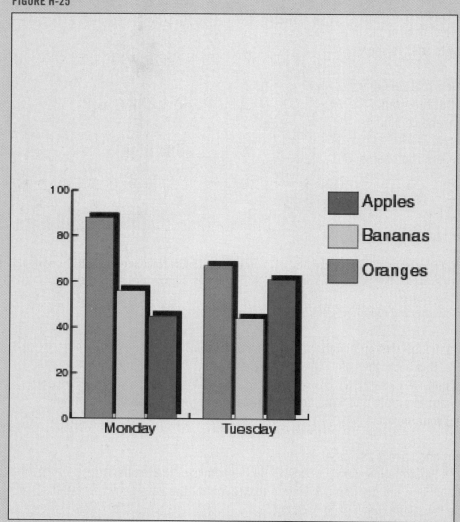

Appendix A

Export Options Windows and Macintosh

File Format Abbreviation	File Format Name	Use
.IFF	Amiga Interchange File Format	In Video Toaster and in transferring files to and from the Commodore Amiga system
.DWG	AutoCAD Drawing	
.DXF	AutoCAD Interchange File	
.BMP	Bitmap	In Paint and image-editing software, such as Adobe PhotoShop; can be imported into Microsoft PowerPoint or Macromedia Director for on screen presentations
.CGM	Computer Graphics Metafile	
.EMF	Enhanced Metafile	
.SWF	Flash	Used in Flash software for Web animation
JPEG	Joint Photographic Experts Group	In HTML, retains all color information but reduces file size by eliminating data that is not essential to display the image; used for photographic images or continuous tones.
.PCT	Macintosh PICT	For placing a bitmap in the Macintosh version of Illustrator
.PCX	PCX	In Z-Soft Paintbrush software on IBM PC compatible computers
.PSD	Photoshop 5	In Adobe Photoshop, a photo manipulation and digital imaging software program
.PXR	Pixar	
.SVG	SVG	
.SVGZ	SVG Compressed	
.TGA	Targa	
.TXT	Text format	For use in word processing and desktop publishing software programs
.TIF	TIFF	For use in word processing and desktop publishing software programs
.WMF	Windows Metafile	

Appendix B

Quick Keys Macintosh

File Menu

New	[Command]+[N]
Open	[Command]+[O]
Close	[Command]+[W]
Save	[Command]+[S]
Save As	[Command]+[Shift]+[S]
Save a Copy	[Command]+[Option]+[S]
Save for Web	[Command]+[Shift]+[Alt]+[S]
Document Setup	[Command]+[Option]+[P]
Print Setup	[Command]+[Shift]+[P]
Print	[Command]+[P]
Exit	[Command]+[Q]

Edit Menu

Undo	[Command]+[Z]
Redo	[Command]+[Shift]+[Z]
Cut	[Command]+[X]
Copy	[Command]+[C]
Paste	[Command]+[V]
Paste in Front	[Command]+[F]
Paste in Back	[Command]+[B]
Select All	[Command]+[A]
Deselect All	[Command]+[Shift]+[A]

Object Menu

Transform Again	[Command]+[D]
Move	[Command]+[Shift]+[M]
Transform Each	[Command]+[Option]+[D]
Bring to Front	[Command]+[Shift]+[]]
Bring Forward	[Command]+[]]
Send Backward	[Command]+[[]

Object Menu (continued)

Send to Back	[Command]+[Shift]+[[]
Group	[Command]+[G]
Ungroup	[Command]+[Shift]+[G]
Lock	[Command]+[2]
Unlock All	[Command]+[Option]+[2]
Hide Selection	[Command]+[3]
Show All	[Command]+[Option]+[3]
Mask, make	[Command]+[7]
Mask, release	[Command]+[Option]+[7]
Compound Path, make	[Command]+[8]
Compound Path, release	[Command]+[Option]+[8]

View Menu

Outline/Preview	[Command]+[Y]
Overprint Preview	[Command]+[Option]+[Shift]+[Y]
Pixel Preview	[Command]+[Option]+[Y]
Zoom In	[Command]+[+]
Zoom Out	[Command]+[-]
Fit In Window	[Command]+[0]
Actual Size	[Command]+[1]
Hide/Show Edges	[Command]+[H]
Hide/Show Rulers	[Command]+[R]
Hide/Show Bounding Box	[Command]+[Shift]+[B]
Hide/Show Transparency Grid	[Command]+[Shift]+[D]
Hide/Show Template	[Command]+[Shift]+[W]
Hide/Show Guides	[Command]+[;]
Lock Guides	[Command]+[Option]+[;]
Make Guides	[Command]+[5]
Release Guides	[Command]+[Option]+[5]
Smart Guides	[Command]+[U]
Show Grid	[Command]+[ ]
Snap to Grid	[Command]+[Shift]+[ ]
Snap to Point	[Command]+[Option]+[ ]
Help	F1

Appendix C

Quick Keys Windows

File Menu

New	[Ctrl]+[N]
Open	[Ctrl]+[O]
Close	[Ctrl]+[W]
Save	[Ctrl]+[S]
Save As	[Ctrl]+[Shift]+[S]
Save a Copy	[Ctrl]+[Alt]+[S]
Save for Web	[Ctrl]+[Shift]+[Alt]+[S]
Document Setup	[Ctrl]+[Alt]+[P]
Print Setup	[Ctrl]+[Shift]+[P]
Print	[Ctrl]+[P]
Exit	[Ctrl]+[Q]

Edit Menu

Undo	[Ctrl]+[Z]
Redo	[Ctrl]+[Shift]+[Z]
Cut	[Ctrl]+[X]
Copy	[Ctrl]+[C]
Paste	[Ctrl]+[V]
Paste in Front	[Ctrl]+[F]
Paste in Back	[Ctrl]+[B]
Select All	[Ctrl]+[A]
Deselect All	[Ctrl]+[Shift]+[A]

Object Menu

Transform Again	[Ctrl]+[D]
Move	[Ctrl]+[Shift]+[M]
Transform Each	[Ctrl]+[Alt]+[D]
Bring to Front	[Ctrl]+[Shift]+[]]
Bring Forward	[Ctrl]+[]]

Object Menu (continued)

Send Backward	[Ctrl]+[[]
Send to Back	[Ctrl]+ [Shift]+[[]
Group	[Ctrl]+[G]
Ungroup	[Ctrl]+[Shift]+[G]
Lock	[Ctrl]+[2]
Unlock All	[Ctrl]+[Alt]+[2]
Hide Selection	[Ctrl]+[3]
Show All	[Ctrl]+[Alt]+[3]
Mask, make	[Ctrl]+[7]
Mask, release	[Ctrl]+[Alt]+[7]
Compound Path, make	[Ctrl]+[8]
Compound Path, release	[Ctrl]+[Alt]+[8]

View Menu

Outline/Preview	[Ctrl]+[Y]
Overprint Preview	[Ctrl]+[Shift]+[Alt]+[Y]
Pixel Preview	[Ctrl]+[Alt]+[Y]
Zoom In	[Ctrl]+[+]
Zoom Out	[Ctrl]+[−]
Fit In Window	[Ctrl]+[0]
Actual Size	[Ctrl]+[1]
Hide/Show Edges	[Ctrl]+[H]
Hide/Show Rulers	[Ctrl]+[R]
Hide/Show Bounding Box	[Ctrl]+[Shift]+[B]
Hide/Show Transparency Grid	[Ctrl]+[Shift]+[D]
Hide/Show Template	[Ctrl]+[Shift]+[W]
Hide/Show Guides	[Ctrl]+[;]
Lock Guides	[Ctrl]+[Alt]+[;]
Make Guides	[Ctrl]+[5]
Release Guides	[Ctrl]+[Alt]+[5]
Smart Guides	[Ctrl]+[U]
Show Grid	[Ctrl]+[_]
Snap to Grid	[Ctrl]+[Shift]+[_]
Snap to Point	[Ctrl]+[Alt]+[_]
Help	F1

Project Files List

To complete many of the lessons and practice exercises in this book, students need to use a Project File that is supplied by Course Technology. Below is a list of the files that are supplied and the unit or practice exercise to which the files correspond. Information on how to obtain Project Files are on the inside cover of this book. The following list only includes Project Files that are supplied; it does not include the files students create from scratch or the files students create by revising the supplied files.

UNIT	File Name	Location
C	AI C-1	Lesson 1
C	AI C-2	Skills Review
C	AI C-3	IND CH. 1
C	AI C-4	IND CH. 3
D	AI D-1	Lesson 1
D	AI D-2	Lesson 3
D	AI D-3	Skills Review
D	AI D-4	Skills Review
D	AI D-5	IND CH. 1
D	AI D-6	IND CH. 3
E	AI E-1	Lesson 1
E	AI E-2	Skills Review
E	AI E-3	IND CH. 2
E	AI E-4	IND CH. 3
F	AI F-1	Lesson 1
F	AI F-2	Skills Review
F	AI F-3	IND CH. 1
F	AI F-4	IND CH. 2
F	AI F-5	IND CH. 3
G	AI G-1	Lesson 1
G	AI G-2	Lesson 4
G	AI G-3	Skills Review
G	AI G-4	IND CH. 1
G	AI G-5	IND CH. 2
G	AI G-6	IND CH. 3
H	AI H-1	Lesson 1
H	AI H-2	Lesson 6
H	AI H-3	Skills Review
H	AI H-4	Skills Review
H	AI H-5	IND CH. 1
H	AI H-6	IND CH. 2

Glossary

Illustrator 9.0

Align The ability to arrange objects by their tops, bottoms, left or right sides, or centers.

Anchor points Smooth, straight corner, curved corner, or combination corner points that join line segments in an open or closed path.

Area Type Tool One of the Illustrator Type tools used to fill the inside of a closed path with text.

Artboard The area, bounded by a solid line, in which you create your artwork.

Bitmap graphics A type of computer-generated graphics which are composed of pixels, small squares used to display a digital image on the rectangular grid of a computer screen.

Bounding box A box that surrounds an object when it is selected. The bounding box contains eight white squares called selection handles.

Category labels Labels entered in the first row of the Graph Data palette.

Clipping mask A closed path that is placed on top of a bitmap or a vector illustration and is used to crop the image below it.

Closed paths One continuous line without any endpoints.

Color stop A symbol at the bottom of the gradient slider indicating a new color in the gradient.

Combination graph A graph that uses two graph styles to plot numeric data.

Compound path A group of two or more overlapping closed paths in which the objects on the top become transparent where they overlap the objects underneath them.

Create outlines An Illustrator feature that converts text into individual vector objects

Custom graph design A picture used to replace traditional columns, bars, or markers in an Illustrator graph.

Digital images Also known as bitmap images or bitmaps and are illustrations or photographs that have been scanned or taken with a digital camera.

Direct Selection Tool An Illustrator tool that allows you to select parts of a grouped object.

Direction line A thin line attached to an anchor point that defines the direction, length, and slope of line segments entering and exiting the anchor point.

Direction point A round black dot connected to an anchor point by a direction line.

Distort filters A category of Illustrator filters that move the original location of an object's anchor points to new locations, thereby distorting the object.

Distribute The ability to evenly space the tops, bottoms, centers, left or right sides of objects on the artboard.

Endpoints The two points at the end of an open path.

EPS The preferred file format for Illustrator line art because it is based on the PostScript printer definition language and results in crisp, vector-based images.

File formats A version of an Illustrator document that is supported by another software program.

Fill The color, pattern, or gradient that occupies the inside area of an object.

Filters Special effects in Illustrator that can be applied to both vector and bitmap graphics.

GIF A file format that is ideal for vector art and large areas of flat color to be used on Web sites.

Global colors Colors that, if modified, will be updated every place on the artboard where they have been applied.

Gradients Multicolor fills used to fill the inside of a closed path.

Graph A diagram of data that shows a quantitative relationship among a set of numbers.

Group The ability to combine two or more objects.

Guides Non-printing horizontal and vertical lines that are created from the ruler and used to snap objects to on the artboard.

Imageable area The area inside the dotted line on the artboard representing the portion of the page that your default printer can print.

Keyboard increment A unit of measure equal to 0.014 inches or 1 point. The cursor key is the amount a selected object moves on the artboard when one of the for arrow keys on the keyboard is pressed.

Knife Tool An Illustrator tool used for cutting open or closed paths into two or more paths.

Layers The stacking order of Illustrator objects when the Layers palette is used. Objects placed on the same layer will form their own stacking order within that layer.

Legend Similar to a map legend, the legend contains legend labels and small colored boxes that represent the columns on a graph.

Legend labels Labels entered in the first column of the Graph Data palette.

Linear gradients Gradients that consist of gradually blending lines of color.

Marquee A dotted rectangle that appears when you drag the Selection Tool or the Zoom Tool on the artboard. A marquee is used to zoom in on a selected area or to select objects that fall within the marquee.

Menu bar A bar that includes all of the Illustrator menus.

New view An Illustrator feature that allows you to save the views that you will be using frequently.

Open paths Straight or curved lines that do not connect.

Outline The mode in Illustrator that displays objects on the artboard as paths only, without fills or strokes and on the same layer.

Outlines Individual vector objects created using the Create Outlines feature. Used for converting text into vector objects.

Palettes Windows containing features for modifying and manipulating Illustrator objects.

Path Type Tool One of the Illustrator Type tools used to place text along an open or closed path.

Pathfinders Illustrator commands that combine and divide overlapping objects and create new objects in the process.

Paths Open or closed lines that are composed of a series of anchor points.

Pixels Small squares used to display a digital image on the rectangular grid of a computer screen.

Point A unit of type size equal to 0.01384 inches, or approximately 1/72 of an inch.

Preview The mode in Illustrator which displays objects with fills and strokes and recognizes the stacking order of objects.

Process colors Colors that are created using Cyan, Magenta, Yellow, and Black and used for printed materials.

Radial gradients Gradients that consist of gradually blending circles of color.

Rasterize The process of converting a vector object into a bitmap image.

Reference points Points on a selected object that represent the four corners of the bounding box, the horizontal and vertical centers of the bounding box and the center point of the bounding box.

Reflect The ability to flip an object horizontally or vertically.

Repeating design A custom graph design in which a value is assigned to the custom design and repeated as many times as necessary.

Report Text file containing information about an Illustrator document, created using the Document Info dialog box.

Resolution dependent A property of bitmap graphics which refers to the fact that they cannot be resized without losing image quality.

Resolution independent A property of vector graphics which refers to the fact that they can be reduced or enlarged without any loss of quality.

Scratch area The area outside the artboard where you can store objects before placing them on the artboard; objects on the scratch area will not print.

Scroll bars Bars that run along the bottom and right sides of the window used to change the portion of the document that is viewable in the Illustrator window.

Selection handles The eight white squares along the bounding box which are used to resize an object.

Series A set of data that can be represented by a graphic element such as a bar, line or point.

Sliding scale designs A custom graph design in which columns are resized from a specific point on the design.

Splash screen A window that displays details about the software and the names of the programmers who created it.

Stacking order The order that Illustrator objects are arranged on the artboard from top to bottom.

Status bar A bar that contains a list arrow menu from which you can choose a status line with information about the current tool, the date and time, the amount of free memory, or the number of undo operations. The status bar also includes the zoom field.

Stroke The color or style of the border of an object.

Tick marks Short lines that extend from the value axis on a graph.

Title bar A bar that contains the name of the program and your picture, as well as the Minimize, Maximize, and Close buttons.

Toolbox A box containing tools that let you create, select, and manipulate objects in Illustrator.

Transformation tools The Move, Scale, Rotate, Reflect, and Shear Tools used to transform Illustrator objects.

Uniformly scaled designs A custom graph design in which columns are resized horizontally and vertically.

Unite A pathfinder that combines two or more objects into one unit and places one stroke around the perimeter of the new object.

Value axis The vertical line to the left of the graph that displays the minimum and maximum graph values.

Vector graphics Mathematically calculated objects that are composed of anchor points and straight or curved line segments.

Vertically scaled designs A custom graph design in which columns are resized vertically.

X and Y coordinates The horizontal and vertical location of a reference point of an Illustrator object, measured from the bottom-left corner of the artboard.

Zoom box A box in the lower-left corner of the Illustrator window that displays the current magnification level.

Illustrator 9.0

Index

Index

Index

text
   entering, A-8, A-9
tick marks
   graphs, H-8, H-9
title bar, A-6, A-7
toolbox, A-6, A-7
Transform Again command, B-8
transformation tools, B-8, B-9, E-6.
   See also specific tools
Transform palette, B-14–15
type size, A-4, C-6
Type Tool, F-13
Type tools, F-12, F-13

▶U
undo levels, A-11
ungrouping objects, C-10

uniformly scaled designs
   graphs, H-14
Unite command, F-10–11
unlocking bitmap images, D-6, D-7

▶V
value axis, H-8
vector graphics, A-3, D-2
   converting to bitmap objects, G-4–5
Vertical Area Type Tool, F-13
vertically scaled designs
   graphs, H-14
Vertical Path Type Tool, F-13
Vertical Type Tool, F-13
viewing
   Illustrator window, A-6–7
   layers and sublayers, E-10, E-11

▶W
Web Swatch library
   choosing colors, B-12–13

▶X
X coordinate, B-15

▶Y
Y coordinate, B-15

▶Z
Zoom command, C-14–15
zooming in, G-6, G-7
Zoom menu, A-7
Zoom slider, C-15
Zoom text box, A-6, A-7